W9-BHL-092

FERGUSON

CAREER
COACH

MANAGING YOUR CAREER IN

Theater and the
Performing Arts

The Ferguson Career Coach Series

Managing Your Career in the Health Care Industry
Managing Your Career in the Music Industry
Managing Your Career in the Sports Industry
Managing Your Career in Theater and the Performing Arts

FERGUSON

CAREER COACH

MANAGING YOUR CAREER IN

Theater and the Performing Arts

Shelly Field

Ferguson
An imprint of Infobase Publishing

Ferguson Career Coach: Managing Your Career in Theater and the Performing Arts

Copyright © 2008 by Shelly Field

Ferguson
An imprint of Infobase Publishing, Inc.
132 West 31st Street
New York NY 10001

Library of Congress Cataloging-in-Publication Data

Field, Shelly.
  Ferguson career coach : managing your career in theater and the performing arts / Shelly Field.
    p. cm. — (The Ferguson career coach series)
  Includes bibliographical references and index.
  ISBN-13: 978-0-8160-5354-4 (hardcover)
  ISBN-10: 0-8160-5354-5 (hardcover)
  1. Performing arts—Vocational guidance. I. Title.
  PN1580.F53 2008
  791.023—dc22   2007036655

Ferguson books are available at special discounts when purchased in bulk quantities for businesses, associations, institutions, or sales promotions. Please call our Special Sales Department in New York at (212) 967-8800 or (800) 322-8755.

You can find Ferguson on the World Wide Web at http://www.fergpubco.com

Text design by Kerry Casey
Cover design by Takeshi Takahashi

Printed in the United States of America

VB Hermitage 10 9 8 7 6 5 4 3 2 1

This book is printed on acid-free paper and contains 30% post-consumer recycled content.

Disclaimer: The examples and practices described in this book are based on the author's experience as a professional career coach. No guarantee of success for individuals who follow them is stated or implied. Readers should bear in mind that techniques described might be inappropriate in some professional settings, and that changes in industry trends, practices, and technology may affect the activities discussed here. The author and publisher bear no responsibility for the outcome of any reader's use of the information and advice provided herein.

CONTENTS

1   Introducing Your Career Coach   7
2   Focusing on a Great Career in Theater or
     the Performing Arts   19
3   Plan For Success in Theater and the Performing Arts   38
4   Get Ready, Get Set, Go: Preparation   56
5   Job Search Strategies   76
6   Tools for Success   92
7   Getting Your Foot in the Door   124
8   The Interview   149
9   The Theatrical Audition   165
10   Marketing Yourself for Success   177
11   Succeeding in the Workplace   193
12   Succeeding on the Talent End of the Industry   207
13   Success Is Yours for the Taking   234

Appendix I: Trade Associations, Unions,
     and Other Organizations   246
Appendix II: Theater and Performing Arts
     Web Sites   258
Bibliography   263
Index   276

1

INTRODUCING YOUR CAREER COACH

Do you truly believe that there is no business like show business? Does just the thought of performing make your heart beat faster and put a smile on your face? When you daydream, do you see yourself on stage? If you let yourself really dream, can you see yourself on Broadway, at Lincoln Center, Madison Square Garden, or headlining in Las Vegas? Do you look at others working in various aspects of the performing arts and wish you had their job? If you are dreaming and wishing for a career in theater and the performing arts or if you're already working in the field and want to climb the career ladder to the next level, then you are in luck!

This book is for you.

The first careers in theater and the performing arts that often come to mind are those of actor, singer, musician, dancer, and other performance parts, but they are by no means the only career options. The performing arts encompass a plethora of career possibilities. One of them can be just right for you.

Think about it. What is *your* dream career? Is it acting on stage, bringing a character to life? Is it being a rock or country music singer making hit records and touring for thousands of adoring fans? Is it soloing as the star in a classic opera or playing the lead in a hot Broadway musical? Is

your passion playing a musical instrument? Do you dream about being a conductor? How about a musician in a symphony or the orchestra of a stage production? Do you want to be a musician in a top touring act or would you rather perform on recordings, work as a musical director, or teach others how to play better? The choices are endless.

Is your dream to be a playwright writing the next Tony-winning Broadway play or a librettist writing the next great opera? Is your passion songwriting or composing music?

Do you fantasize about working in the technical end of theater, putting your imagination to work behind the scenes designing costumes, sets, lights, or sound to help create the magical atmosphere of theater? Is your passion working on the business side of the industry? How about a career supporting the efforts of others on the talent end of the performing arts? The choice is yours.

The performing arts industry is exciting, glamorous, and fun. Whether you want to be out in front, backstage, or in the business or support area, the business can be very competitive. Are you ready for the challenge? Will you be the next star or top producer? Are you going to be the one to succeed?

I'm betting you will, and I want to help you to get there. This book can be your guide to success whether you've recently decided to pursue your dream career in the performing arts or you're already part of it and you want to get the edge in advancing. Throughout the pages of this book, I'm going to be your coach. I'm going to help you get where you want to be because I want you to succeed.

Why? Because I can identify with your struggles. I've been where you are, and I understand your challenges. I, too, wanted to work in the entertainment industry. As far back as I can remember, my dream was to be in the music business. I wanted to be part of it, and most of all be successful in it.

My road to success was not easy. At the time I was trying to get into the industry, I didn't know anyone in the business. I didn't live in one of the major music capitals. I struggled to get my foot in the door. And while I faced challenges in attaining success, I eventually did get there. Why? Because I had a burning desire to be in the music industry and knew I wasn't going to quit until it happened.

Almost every area of the performing arts industry has a reputation of being difficult to enter and even more difficult to navigate to the top. The music business is no exception.

I wish there had been a book to give me advice on how to move ahead, to guide me toward my goals and give me insider tips. Unfortunately there wasn't. I wish that I'd had a mentor or a coach or someone who really knew what I should be doing and could tell me what it was. Unfortunately, I didn't have that either.

Did anyone ever help me? It wasn't that no one wanted to help, but most of the people in my network at that time just didn't have a clue about the entertainment industry.

A few times I did run into some entertainment industry professionals who tried to help. A few months after I started job hunting, I landed an interview at a large booking agency. I arrived for my appointment and sat waiting for the owner of the agency to meet with me. I sat and sat and sat.

A recording artist who was a client of the agency walked over to me after his meeting with the agent and asked how long I had been there. "Close to three hours," I replied. My appointment was for 1 p.m. and it was almost 4 p.m. "What are you here for?" he asked. "I want to be in the music industry," was my answer. "I want to be a tour manager."

"Someday," he said, "you'll make it and this joker [the agency owner] will want something from you and you can make *him* wait. Mark my words; it will happen." He then stuck his head inside the agency owner's door and said, "This woman has been sitting out here for hours; bring her in already." As I walked into the office I had a glimmer of hope. It was short lived, but it was hope just the same.

The agency owner was very nice. During our meeting he told me something to the effect of, if he ever needed someone with my skills and talents, he would be glad to give me a call and I should keep plugging away. In other words, thanks for coming in. I talked to you; now please leave. Don't call me; I'll call you.

He then explained in a hushed voice, "Anyway, you know how it is. Most managers don't want *girls* on the road with their acts." Not only was I being rejected because of my skills and talents, but now it was because I was a *girl*. (Because my name is Shelly, evidently many people incorrectly assumed that I was male instead of female when their secretaries were setting up appointments. The good news is that this got me into a lot of places I probably wouldn't have had a chance to otherwise. The bad news? Once I got there, they realized I was not a man.)

I smiled, thanked the agent for meeting with me, and left wondering if I would ever get a job doing what I wanted. Was it sexual discrimination? Probably, but in reality the agent was just telling me the way it was at that time. He actually believed he was being nice. Was it worth complaining about? I didn't think so. I was new to the industry, and I wasn't about to make waves before I even got in. The problem was, I just couldn't find a way to get in.

On another occasion, I met a road manager at a concert and told him about how I wanted to be a road or tour manager. He told me he knew how hard it was to get into the industry, so he was going to help me. "Call me on Monday," he told me Saturday. I did. "I'm working on it," he said. "Call me Wednesday." On Wednesday he said, "Call me Friday." This went on for a couple of weeks before I realized that he was trying to be nice but he really wasn't going to do anything for me.

⭐ Tip from the Top

During that interview I learned two important lessons. One, use what you have to get your foot in the door. If someone thought I was a man because of my name, my idea was not to correct them *until* I got in the door. At least that way I could have a chance at selling myself.

The second lesson was to choose your battles wisely. Had I complained about sexual discrimination at that point, I might have won the battle, but I would have lost the war.

I decided that if I were ever lucky enough to break into the music industry, I would help as many people as I possibly could who wanted a job doing *anything* to fulfill their dreams. I wasn't sure when I'd make it, but I knew I would get there eventually.

Like many others I dreamed about standing on a stage in front of thousands of adoring fans singing my number-one song. In reality, though, I knew that was not where my real talent was. While at the time, I had a couple of dreams, I knew that I did have the talent to make it on the business end of the industry.

I did all the traditional things to try to get a job. I sent my resume, I searched out employment agencies that specialized in the music industry, I made cold calls, and I read the classifieds.

And guess what? I still couldn't land a job. Imagine that. A college degree and a burning desire still couldn't get me the job I wanted. I had some offers, but the problem was that they weren't offers to work in the music industry. I had offers for jobs as a social worker, a teacher, a newspaper reporter, and a number of other positions I have since forgotten. Were any of these jobs I wanted? No! I wanted to work in the music business, period, end of story.

Like many of you might experience, I had people telling me I was pipe dreaming. "The entertainment industry," I was told, "is for *the other people*. You know, the *lucky ones*. The ones who have connections in the industry." I was also told consistently how difficult the entertainment industry was to get into and, once in, how difficult it was to succeed.

Want to hear the good news? I eventually did get into the entertainment industry. I'll share the story of how I did it later in the book, but basically I had to "think outside of the box" to get there. The important thing was that I found

⭐ Tip from the Coach

Despite the scope of the industry, the world of entertainment is really very small. That means that everyone knows everyone else. What does that have to do with you? It's always important that you leave a good impression, and realize that you might run into people again. Remember what the recording artist at the booking agency told me? A number of years after I broke into the industry, his words actually did come true. At the time I was working on a project booking the talent for a big music festival overseas, and the booking agent heard about it. He put in a call to me to see if I'd consider using his talent for the show. "Hi, Shelly, it's Dave. It's been a long time," said the voice mail. "I heard you were booking a new show and wanted to talk to you about having some of my acts appearing on it. Give me a call." As soon as I heard his name, the words of that recording artist came flooding back into my mind. This was a true "mark my words" moment.

I was busy, so I couldn't call him right away. He kept calling back. He really wanted his acts on the show. I finally took his call and told him we'd get back to him. He must have called 25 times in a two-day period to see if we'd made up our mind. He finally said, "How long do you expect me to wait?"

I then reminded him of the day I sat in his office and waited and waited for him to see me. He, of course, didn't even remember the moment, but to his credit, he apologized profusely and promised never to have me wait again. I accepted his apology and told him, he'd only have to wait . . . a little bit longer.

a way to get into the exclusive entertainment industry! Want to hear some more good news? You can too! As a matter of fact, not only can you get in, but you can succeed.

Remember when I said that if I got in, I'd help every single person who ever wanted a job doing anything? Whether you want to work in theater or any of the other performing arts, I want to help you get there.

I give seminars around the country on entering and succeeding in various career areas including theater, the performing arts, and the music industry, and I'm a personal coach and stress management specialist to many celebrities, entertainers, and executives in the entertainment industry. Unfortunately, I can't be there in person for each and every aspiring performing arts professional. So, through the pages of this book, I'm going to be your personal coach, your cheerleader, and your inside source to getting into and succeeding in a career in theater or any of the other performing arts.

A Personal Coach—What's That?

The actual job title of "personal coach" is relatively new, but coaches are not. Athletes and others in the sports industry have always used coaches to help improve their game and their performance. You may already be familiar with vocal coaches and acting or drama coaches who help people improve and perfect their performance skills. Over the past few years, coaches have sprung up in many other fields as well.

There are those who coach people toward better fitness or nutrition and etiquette coaches to help people learn how to act in every situation. There are parenting coaches to help people parent better, retirement coaches to help people be successful in retirement, and time management coaches to help people better manage their time. There are stress management coaches to help people better manage their stress; executive business coaches to help catapult people to the top; life coaches to help people attain a happier, more satisfying life; and career coaches to help people create a great career. Personal coaches often help people become more successful and satisfied in a combination of areas.

"I don't understand," you might be saying. "Exactly what does a coach do and what can he or she do for me?" Well, there are a number of things, depending on exactly what you want to do.

A coach can help you find your way to success faster. He or she can help motivate you, help you find what really makes you happy, get you on track, and help you focus your energies on what you really want to do. Unlike some family and friends, coaches aren't judgmental. You, therefore, have the ability to freely explore ideas with your coach without fear of them being rejected. Instead of accepting your self-imposed limitations, coaches encourage you to reach your full potential and improve your performance.

Coaches are objective, and one of the important things they can do for you is to point out things that you might not see yourself. Most of all, a coach helps you find the best in you and then shows you ways to bring it out. This, in turn, will make you more successful.

As your coach, what do I hope to do for you? I want to help you find your passion and then help you go after it. If working in theater or one of the other performing arts is what you want, I not only want you to get in, I want you to be successful.

Do you want to be an actor? A comedian? Do you want to be part of a top musical touring act or a show group? How about singing opera? Singing in a musical? Do you want to be a ballet dancer? A modern dancer?

How about a classical artist playing in a major orchestra? A conductor? What about a member of a rock band, country group, or R&B act?

Do you dream of being a costume designer? A scenic designer? A lighting designer or a sound designer? What about a casting director, a producer, or director?

If your career aspiration is in the talent end of the industry, we're going to work on finding ways to catapult you to the top. If your career aspirations are more in the creative end of the industry, we'll work on ways you can get into the industry and succeed. If, on the other hand, you want to work in the business end of the industry or performing arts administration, we'll work on finding ways for you to get your foot in the door. If you're already in, we'll work on ways to help you climb the career ladder to your dream position.

Look at me as your personal cheerleader and this book as your guide. I want you to succeed and will do as much as possible to make that happen. No matter what anyone tells you, it is possible to get into the performing arts and succeed. Thousands of people have done so and now you can be one of them!

Did you ever notice that some people just seem to attract success? They seem to get all the breaks, are always at the right place at the right time, and have what you want? It's not that you're jealous; you just want to get a piece of the pie.

"They're so lucky," you say. Well, here's the deal. You can be that lucky too. Want to know why? While a little bit of luck is always helpful, it's not just chance. Some people work to attract success. They work to get what they want. They follow a plan, keep a positive attitude, and they know that they're worthy of the prize. Others just wait for success to come, and when all you do is wait, success often just passes you by.

The good news here is that you can be one of the lucky ones who attracts success if you take the right steps. This book will give you some of the keys to control your destiny; it will hand you the keys to success in your career and your life.

Through the pages of this book, you'll find the answers to many of your questions about theater and the performing arts in both the business and talent areas. You'll get the inside scoop on how the business works, key employment issues, moving from amateur to pro, and finding opportunities.

You'll find insider tips, tricks, and techniques that worked for others who have succeeded in the industry. You'll discover secrets to help you get in the door and up the ladder of success, as well as the lowdown on things I wish I had known when I was first beginning my quest for success in the entertainment industry.

If you haven't already attended one of my Making It in Theater, Making It in the Performing Arts, or Making It in Music seminars, or any of the entertainment industry, stress management, or career workshops I offer, you will get the benefit of being there by simply reading this book. If you have attended one, here is the book you've been asking for!

Change Your Thinking, Change Your Life

Sometimes the first step in getting what you want is just changing the way you think. Did you know that if you think you don't deserve something, you usually don't get it? Did you know that if you don't think you're good enough, neither will anyone else? Did you know that if you think you deserve something, you have a much better chance of getting it? Or that if you think you are good enough, your confidence will shine through?

When you have confidence in yourself, you start to find ways to get what you want. And guess what? You succeed!

And while changing your thinking can change your life, this book is not just about a positive attitude. It's a book of actions you can take.

While a positive attitude is always helpful in order to succeed in whatever part of the industry you're interested in pursuing, you need to take positive actions too.

I am living my dream and love what I do. I want everyone else who has a dream to live their dream as well. If all it took for you to be successful was for me to tell you what you needed to do or even do it for you, I would. Unfortunately, that's not the way it works.

Here's the reality of the situation. I can only offer advice, suggestions, and tell you what you need to do. You have to do the rest. Talking about what you can do or should do is fine, but without your taking action, it's difficult to get where you want to go.

This is your chance to finally get what you want. You've already taken one positive step toward getting your dream career simply by picking up this book. As you read through the various sections, you'll find other actions to take that will help get you closer—whether you choose the talent, support, or business end of theater and the performing arts.

As you read through the book we'll talk about creating your own personal action plan. This plan can help you focus on exactly what you want and then show you the actions needed to get it.

Your personal action plan is a checklist of sorts. Done correctly it can be one of the main

The Inside Scoop

It is never too late to be what you might have been.

–George Eliot

keys to your career success. It will put you in the driver's seat and give you an edge over others who haven't prepared a plan themselves.

We'll also discuss putting together a number of different kinds of journals to help you become more successful in your career. For example, one of the problems many people experience when they're trying to get a new job, move up the career ladder, or accomplish a goal is that they often start feeling as though they aren't accomplishing anything. A career journal is a handy tool to help you track exactly what you've done to accomplish your goals. Once that is in place, you know what else needs to be done.

Is This the Right Career for Me?

Unsure of exactly what you want to do in the performing arts? As you read through the book, you'll get some ideas.

"What if I'm already working at a job in another industry?" you ask. "Is it too late? Am I stuck here forever?" Here's the deal. It is never too late to change careers, and going after something you're passionate about can drastically improve the quality of your life.

Thousands of people stay in jobs because it's easier than going after what they want. You don't have to be one of them.

We all know people who are in jobs or careers that they don't love. They get up every day waiting for the workweek to be over. They go through the day, waiting for it to be over. They waste their life waiting and waiting. Is this the life you want to lead? Probably not. You now have the opportunity to get what you want. Are you ready to go after it? I'm hoping that you are.

If theater or the other performing arts is where you want to work, there are countless op-

portunities in the talent, creative, support, and business areas. In addition to the traditional careers most people think of, there is an array of others for you to explore. No matter what your skill or talent, you can almost always find a way to parlay them into your performing arts career.

"Really?" you ask. "What if I'm a nurse? What if I'm a hairstylist? What if I work in a bank? What if I'm a teacher? What do any of those have to do with the performing arts industry?"

Here's the good news. If you think in a creative manner, you probably can use any of your skills to get a job at least around the performing arts.

A number of years ago I was on a radio call-in show about getting into the music industry. A woman called and said, "I really want to work in the music business."

"What do you do now?" I asked.

"I'm a nurse," she replied.

"Use your skills," I told her.

"No," she said. "You didn't hear me. I'm a nurse."

"I heard you," I said. "Here's an idea. Why don't you put a small ad in the trades? There might be some touring acts who are dealing with drug rehab or medical issues who need a nurse on the road with them."

Four months later she called me again. She had placed an ad in the trade journals and didn't get a response. She had, however, won tickets from a local radio station to a concert and "meet and greet" event for a major recording act appearing in her area. She went and enjoyed the show and met the act. In a conversation with the group's road manager, she told him how excited she was to meet the group and happened to mention that she had just placed an ad in the trades for going on the road but that it hadn't brought in any response. A couple of weeks later she got a call from the group's management asking if she was interested in going on the road with the group to handle minor medical needs. They located her number by calling the local radio station that had sponsored the contest she had won. While being in the right place at the right time certainly helped, had she not "thought outside of the box," she might not have been living her dream.

At one of my Making It in Theater seminars, one of the attendees raised her hand and asked how she could make the transition from being a cabaret singer in New York City hotel lounges to working in theater. She had recently fired her agent and was booking herself.

I asked her if she had any contacts in the theater industry and she said she didn't. "My only professional contacts are in music," she replied. "That's it unless you count a couple of people I know in magazine publishing."

"Who do you know in publishing?" I asked.

"Just a couple of editors at some women's and fashion magazines," she said. "A couple of years ago, I was looking into new ways to meet people and went to one of those parties where you meet people and spend 8 or 9 minutes with them and then move on to the next person. One of the women at the party was an editor at a magazine. We were comparing notes and got to talking and I ended up writing a couple of articles on Internet dating."

"Why don't you give her a call and see if they might be interested in an article on tips for getting auditions for young actors and actresses," I suggested. "That way you'll have a reason to call potential casting agents, managers, and other people in theater. You'll be calling and meeting people in the industry who will see you on a different level. The process will help give you entrée into the industry where people remember you for something other than you wanting to be one of a hundred other people trying to be an actress. Then, after you meet them and develop a relationship, you will have an easier time contacting them and saying something like, 'Hi, this is Jane Brown. We spoke when I was researching the magazine article on getting auditions. You made the whole experience sound so interesting, I wanted to give it a try. I've been singing cabaret, but my dream is to work in theater. Do you have any suggestions on whom I might contact to audition for a musical?'"

The woman resisted the idea. "What if the people I speak to don't remember me?" she asked. "What if they say they don't know anyone who can help? Do I have to wait for the article to come out?"

"Just try it," I urged. "You might just get lucky and meet someone who can help you in your career."

About a year later, I went to see a Broadway show with a friend. Somewhere in the second

---

⭐ Words from the Wise

Always carry business cards with your phone number and other contact information. Make it easy for people to find you when an opportunity presents itself.

act, I recognized the woman from my seminar singing in the chorus. After the show, I sent a note backstage with my card congratulating her. By the time I got into my office on Monday, there was a message on my voice mail.

Evidently she did call her friend at the magazine about the article and got the assignment. She made contact with a number of agents, producers, directors, and actors while researching the piece, and although the article never made it to print, it brought the woman a stroke of luck.

She had mentioned to one of the directors she was interviewing for the article that she needed to reschedule because she had to sing at an event at one of the hotels where she worked. The director, who was going to be in the area, suggested that they meet in between shows. He heard her sing while waiting and her voice impressed him. At the time he was working on an off-Broadway show that needed singers. He invited her to audition and she got the part. The show closed down shortly after, but one of the other singers in the cast gave her a lead on an audition for a Broadway musical. She auditioned and once again got the part!

Could she have reached that goal without looking outside the box? She might have, but being creative helped move her along by giving her ideas to make new contacts within the industry.

Want to hear another story of how creativity helped someone live their dream? During a radio interview one day, a call came in from an attorney. "I hate what I do," he said. "I don't know why I ever went into law. I'm so unhappy."

"What was the last thing you did that made you happy?" I asked. "What did you do when you were growing up that you liked?"

"I saw a couple of Broadway plays last month. I enjoyed that," he said. "I come from

New York City so I grew up going to theater and Broadway shows."

"Did you ever want to be an actor?" I asked.

"When I was in college I used to be in the drama club productions. I kind of liked acting, but I was really not great at it."

"So we know you probably don't want to be an actor," I said.

"You're right," he said. "A number of my friends are actors and actresses. A couple of them are even on Broadway, but it's not for me. I would love to work in the performing arts in some manner, but I'm not sure where I would fit."

"Is it that you don't like practicing law or that you don't like your job?" I prodded.

"I don't really hate practicing law, I just don't like the type of law I'm doing," he said. "I like my company. I like my boss and I like my colleagues. I work at a large firm in New York City. I've been there for a couple of years now and I think they like me too, because I just got a nice raise."

"Do you think you might like working in entertainment law?" I asked. "Do you think you might be interested in dealing with contracts and negotiations in that industry?"

"If I had a job like that, I wouldn't be calling you," he said. "How difficult are jobs like that to get? Where can I look?"

"Well, you can go look for a firm that specializes in entertainment law and try to get a job with them," I said. "Or if you like where you currently work, but not exactly what you do there, you can try to get creative with the job you have. Do you want to hear that option?"

"Definitely," he said excitedly.

"Go take some classes in entertainment law, the performing arts, theater business, contracts, things like that. Network as much as you can. During this process, sit down and work out a plan on paper for adding an entertainment arm to your law firm."

"But they don't handle entertainment," he said.

"They might not now, but they might consider it if they see the idea as a good one. Do some research and develop a plan. Do it in writing so you can see any holes. Then set up a meeting with your supervisor and anyone else who can help make a decision. Tell them all the positive things it can do for your company, how the addition of an entertainment specialty can attract clients and increase business. The only thing you have to remember is to make sure they know you want to be a part of the entertainment division."

"It's a good idea," the man said, "but it will never work. I doubt my firm will go for it."

"Well, you can always go the traditional way and look for a job in a law firm which already specializes in the entertainment industry," I said. "Either way, take some classes so you're knowledgeable about the industry. If you're really interested, you should give it a try. What's the worst that can happen? Let me know how it works out."

Over the next few months, I received a number of e-mails from the man updating me on his progress. He took some continuing education, went to seminars, and even attended a few entertainment conferences and conventions. Soon after he put together his plan in writing and set up a meeting with his supervisor and one of the firm's partners.

They listened to his presentation and told him that they would get back to him. They wanted to bring the idea to the other partners. A few weeks later, they called the man in. He was told that while the idea was good, they didn't want the firm to go in that direction.

The man was understandably devastated. He had worked hard taking classes, networking, and putting the plan together, and he was still no

further ahead. He went home that night, despondent, when he checked his voice mail. There was a message from an attorney he met at one of the entertainment conferences asking him to call.

To make a very long story short, the man was so excited about his plan to bring an entertainment law division to his company, that he mentioned it to almost everyone he met. One of the attorneys who he talked to at a conference was a partner in a law firm that handled a large number of clients from the theater and performing arts industry. After a couple of interviews, he not only offered the man a very lucrative job, but he also promised that after a short time, he would have the opportunity to become a partner.

A Job versus a Career: What's the Difference?

What do you want in life? Would you rather just have a job or do you want a career? What's the difference? A job is just that. It's something you do to earn a living. It's a means to an end. A career, on the other hand, is a series of related jobs. It's a progressive path of achievement, a long-term journey. A career is something you build using your skills, talents, and passions.

You might have many jobs in your career. You might even follow more than one career path. The question is what do you want?

If all you want is to go to work, day after day, week after week just to get paid, a job is all you need, and there is nothing wrong with that. On the other hand, if you would like to fill your life with excitement and passion while getting paid, you are a prime candidate for a great career.

How can you get that? Start planning now to get what you want. Define your goals and then start working towards them.

Not everyone starts off with a dream job. If you just sit and wait for your dream job to come to you, you could be sitting forever. What you can do, however, is to take what you have and make it work for you until you get what you want.

What does that mean? It means that you can make whatever you do better at least for the time being. The trick in this whole process is finding ways to give the job you have some meaning. Find a way to get some passion from what you're doing. If you get that mind set you'll never have a bad job. Focus on your ultimate career goal and then look at each job as a benchmark along the way to what you want.

How to Use This Book to Help You in the Theater and Performing Arts

Ideally, I would love for you to read this book from beginning to end, but I know from experience that that's probably not the way it's going to happen. You might browse the contents and look for something that can help you *now*, you might see a subject that catches your eye, or you might be looking for an area of the book that solves a particular problem.

For this reason, as you read the book, you might see what appears to be some duplication of information. In this manner, I can be assured that when I suggest something that may be helpful to you in a certain area that you will get all the information you need, even if you didn't read a prior section.

You should be aware that even if you're interested in working on the talent end of the industry as an actor, actress, singer, dancer or musician, knowing about the business end will be helpful to succeeding in your career and vice versa.

If you're on the talent end of the industry, understanding how the business end works, for example, will help assure that you are treated fairly, don't get ripped off, and know where the monies come from and go. If you're on the business end of the industry, understanding as much as possible about the talent area can help you be more effective in your job.

There's a great mystique to the entire entertainment industry, and theater and the performing arts are no exception. Many would have you think that the performing arts industry is impossible to break into, impossible to succeed in. Trust me—it is not. If you're willing to put some effort into the process, you can make it.

You might have heard the saying that knowledge is power. This is true. The more you know about the theatrical world and the performing arts and how it works, the better your chances are of succeeding. This book is full of information to help you learn everything you need to know about the industry and how it works. I almost guarantee that you will refer to information in this book long after you've attained success.

As you read through the various sections, you'll find a variety of suggestions and ideas to help you succeed. Keep in mind that every idea and suggestion might not work in every situation and for every person. The idea is to keep trying things until one of them works. Use the book as a springboard to get you started. Just because something is not written here doesn't mean that it's not a good idea. Brainstorm to find solutions to barriers you might encounter in your career.

My job is to lead you on your journey to success in theater and the performing arts. Along the way you'll find exercises, tasks, and assignments that will help get you where you want to be faster. No one is going to be standing over your shoulder to make you do these tasks. You alone can make the decision on the amount of time and work you want to put into your career. While no one can guarantee you success, what you should know is that the more you put into your career, the better your chances of having the success you are dreaming about.

Are you worth the time and effort? I think you are! Is a career in theater or the performing arts worth it? If this is *your* dream, it is! Aside from the opportunity to make a good living and fulfill your dreams, you can impact the entertainment others enjoy.

No matter what level you're currently at in your career in theater or the performing arts and in whatever capacity, this book is for you. You might not need every section or every page, but I can guarantee that parts of this book can help you.

Whether you're just starting out in the business or support area of the performing arts or at the top of your field; whether you're a struggling actor or actress, songwriter, singer, or musician, or are performing to rave reviews, this book can help you experience more success in your career and a happier, more satisfying, and stress-free life.

A Sampling of What This Book Covers

This informative, handy guide to success in the performing arts is written in a friendly, easy-to-read style. Let it be your everyday guide to success. Want to know how the theater and performing arts industry works? Need an overview of the industry? How about focusing on what you really want to do? Check out the book!

Want to learn how to plan and prepare for your dream career? Do you want to know the best places to be for performing arts careers? Do you want to focus on search strategies especially for theater or the performing arts or even performing arts management? How about tips for making those important industry contacts, networking, and creating the ideal industry-specific resume or cover letter? Check out the book!

Do you need to know how to develop your bio or resume, or how to put together your press kit? Do you want to get your portfolio together? Want to know what business cards can do for you and your career? What type of photographs you need? Check out the book!

Want to learn how to get your foot in the door? How about checking out tried-and-true methods to get people to call you back? Do you want to learn the best way to market yourself and why it's so important? Do you want to learn how to succeed in the workplace, deal with workplace politics, keep an eye out for opportunities, and climb the career ladder? You know what you have to do: Check out the book!

Do you want to know how to move from the small stage to the big stage or the garage to the recording studio? How to find gigs? How to generate auditions? Do you want to know about contracts, dealing with managers, agents, lawyers, casting directors, and more? Are you interested in learning how to deal with the media, get exposure, and protect yourself? You got it. You need to read the book!

Do you need important contact information so you can move your career forward? Check out the listings of organizations, associations, and unions.

Although this book won't teach you how to act, produce, direct, or write a play, compose a hit tune, sing a popular song, or play an instrument better, it will help you find ways to garner success, whether your passion is the talent or business area.

If you dream of working in the theater and the performing arts and don't know how to make that dream a reality, this book is for you. Have fun reading it. Know that if your heart is in it, you can achieve anything.

Now let's get started.

2

FOCUSING ON A GREAT CAREER IN THEATER OR THE PERFORMING ARTS

Focusing on What You Really Want to Do

Do you wake up every morning dreading going to work? Do you ask yourself, "What should I be?" How about, "What should I do for the rest of my life?" Do you daydream about working in theater or one of the performing arts? Do you wonder how you're going to make it in the industry?

Unless you're independently wealthy or just won the megamillion-dollar lottery, you, like most people, have to work. Just in case you're wondering, life is not supposed to be miserable. Neither is your job.

Life should have purpose. That purpose is not sleeping, getting up, going to a job that you don't particularly care about, coming home, cooking dinner, and watching TV only to do it all over again the next day.

To be happy and fulfilled, you need to enjoy life. You need to do things that give you pleasure. As a good part of your life is spent working, the trick is to find a career that you love and that you're passionate about—the career of your dreams.

This is not something everyone does. Many people just fall into a career without thinking ahead of time about what it will entail. Someone who needs a job hears of an opening or answers an ad and then goes for it without thinking about the consequences of working at something for which they really have no passion. Once hired, either it's difficult to give up the money or just too hard to start job hunting again, or they don't know what else to do, so they stay. They wind up with a career that is okay but one they're not really passionate about.

Then there are the other people. The ones who have jobs they love, the lucky people. You've seen them. They're the people who have the jobs and life you wish you had.

Tip from the Coach

Okay is just that: It's okay. Just so you know, you don't want just okay; you don't want to settle; you want *great!* That's what you deserve and that's what you should go after.

Have you noticed that people who love their jobs are usually successful not only in their career but in other aspects of life as well? They almost seem to have an aura around them of success, happiness, and prosperity. Do you want to be one of them? You can!

Finding a career that you want and love is challenging but possible. You are in a better position than most people. If you're reading this book, you've decided that theater or one of the other performing arts is what you're passionate about. Now all you have to do is determine exactly what you want to do in the industry.

What's your dream career? What do you really want to do? This is an important question to ask yourself. Once you know the answer, you can work toward achieving your goal.

If someone asks you right now what you really want to do, can you answer the question? Okay, one, two, three: "What do you want to do with your life?"

If you're saying, "Uh, um, well . . . What I really want to do is . . . well, it's hard to explain," then it's time to focus in on the subject. Sometimes the easiest way to figure out what you want to do is to focus in on what you don't want.

Most people can easily answer what they don't want to do. "I don't want to be a teacher. I don't want to work in a factory. I don't want to work in a store. I don't want to work with numbers," and the list goes on. The problem is that just saying what you don't like or don't want to do doesn't necessarily get you what you want to do. You can, however, use this information to your advantage.

It may seem simple, but sometimes just looking at a list of what you don't like or don't want to do will help you see more clearly what you do like.

Sit down with a sheet of paper or fill in the "Things I Don't Want to Do" worksheet on page 21 and make a list of work-related things you don't like to do. Remember that this list is for you. While you can show it to someone if you want, no one else really has to see it, so try to be honest with yourself.

Here's an example to get you started. When you make your list, add your personal likes and dislikes.

- ◎ I don't want to be cooped up in an office all day.
- ◎ I don't want to sing in front of a live audience.
- ◎ I don't want to have to commute for an hour each way every day.
- ◎ I don't like to be in the limelight.
- ◎ I don't want to be just one of the crowd.
- ◎ I don't want to make decisions.
- ◎ I don't like getting up early in the morning to go to work.
- ◎ I don't want to work in retail sales.
- ◎ I don't want to have to travel for work.
- ◎ I don't like working with numbers.
- ◎ I don't want to do the same thing day after day.
- ◎ I don't like taking risks.
- ◎ I don't like working under constant pressure.
- ◎ I don't like not knowing where my next paycheck is coming from.

We now know what you don't like and don't want to do. Now use this list as a starting point to see what you do like. If you look closely, you'll find that the things you enjoy are the opposite of the things you don't want to do.

You might want to make another list using the "Things I Enjoy Doing" worksheet on page 23. Remember that the reason you're writing

Things I Don't Want to Do

_____

_____

_____

_____

_____

_____

_____

_____

_____

_____

_____

_____

_____

_____

everything down is so you can look at it, remember it, and focus in on getting exactly what you want. Here are some examples to get you started.

◎ I don't like being cooped up in an office all day.
  ▫ But I'd really like to work on the road.
◎ I don't like singing in front of a live audience.
  ▫ But I'm a really good singer. Maybe I'll look into working as a background singer in a studio.
◎ I don't want to have to commute for an hour each way every day.
  ▫ But if I find a job in the city, perhaps I can find an apartment close by.
◎ I don't like to be in the limelight.
  ▫ But I really like supporting others who are there. I think I would like helping others become successful.
◎ I don't want to be just one of the crowd.
  ▫ But I love getting attention. I want to be a star!
◎ I don't like making decisions.
  ▫ I like working in a situation where I'm given direction.
◎ I don't want to work in retail sales.
  ▫ But I'm really good at selling. I think I might be interested in working in the marketing department of a symphony, ballet, or theater company.

As you can see, once you've determined what you don't like doing, it's much easier to get ideas on what you'd like to do. It's kind of like brainstorming with yourself. Many people in this world don't like what they do or are dissatisfied with their career. The good news is you don't have to be one of them.

You and you alone are in charge of your career. Not your mother, father, sister, brother, girlfriend, boyfriend, spouse, or best friend. Others can care, others can help, and others can offer you advice—but in essence, you need to be in control. What this means is that the path you take for your career is largely determined by the choices you make.

The fastest way to get the career you want is by making the choice to take actions now and going after it! You *can* have a career you love and you *can* have it in the performing arts. And when you're doing something you love, you'll be on the road to a great career and a satisfied and fulfilled life.

At this point you might be in a number of different employment situations. You might still be in school planning your career; just out of school beginning your career; or in a job that you don't really care for. You might be in your late teens, 20s, 30s, 40s, 50s, or older.

"Older? Did you say older?" you ask. "Can I start a career in the performing arts even if I'm older?"

Yes! If you have a dream, it is never too late not only to pursue it, but to succeed. And it doesn't matter what branch of the performing arts interests you.

Estelle Getty, the Emmy award-winning actress who starred for 10 years as Sophia Petrillo in the sitcom *The Golden Girls*, didn't experience real success until she was in her 60s.

Jackie Mason gave up his job as an ordained rabbi when he was 28 and became a comedian. In the 1960s Mason was one of the hottest stand-up comedians around. He never let aging stop him. In 1986 Mason, in his fifties, opened on Broadway in his own one-man show, *The*

Things I Enjoy Doing

_____

_____

_____

_____

_____

_____

_____

_____

_____

_____

_____

_____

_____

World According To Me. The show earned Mason a Tony, an Outer Critics Circle Award, an Ace Award, an Emmy Award, and a Grammy nomination. But he wasn't done. Between 1990 and 2002, Mason had five more critically acclaimed Broadway hits. In 2005, Mason, in his mid-seventies, was on Broadway again with another megahit: *Jackie Mason: Freshly Squeezed.* While many comedians quietly disappeared over the years, Mason not only kept going but kept going strong.

Alan Alda is another example. After a successful career as a television actor in *M*A*S*H,* Alda once again hit the big time in his seventies starring in a feature film as well as earning accolades on the Broadway stage in *Glengarry Glen Ross.*

The list goes on. The point that I'm making is that it's never too late to go after your dreams.

Okay, you've decided that the performing arts is the industry for you, but do you know what your dream career is? There are hundreds of exciting career choices whether you want to be in the business end, talent area, or somewhere in between. It's up to you to decide which one you want to pursue.

What's Your Dream?

I bet that you have an idea of what your dream job is and I bet that you have an idea of what it should be like. I'm also betting that you don't have that job yet—or if you do, you're not at the level you want to be. So, what can we do to make that dream a reality?

One of the challenges many people have in getting their dream job is that they just don't think they deserve it. Dream jobs are something many people talk about and wish they had, but just don't. Many people think that dream jobs are for the lucky ones.

Well, I'm here to tell you that you are the lucky one. You can get your dream job, a job you'll love, and it can be in theater or the performing arts!

If I had a magic wand and could get you any job you wanted, what would it be? Do you want to be an actor on Broadway? A singer? A section member of a major symphony? A dancer in a popular ballet?

Do you want to be a comedienne? What about a magician? Do you want to book acts into a major venue? Or is it your dream to be a successful playwright or write the next great libretto?

Do you want to manage others' careers? Is your dream to coordinate the press and media for Broadway productions? How about handling the publicity or fund-raising for a symphony, ballet, or opera company? Maybe your dream is to be the executive director of a major performing arts organization.

Have you always dreamed of designing the elaborate sets that grace Broadway stages or is it your vision to design intricate period costumes for a show?

Not sure what you want to do? Then read on!

Determining what you really want to do is not always easy. Take some time to think about it. Throughout this process be as honest with yourself as possible. Otherwise you stand the chance of not going after the career you really want.

Let's get started with another writing exercise. You might wonder why you're doing all this work, but if you follow through, you will find it easier to attain your dream.

★ Tip from the Coach
Recognize your natural talents and then use them every chance you get.

⭐ The Inside Scoop

When Estelle Getty was a young girl, her parents took her to see a vaudeville show. From that point on, she wanted to be an actress. She spent a good portion of her life trying to achieve her dream. I was fortunate enough to hear a few of the stories about her journey firsthand because my parents were friends with another couple who had been longtime friends with Getty and her husband. Getty visited our home on a couple of occasions. The first was a number of years before she landed her starring role in *The Golden Girls.* Getty and her husband were visiting their friends and they all stopped by for coffee on their way through town. My parents' friends introduced Getty, saying she was an aspiring actress. At the time she worked as a secretary in New York City, and her boss was flexible so that she could go on auditions.

At the time she had done a little acting in regional theater, or maybe even a commercial or two, but her biggest break had been getting on a game show where, she said, she didn't do very well.

"There aren't a lot of parts for mature women," I recall her saying. "But I'm not giving up."

And she didn't. The next time they all stopped by our house, things had changed dramatically. Getty was now a star. Evidently she had run into playwright Harvey Fierstein a number of times in New York City and told him there were no good parts for older women. She challenged him to write a part for her in one of his productions.

She must have made an impact on him, because one day she got a call to audition for the part of Fierstein's nagging mother in the Broadway production of *Torch Song Trilogy.* The rest is, as they say, history. Getty got the part and became a Broadway star.

She excitedly told us of all the perks of starring in a Broadway show. They sent a car for her every day to bring her to the theater as well as bring her back home, fans waited after the show to get autographs, she could always get a seat in a restaurant, people recognized her, and the list went on. It seems, however, that for her the biggest perk was that she was able to pursue her passion for performing.

That was the last time Getty visited my family, but I always followed her career. She parlayed her triumphs in *Torch Song Trilogy* into a successful run in films and television and became a megastar in the entertainment industry.

Had she given up because she thought she was too old or because she just didn't think success would ever come her way, Getty would never have lived her dreams.

Get a pad of paper and a pen and find a place where you can get comfortable. Now all you have to do is sit down and daydream for a bit about what you wish you could be and what you wish you were doing.

"Why daydream?" you ask.

When you daydream your thinking becomes more free. You stop thinking about what you *can't* do and start thinking about what you *can* do. What is your dream? What is your passion? What do you really want to do? Admit it now or forever hold your peace.

Many people are embarrassed to admit when they want something because they fear looking stupid if they don't get it. They worry people are going to talk badly about them or call

⭐ Tip from the Coach

What are your dreams? Are you ready to turn them into reality? You increase your chances of success if you have a deep belief in yourself, your vision, and your ideas.

them a failure. Is this what you worry about? Do you really want to be a singer, but you're afraid you'll fail? Is your dream to be a record executive, but you don't think you'll make it?

First of all, don't ever let fear of failure stop you from going after something you want. While no one can guarantee you success, I can guarantee that if you don't go after what you want, it is going to be very difficult to get it.

One thing you never want to do is get to the end of your life and say with regret, "I wish I had done this" or "I wish I had done that." Will you get each and every thing you want? I'd like to say a definitive yes, but that probably wouldn't be true. The truth of the matter is you might not succeed at everything. But even if you fail, when you try to do something, it usually is a stepping-stone to something else. And that something else can be the turning point in your career.

Later in the book, I'll discuss my story of doing stand-up comedy. I mention it here to illustrate the point that although I didn't turn into a megastar stand-up comedienne, performing comedy was a major stepping-stone for me to do other things I wanted to accomplish in my career. Had I been too scared to try it or not wanted to take the risk for fear I would fail, I would have missed out on important opportunities. I also would have always looked back and said, "I wish I had."

Your dream might not be to become a comedienne. Your dreams are probably totally different. What you need to take from the story is

Words from the Wise
The only thing we have to fear is fear itself.

—Franklin Delano Roosevelt

Tip from the Coach
If there is something that you want to do or try in your career or your life, my advice is to go for it. No matter what the risk, no matter how scared you are, no matter what. Your life and career will benefit more than you can imagine and you'll never look back with regrets. Even if it doesn't work out, you'll feel successful because you tried.

the concept that taking risks and pursuing your dreams can lead to wonderful things.

Think about things that make you happy. Think about things that make you smile. Continue to indulge your passions as you daydream. As ideas come to you, jot them down on your pad. Remember: Nothing is foolish, so write down all the ideas you have for what you want to do. You're going to fine-tune them later.

Here's an example to get you started.

◎ I want to act in a Broadway show. As a matter of fact, I want to star in a Broadway hit. Now that I think about it, I want to win a Tony for my performance.
◎ I want to develop and write theatrical productions. I want to win a Tony for best play of the year.
◎ I want to conduct a symphony.
◎ I want to play in a world-class orchestra.
◎ I want to be a successful stand-up comedian.
◎ I want to work in the business end of the performing arts.
◎ I want to be a theatrical press agent promoting Broadway plays.
◎ I think it would be fun to help make other people famous. I want to be a publicist.

◎ I want to work for an arts council and bring the performing arts to a community.

◎ I want to design the costumes for theatrical performances.

◎ I want to design the sets for a Broadway play.

◎ I want to choreograph a Broadway musical.

◎ I want to find all the right talent for theatrical productions. I want to be a casting director.

Do you need some help focusing on what you really want to do in the performing arts? To choose just the right career, pinpoint your interests and what you really love doing. What are your skills? What are your personality traits? What are your interests? Fill in the following worksheet to help you zero in even more.

What's Stopping You from Getting What You Want?

Now that you have some ideas written down about what you want to do, go down the list. What has stopped you from attaining your goals? Is it that you told people what you wanted to do and they told you that you couldn't do it? Did they tell you it was too difficult and your chances of making it were slim? Is it that you don't have the confidence in yourself to get what you want? Or is it that you need more education or

⭐ The Inside Scoop

When you write down your ideas you are giving them power. You now have them down on paper, making it easier to go over them, look at them rationally, and fine-tune them.

training? Perhaps it's because you aren't in the location most conducive to your dream career. If you can identify the obstacle, you usually can find a way to overcome it, but you need to identify the problem first.

Do you know exactly what you want to do but can't find an opening? For example, do you know you want to work on the administrative end of a symphony but can't find a job? If this is the case, don't just keep looking, but look outside the box. Try to find ways to get your foot in the door, and once it is in, don't take it out until you get what you want.

Have you found the perfect job and interviewed for it, but then the job wasn't offered to you? While at the time you probably felt awful about this, there is some good news. Generally when one door closes, another one opens. Hard to believe? Maybe, but if you think about it, you'll see that it's true. Things work out for the best. If you lost what you thought was the job of your dreams, a better one is out there waiting for you. You just have to find it.

Sometimes while you know exactly what type of job you want, you just can't find a job like that available. Don't give up. Keep looking. Keep thinking outside of the box to get what you want.

Perhaps you're just missing the skills necessary for the type of job you're seeking. This is a relatively easy thing to fix. Once you know the skills necessary for a specific type of job, take steps to get them. Take classes, go to workshops, attend seminars, or become an apprentice or intern.

"But," you say, "I'm missing the education necessary for the job I want. The ad I read said I needed a bachelor's degree and I don't have one."

While you can't get a job as an attorney unless you have gone through law school and you

Focusing on the Job of Your Dreams

Finish the following sentences to help you pinpoint your interests and find the job of your dreams.

In my free time I enjoy

_____

In my free time I enjoy going

_____

My hobbies are

_____

Activities I enjoy include

_____

When I volunteer the types of projects I do are

_____

When I was younger I always dreamed of being a

_____

My skills are

_____

My talents are

_____

My best personality traits include

_____

My current job is

_____

Prior types of jobs have been

_____

The subjects I liked best in school were

_____

If I didn't have to worry about any obstacles, the three jobs I would want would be

_____

What steps can I take to get one of those jobs?

_____

Tip from the Coach

Start training yourself to practice finding ways to turn "can'ts" in your life into "cans."

---

can't get a job as a CPA without the required education, educational requirements may be negotiable in many cases.

Just because an ad states that a job has a specific educational requirement doesn't mean you should just pass it by if your education doesn't meet that requirement. First of all, advertisements for jobs generally contain the highest hopes of the people placing the ads, not necessarily the reality of what they will settle for. Secondly, many companies will accept experience in lieu of education. Lastly, if you're a good candidate in other respects, many companies will hire you while you're finishing the required education.

Is a lack of experience stopping you from entering your dream career? If you can't get experience in the workplace, volunteer. See if you can find an internship. Experience is transferable.

Do you need experience performing? If your dream is a career as an actor, singer, comedian, dancer, musician, or any other performing artist, keep in mind that experience is almost always necessary. While there are exceptions of overnight sensations, generally most people who make it have performed every chance they get.

To get experience take every opportunity that presents itself. Offer to provide the entertainment for local not-for-profit events. Propose singing the national anthem at a local sporting event. Get involved in community theater.

Go to a local club or restaurant and suggest they put together an amateur night. Go to your neighborhood florist or gift shop and see if they might be interested in offering singing telegrams with you as the singer.

Depending on where you live, you might need to get creative. Most importantly, if you want to work in the talent end of the performing arts, don't ever let a chance to perform pass you by. You can never tell who might be in the audience.

Is one of the obstacles you're facing that you aren't in the geographic location for the opportunities you want? Do you, for example, aspire to a career on Broadway, yet you live in Cincinnati? Instead of just giving up, look for a solution. If you're not prepared to move, start your career working in some capacity with a theater where you live.

There's no question that living in an area that doesn't have the opportunities you're looking for makes your job more difficult. If this obstacle is what is holding you back, put some time into developing a solution and find a way to move forward.

Is what's holding you back that you don't know anyone in the industry? Is it that you don't have any contacts? Find ways to make contacts. Take classes, seminars, and workshops in subject areas related to the performing arts. Volunteer. Make cold calls. Attend events and network. Put yourself in situations where there are people in the industry and sooner or later you will meet them.

What else is standing between you and success?

"The only thing between me and success," you say, "is a big break." Getting your big break may take time. Keep plugging away. Don't give up. Your break will come when you least expect it.

Are you just scared about going after what you want? Are you not sure you have the talent? If you start doubting yourself, other people might do the same. Don't let fear stop you.

Whatever you do, don't let anyone burst your bubble. What does that mean? You know how it is when you get so excited about doing something that you just can't keep it to yourself? So you share your ideas of what you want to do with your family and friends. If they start trying to destroy your dream by pointing out all the problems you might encounter, don't let them undermine you. It's not that they're trying to be unsupportive, but for some people it seems to be their nature to try to shoot down other people's dreams. Why? There are a number of reasons. Let's look at a few scenarios.

Scenario 1—Sometimes people are just negative. "You'll never make it," they tell you. "Do you know how many people want to work in theater?"

"Well," you say, "I'm talented."

"There are a lot of talented people who never make it," they say. "Why don't you just act in community theater until you get it out of your system. Be smart. Get a real job."

Scenario 2—Sometimes people are jealous. They might hate their job and be jealous that you are working toward finding a great career. Others might be trying to make it in some segment of the performing arts and be jealous that you have a plan or worry you might make it before them.

Scenario 3—Sometimes people are scared of change. In many cases friends or family are concerned about your well-being and are just scared of change. "You have a job working in a bank," your girlfriend may say. "Why don't you stay there so you know you'll have a solid income? You don't want to lose that by going on auditions which will never pan out."

Scenario 4—Sometimes people just think you're pipe dreaming. "You're a pipe dreamer," your family may say. "What you need is a dose of reality. Just because you got one paying role does

> ### Tip from the Coach
> Everything good in life including your career starts with a dream. Go after yours!

not mean that you're going to make it big. There are thousands of people who want to work in the theater. You're just one in a million. The odds are not good."

Scenario 5—Sometimes people really think that you can't make a living doing something you love. "Nobody likes their job," your family may say. "It's just something you have to do."

Scenario 6—Sometimes people are under the impression that you can't make it if you don't have any connections. "You don't know anyone in the business," your friend says. "Don't be an idiot. You can't make it if you don't know anyone. You need connections."

Whatever the scenario, you may start to question yourself. Well, stop! No matter what anyone says, at least *you* are trying to get the career you want. At least *you* are following your dream.

I can't promise you that you will definitely achieve every one of your dreams, but I can promise you that if you don't go after your dream, it will be very difficult to achieve. So don't listen to anyone and keep working toward what you want.

What Gives You Joy? What Makes You Happy?

Let's zero in further on what you want to do. Let's talk about what gives you joy. What makes you happy? Have you ever noticed that when you're doing something that you love, you smile? It's probably subconscious, but you're smiling. You're happy inside. And it's not only that you're happy, you make others around you happy.

So let's think about it. What makes you happy? What gives you joy? Is it acting? Is it singing? Is it playing an instrument? Is it dancing? Is it writing a song? Is it writing a play? It is a combination of things?

Does the thought of seeing a review you wrote in the newspaper make you smile? When you close your eyes, can you see yourself planning a press conference for one of your new theatrical clients? Can you almost hear the song you wrote being played on the radio? Can you see yourself getting a standing ovation opening night at a Broadway play? Are you smiling as you think about seeing your name in a positive review after opening night? Then maybe that's what would make you happy.

Keep dreaming. Keep asking yourself what makes you happy and gives you joy. Are you having a hard time figuring it out? Many of us do. Here's an idea to help get your juices flowing.

Take out a pad and pen again. Make a list of any jobs or volunteer activities you've done, things you do in your "off time," and hobbies. If you're still in school, you might add extracurricular activities in which you've participated.

Note what aspects of each you like and what you don't like. This will help you see what type of job you're going to enjoy.

What are your special talents, skills, and personality traits? Have you performed in every theatrical production in your community since you were a young child? Is your special talent acting?

Have you been part of your church choir? Is your special talent singing? Are you always volunteering to do the publicity for a charity? You might really love doing the publicity for a symphony or theatrical production. You might

also really enjoy a career as a publicist for a record label or performing artist.

Do you thrive on the excitement of putting together events? You might love a job as a special events coordinator at a nightclub, concert hall, or coordinating opening night galas and special events for a ballet, symphony, or opera company.

I got a call about a year ago from someone who had heard an interview I did on radio. "I was driving the other morning and caught the end of your interview," the woman said. "I always wanted to work in the performing arts, but I just don't have any talent. Any ideas?"

"Everyone has talent," I said. "Sometimes it just isn't in the performing area. What do you do now? What kind of job do you have?"

"Nothing that is the least related to the performing arts," she said. "I work for a not-for-profit hospital in the fund-raising and development office. Not very exciting."

"Do you have any hobbies?" I questioned. "Do you do any volunteer work?"

"I volunteer raising funds for our local animal shelter," she said. "And of course I go to the symphony and theater."

"Do you like fund-raising?" I asked. "You do it in your job at the hospital and volunteer work."

"Yes," she said. "I love the challenges involved and I'm good at it."

"Did you ever consider a job in the development office of a symphony or ballet," I asked. "They often look for talented fund-raisers."

"I thought that was a volunteer job," she said. "I didn't know people got paid for that."

"You live in an area where you're close to a large number of orchestras and ballet companies," I said. Do you know anyone in the administration or the boards of any of the companies?"

"I do," she said. "One of the hospital board members is also on the board at the symphony. He was just at one of our events."

"Why don't you call him and see if there are any opportunities to volunteer in fund-raising?" I suggested. "Tell him it's something you always wanted to do. That way you're not putting your job in jeopardy. Instead what you're doing is planting a seed. He already knows what a good job you do at the hospital. If an opening happens to present itself in the orchestra, he'll think of you. You can also check out some of the other orchestras if you don't mind traveling a bit."

"I doubt that anyone would give up a job there," she said, "but even volunteering would be great."

About six months later the woman called back. "Do you remember me?" she asked. "I was the one who wanted to work in the performing arts, but had no talent and you told me I did. Well, I did what you told me. I called the board member from the hospital who was also on the symphony's board of directors. He told me that the director of development would call me, but he never did and I felt funny about calling back. But guess what happened? Someone from one of the larger symphonies called me and told me they were looking for a director of development and asked me to interview, and I did and I got the job. I start next month. I had to give notice at the hospital and I need to find an apartment and get settled."

"That's great," I said. "How did they hear about you?"

"That's what was so neat," she said. "It was the board member from the hospital. He must have been at a meeting or function or something and ran into someone from the other orchestra who was looking for a director of development and he mentioned my name. I'm so happy. I can't wait to start my job."

"Congratulations," I said. "Thanks for letting me know. Keep me posted on your career."

What Are Your Talents?

It's important to define what your talents are. Sometimes we're so good at something that we just don't even think twice about it. The problem with this is that often we don't see the value in our talent. What does this mean? It means that we may overlook the possibilities associated with our own talents.

It is also important to know that you can have more than one talent. Just because you can sing, doesn't mean you aren't also a talented writer. Just because you can play an instrument doesn't mean you couldn't be a talented publicist. Most of us have more than one talent. The trick is making sure you know what *your* talents are and using them to your advantage.

Can you identify your talents? Do you know what they are? Sit down and start writing. Write down everything that you're good at. Write down all your talents—not just the ones you think are related to the performing arts industry.

This is not the time to be modest. Remember, this list is for you, so be honest with yourself.

Whatever your talents, there is usually a way you can use them to help your career.

Getting What You Want

You hear opportunity knocking. How do you get what you want? How do you turn your dream into reality? One of the most important things you need to do is have faith in yourself and your dream. It is essential that you believe that you can make it happen in order for it to happen.

As we've discussed, you need to focus on exactly what you really want. Otherwise you'll be going in a million different directions. Remember that things may not always come as quickly as you want. As we've mentioned previously, no matter how it appears, most people in the performing arts are not overnight successes.

You, like others in the industry, will probably have to "pay your dues." What does that mean? On the most basic level it means you probably have to start small to get to the big time. Before you get to ride in the limo, you're going to have to drive a lot of Chevys. (There's nothing wrong with a Chevy; it's just not the same as having a chauffeured limo.)

It might mean acting in community theaters, dinner theaters, and regional theaters before you work on Broadway. It might mean having to dance on a lot of smaller stages before you get to the American Ballet Theatre. It might mean singing the national anthem at a local sports event before you're invited to sing it at the Super Bowl.

Paying your dues means you may have to pound on a lot of doors before the right one opens. On the business end of the industry, you may have to take jobs that are not your perfect choice to get experience so you can move up the career ladder and get the job of your dreams. You may have to do a lot of the grunt work and stay in the background while others get the credit. While all this is going on, you have to be patient with the knowledge that everything you do is getting you closer to your goal.

If you look at every experience as a stepping-stone to get you to the next level of your career, it's a lot easier to get through the trying things you may have to go through.

Want to hear another story? Let me share how I finally got into the entertainment industry. Perhaps my experience will help you in your quest for success.

I wanted to be in the music business for as long as I can remember. I thought I knew what I wanted to do. My dream job was to be a road or tour manager. It wasn't the most glamorous job, but that's what I thought I wanted to do. I mentioned earlier how at that time no one wanted a woman as a road manager with a male acts. Did that stop me? Not at all.

After dealing with disappointment after disappointment, interview upon interview, letter upon letter, and countless unreturned phone calls, I decided my traditional job search just wasn't working quickly enough. I was sure that I wasn't going to let the lack of a job offer stop me from working in the industry I wanted to be in. I decided to look "outside of the box."

I tried a number of things. I looked at my talents, I looked at my skills, and then I tried to find a way to use them. I knew I was a good writer. I had been a part-time reporter/photographer for my local biweekly newspaper during summer vacations and stayed on part time after I had graduated from college. I knew how to do public relations and publicity. My parents had their own public relations and marketing firm. I had literally grown up with press releases.

I knew I wanted to be a road manager, maybe even a tour manager, because I wanted to be on the road with music acts. Yet, I already had experienced that management often didn't feel comfortable having a woman on the road with their male acts. I also knew that no matter how many record labels, agents, or management companies I talked to, right or wrong, I might have the same problem with all of them.

What could I do? I had landed interviews, yet no one had hired me. I had made contacts, yet I still couldn't get a job.

I had a lightbulb moment. I knew what I had to do. I don't know why I hadn't thought of it before. I actually did know one person who would hire me, a person who thought I would be great at whatever I did. And not only did I know this person, I knew her very well. Guess what? It was me!

I decided to start my own business, a music industry public relations and publicity firm, and hired myself. My specialty would be "on the road" publicity. For some reason, no one seemed to mind my presence on the road if I was getting the act media exposure. As a matter of fact, they were happy I was there to make sure everything went well.

"Well, anyone can do that," you say.

Technically you're right. Anyone can start their own business. Sometimes it's the right move and sometimes it's not. For me it was right. For you it may or may not be the correct path. The idea wasn't without problems. The challenge once you start a business is getting clients to utilize your services. I wasn't sure exactly where I was going to get clients, but I knew I would find a way to get them.

One of the main things I had going for me was the faith I had in myself that I *would* do it.

No matter what obstacle anyone put in my way, I knew I could find a way around it. I also knew I wasn't going to quit until I got what I wanted. Could I have failed? Absolutely not. Once I made a commitment to myself, failure was not an option.

To make a very long story short, I hustled to get my first clients and I was on my way to living my dream career.

"Well," you might be saying, "that's you. You were lucky."

Yes, I was lucky, but it was luck put together with focus, a lot of hard work, a huge commitment, and knowing I wasn't giving up no matter what. Just so you know, I am no different from you. That means if I can do it, you can do it too. If I could find a way, you can find a way. Whether your dream is to work on the business end or the talent end of the performing arts, if you focus on just what you want, use your talents, and don't give up, the dream can be yours.

Setting Goals

Throughout this process, it's essential to set goals. If you don't have goals, it's hard to know where you're going. If you don't know where you're going, it's very difficult to get there. You might want to look at goals as the place you arrive at the end of a trip. Actions are trips you take to get to your destinations. Your action plan is your roadmap.

What's the best way to set goals? To start with, be as specific as you can. Instead of your goal being, "I want to be an actor," your goal might be, "I want to work on Broadway as a featured actor in a musical." Instead of your goal being, "I want to be a comedienne," your goal might be, "I want to be a successful comedienne playing to sell-out crowds in cities throughout the country and appearing regularly on all the popular late-night shows."

Instead of your goal being "I want to work at a symphony," it might be "I want to be the director of development at a major symphony." Instead of your goal being "I want to be a singer," your goal might be, "I want to be a singer creating a steady stream of hot number-one CDs." Instead of "I want to make a million dollars," your goal might be, "I want to make millions of dollars by writing and producing a series of award-winning Broadway plays."

Notice that the specific goals have actions attached to them. For example, in the goal, "I want to work on Broadway as a featured actor in a musical," the action would be working on Broadway as a featured actor.

Make sure your goals are clear and concise. You'll find it easier to focus in on your goals if you write them down. Writing down your goals will help you see them more clearly. It also gives them power, and power is what can make it happen.

So take out your pad or notebook and get started. As you think of new ideas and goals, jot them down. Some people find it easier to work toward one main goal. Others find it easier to develop a series of goals leading up to their main goal.

To help you do this exercise, first develop a number of long-term goals. Where do you think you want to be in your career in the next year?

Tip from the Top

Successful people continue setting goals throughout their career. That ensures their career doesn't become stagnant and they always feel passion for what they do.

Tip from the Coach

Goals are not written in stone. Just because you have something written down does not mean you can't change it. As you change, your goals might change as well. This is normal.

How about the next two years, three years, five years, and even 10 years?

Once you've zeroed in on your long-term goals, you can develop short-term goals. Feel free to add details. Don't concern yourself with situations changing. You can always adjust your goals.

When focusing on your goals, remember that there are general work-related goals and specific work-related goals.

- General goal: I want to get a promotion.
  - *Specific goal*: I want to be promoted to the director of the department by the end of the year.
- General goal: I want to work in theater.
  - *Specific goal*: I want to work in a musical on Broadway.
- General goal: I want to be an entertainer.
  - *Specific goal*: I want to be a major touring recording artist with songs on the charts.
- General goal: I want to be a playwright.
  - *Specific goal*: I want a career as a playwright. When I am being interviewed on television and radio or in print radio, I want the title *playwright* under my name. I want my plays to be performed first on Broadway and then tour throughout

the country and maybe the world. I want to win a Tony for best play.

Whether you're interested in a career on the business or talent side of the performing arts, you can use your goals as a road map to help you realize your dreams.

Visualization Can Help Make It Happen

Visualization is a powerful tool for success in all aspects of your career and your life. What is it? Visualization is "seeing" or "visualizing" a situation the way you want it. It's setting up a picture in your mind of the way you would like a situation to unfold.

How do you do it? Simple. Close your eyes and visualize what you want. Visualize the situation that you desire. Think about each step you need to take to get where you want to go in your career and then see the end result in your mind. Want to see how it's done?

Want to be an actor? A rock star? How about a prima ballerina? Perhaps you want to be the next Pavarotti? Visualization can help you get there! How so?

Visualize driving up to the theater in a limo—a long, black stretch limo. On the way there, you see billboards advertising the show you're in. You see the word *starring*, and below it is your name. Then you look up at the theater marquee. Do you see your name there as well? Wow!

As the limo driver opens the car door to let you out, fans are waiting outside trying to get a glimpse of you. They're calling your name. You stop to sign some autographs and go inside the theater.

Now visualize yourself getting ready in your dressing room. The hairstylist, the makeup artist, and your star dresser are there. You hear the words, "Five minutes!" and you know that it's show time.

Visualize yourself as you would like others to see you on stage. The spotlights are on you. Can you feel the energy in the air? Your heart is pounding in a good way. You're in front of an audience now—you're on stage! What a feeling.

Look out into the audience. Browse up to the mezzanine. You open your mouth and your lines just flow. Things are going well. You're bringing your character to life. The next thing you know it's intermission. With intermission over, you start your next scene. Before you know it, the show is over.

As the other actors are taking bows, you hear applause. It's your turn to go out. As you step onto the stage and take your bow, the applause gets louder, becoming almost thunderous. People are cheering. You are getting a standing ovation. What a great night. And it's only one of many. You're a Broadway star! Got the picture? That's visualization!

No matter what you want to do, you can visualize it to help make it happen. Visualize your career working as a set designer, a costume designer, or a prop person. Visualize yourself getting a job in the administrative end of a symphony. See yourself going for the interview, getting the job, and then sitting at your desk. Visualize speaking to coworkers, going to meetings, and doing your work.

The more details you can put into your visualization, the better. Add in the colors of things around you; the fragrance of the flowers on your desk; the aroma of the coffee in your mug; the color of the suit you're wearing; even the bright blue sky outside. Details will help bring your visualization to life.

Whatever your dreams, concentrate on them, think about them, and then visualize them. Here's the great news. If you can visualize

---

The Inside Scoop

Visualization works for more than your career. Use it to help make all your dreams come true in all facets of your life.

---

it, you can make it happen! No one really knows why, but it does seem to work and it works well. Perhaps it's positive energy. Perhaps you're just concentrating more on what you want.

One of the tricks in visualizing to get what you want is actually visualizing all the actions you need to take to achieve your goal. If you don't know what these actions are or should be, an easy exercise that might help you is reverse visualization. In essence, you're going to play the scenes in reverse.

Start by visualizing at the point in your life where you want to be and then go back to the point where you are currently. If your dream is to be a Broadway actor or actress, that's where you're going to start. If you are currently working in community theater, that's where you're going to end up.

There are other ways of visualizing as well. Let's say you want a career as the director of audience development for an orchestra. Think about where you'd like to work. Add your office environment, the office décor. Now add your coworkers. Next put yourself in the picture. Remember to visualize what you're wearing, your accessories, even the color of your suit.

Visualize yourself speaking to colleagues, supervisors, and the board of directors. Feel the excitement of the day. Now go backwards. Visualize yourself driving to work the first day. Keep visualizing. Now you're thinking about getting dressed that morning. Keep going. Remember hearing the alarm buzzing and how you just couldn't wait to get up to go to work.

Keep visualizing in reverse. Hear your cell phone ringing and remember the feeling you had when the voice at the other end told you that you got the job. Go back and visualize the feeling that you had waiting for that call. Visualize the thank-you note you wrote to the human resources director. See the letter in your mind. Now remember leaving the interview. Visualize in detail what you wore, what the experience was like, the questions that you were asked, and the feelings you had at that moment. Remember how much you hoped you would be hired.

Visualize filling out the application and developing and sending in your resume with your perfectly tailored cover letter. Now visualize seeing the job advertised and the excited feeling you had.

Recall all the preparation you did to find that job; the skills you updated, the people you spoke to, the networking. Visualize the internship you went through.

You are now back at the position in the visualization process where you currently are in your career. You have an idea of the steps needed to get where you want to go. This might not be the exact way your situation develops, but it can get you started in the visualization process.

Paint a picture in your mind of what you want to achieve detail by detail. Whether you're using a reverse visualization or a traditional visualization technique, this powerful tool can help you get what you want. Give it a try. You'll be glad you did.

Tip from the Coach

Make a commitment to your dream and stick to it. Without this commitment, your dream will turn into a bubble that will fly away and burst in mid-air.

3

PLAN FOR SUCCESS IN THEATER AND THE PERFORMING ARTS

Take Control and Be Your Own Career Manager

If you want more control over success in your career, a key strategy is becoming your own career manager. What does this mean? It means that you won't be leaving your career to chance. You will be in the driver's seat! *You* will have control and *you* can make your dream career happen!

No one cares about your career as much as you do. Not your mother, your father, your sister, or your brother. Not your best friend, girlfriend, boyfriend, or spouse. Not even people associated with your business. It's not that these people don't care at all. They probably all want you to be successful, but no one really cares as much as you do.

Will it take a lot of work? Yes, being your own career manager can be a job in itself. The payoff, however, will be worth it.

If you look at many successful people in the performing arts, you will notice that most have a tremendous dedication to their career. Of course, they have managers, agents, attorneys, financial professionals, and others who advise

them, but when it comes to the final decision making, they are the ones who take the ultimate responsibility for their career.

Now that you've decided to be your own career manager, you have some work to do. Next on the list is putting together an action plan. Let's get started!

What Is an Action Plan?

Let's look at success a little closer. What's the one thing successful people, successful businesses, and successful events all have in common? While money, luck, and talent all are cer-

---

⭐ **The Inside Scoop**

No matter how dedicated your agent is, he or she can't do everything. At a recent seminar I gave, a man asked what he could do to move his acting career to the next level.

"I have an agent," he said, "and while he gets me some auditions and jobs, certainly not enough for my taste. I appreciate any acting job, but I really want to be auditioning for better parts. He's my agent. He should be working harder for me. What can I do?"

"Good question," I said. "What are you doing to help your career?"

"I told you. I signed with an agent. He's supposed to be helping my career...isn't he?" the man asked.

"Yes, your agent is supposed to help your career, but keep in mind that you are probably not your agent's only client. He is most likely working with a number of actors and actresses. While I'm sure your career is important to him, I can pretty much guarantee you that it's not as important to him as it is to you.

"Just because you have an agent doesn't mean that you shouldn't look for opportunities. It doesn't mean you shouldn't send out cards with your headshot. It doesn't mean you should just sit back and let someone else determine where your career goes. You have to take control of your career. The more you put into it, the more you'll get out of it."

"But let's say I hear someone is casting for a Broadway show," the man said. "And I get the audition on my own and then get a role in a Broadway show, I still have to give him a commission. I don't want to give him a commission when I got the role myself."

The rest of the audience started laughing.

"Okay," I said. "The good news is according to your scenario, you're on Broadway. That's where you want to be isn't it?"

"It's where I want to be, but I don't want to be paying a commission to an agent who didn't have anything to do with me getting there," he said.

"First of all, going back to your scenario, I'm sure some of the jobs he got you probably helped you get your role on Broadway," I told him. "Second of all, look at it like this. Would you rather pay your agent a commission and stay at the career level you're at now, getting roles in dinner theater or regional theater and maybe every now and then doing a role in an off-off-Broadway show or would you prefer to be starring on Broadway, but paying your agent because you heard about the audition first?"

"I get it," he said. "I just never thought of it like that."

"The important thing to remember," I told him, "is that you need to be in charge of your career."

---

tainly part of the mix, generally the common thread most share is a well-developed plan for success. Whatever your goal, be it short range or long range, if you have a plan to achieve it, you have a better chance of succeeding. With that in mind, let's discuss how you can create your own plan for success.

What exactly is an action plan? In a nutshell, an action plan is a written plan detailing all the actions you need to and want to take to successfully accomplish your ultimate goal: success in your chosen career.

How an Action Plan Can Help You Succeed

Success is never easy, but you can stack the deck in your favor by creating your own personal action plan. There are many different things you might want to accomplish to succeed in your career. If you go about them in a haphazard manner, your efforts might not be as effective as they could be. An action plan helps define the direction to go and the steps needed to get the job done. It helps increase your efficiency in your quest for success.

Sometimes seeing a plan in writing helps you see a major shortcoming, or simply makes you notice something minor that may be missing. At that point, you can add the actions you need to take and the situation will be easily rectified.

With an action plan, you know exactly what you're going to be doing to reach your goals. It helps you focus so that everything you need to do is more organized.

Many of us have had the experience of looking in a closet where everything is jumbled up. If you need a jacket or a pair of pants from the closet, you can probably find them, but it may be frustrating and take you a long time. On the other hand, if you organize your closet, you can reach for that jacket or pair of pants and find them in a second with no problem.

One of the main reasons you develop a plan is to have something organized to follow, and when you have something to follow, things are easier to accomplish and far less frustrating. In essence, what you're creating with your action plan is a method of finding and succeeding in your dream career, whether it be in the talent area, one of the creative areas, business area, or

---

Tip from the Coach

When you break large projects up into smaller tasks, they seem more manageable. It's kind of like spring-cleaning. If you look at cleaning the whole house at one time, it can seem impossible. But if you break the job up into cleaning one or two rooms at a time, it seems easier to accomplish. When you look at the ultimate task of finding the perfect career and then becoming successful, it too can seem like a huge undertaking. Breaking up the tasks you need to accomplish will help you reach your goal.

---

somewhere in between. When you put that plan into writing, you're going to have something to follow and something to refer to, making it easier to track your progress.

For the most part, your action plan is going to be composed of a lot of the little, detailed steps you're going to have to accomplish to obtain your goal. Some people make very specific and lengthy action plans. Others develop general ones. You might create a separate action plan for each job you pursue, a plan for your next goal, or even a plan that details everything you're going to need to do from the point where you find yourself now up to the career of your dreams. As long as you have some type of plan to follow, the choice is yours.

Your Personal Action Plan for Success in Theater and the Performing Arts

So you've decided to be your own career manager. It's now up to *you* to develop your personal action plan or plans for success in theater or one

---

Voice of Experience

Once you get the knack of creating action plans, you can use them for everything in your life, not just your career. You'll find everything goes more smoothly with a plan in place.

of the other performing arts. Are you ready to get started?

A great deal of your action plan will depend on what area of the industry you're interested in and exactly what you want to do.

Take a notebook and pen, sit down, and start thinking about your career and the direction you want it to go. Start by doing some research. What do you want to find out? Almost any information can be useful in your career. Let's look at some of the things that might help you.

Your Market

One of the first things to research is your market. What does that mean? Basically it means that you need to determine what jobs or employment situations you are interested in and where they are located. Who and where will your potential employers or clients be?

For example, if you're seeking a career as an actor in theater, you want to know where you can find jobs. While you probably want your stage to be Broadway, it's not the only place to act. If you do some research you'll find opportunities in a variety of other situations in New York City as well as in locations throughout the country. You might find employment in dinner theaters, regional theaters, resident theaters, and stock to name a few. You might find acting jobs in theatrical productions in theme parks, on cruise ships, in touring companies, children's theater, corporate theater, or an array of other situations in almost every geographical area.

If you want to be a songwriter or composer you probably should look into how to develop interest in your songs and compositions. What labels might need songs in the style you write? Which publishers or artists might be possibilities? What theatrical producers might be looking

for new material? What about television shows, films, or commercials? Would any of them be possibilities? The more information you can mine, the better your chances of success.

Let's say your dream is to work in the creative end of theater doing something like costume design, scenic design, lighting, or sound design. Explore the various possibilities. Your research will probably show you that while your first choice might be Broadway, there is an array of other options to earn a living while executing your craft.

Is your dream to have a career on the talent end of a symphony, opera, or ballet company? Or is it working in performing arts administration of one of those companies? While you might determine that the greatest number of major orchestras, operas, and ballet companies are located in large, culturally active cities, through research you may also discover that there are midsized and smaller symphony, opera, ballet, and not-for-profit theater companies that may offer opportunities. These can be especially important if you're just beginning your professional career.

Is the business end of the performing arts where your dream career lies? If so, research potential employers and where they are located. If you're interested in working on your own as an agent, personal manager, or business manager,

---

★ Tip from the Top

While New York City is known as the theatrical capital of the world, it is by no means the only place to find work as an actor. Possibilities exist in almost every culturally active city.

you will also want to research what your best location is to obtain and service clients. While larger areas offer more opportunities, you may find it easier to break into the industry in smaller, less metropolitan areas.

If your dream is to be a singer, dancer, comedienne, magician, or other performing artist, it is equally important for you to explore the various places to perform, who your audiences might be, and how you can bring yourself and/or your act to the attention of the movers and shakers in the entertainment industry.

Why do you have to research your market now? Why do you need this information at all? Because information is power. The more you think about your potential markets now, the more opportunities you may find.

What Do You Need to Do to Get What You Want?

Next, research what you need to do to get the career you want. Do you need additional skills? Training? Education? Experience? Do you need to move to a different location? Make new contacts? Get an internship? Would it help to take some acting classes? How about getting a drama coach? Do you need to take a seminar or two in playwriting? What about attending a songwriting workshop? Do you need to join a union? Do you need to find a way to deal with the anxiety of stage fright? What you need to determine is what is standing in between you and the career you want.

If you are already working in theater or one of the other performing arts in some capacity, you need to determine what is standing in between you and success. How can you climb the ladder of success and perhaps even skip a few rungs?

Spend some time thinking about this. If you can determine exactly what skills, qualifications,

training, education, or experience you're missing or what you need to do, you're halfway there.

It often helps to look at exactly what is standing between you and what you want on paper. Use the form on page 43 to help you clarify each situation and the possible solution.

How Can You Differentiate Yourself?

If you're looking for a career in the performing arts, you are not alone. Thousands of others are seeking stardom. Thousands want to make it as actors, singers, dancers, songwriters, musicians, comedians, magicians, and recording artists.

There are also thousands of people who want to make it as conductors, playwrights, composers, costume designers, lighting designers, sound designers, set designers, producers, and directors.

That doesn't even count all the people who want to make it in the business end of theater and the performing arts—the agents, managers, lawyers, publicists, press agents, literary agents, and more.

I can almost hear you say, "That's a lot of competition. Can I make it? Can I succeed?"

To that I answer a definitive "Yes!" Lots of people succeed in all aspects of theater and the performing arts. Why shouldn't one of them be you?

Here's the challenge: How can you stand out in a positive way? What attributes do you have or what can you do so people choose you over others?

"I don't like to draw attention to myself," you say. "I just kind of like to blend into the crowd."

Well, you're going to have to drop that attitude, especially in this industry. Why? Because the people who get the jobs in both the business and talent areas—the ones who succeed, the ones who make it—are the ones who have found a way to set themselves apart from others.

What Stands Between Me and What I Want?	Possible Solution

How? Perhaps it's your personality or the energy you exude. It might be the way you bring a character to life when you're acting on stage. Maybe it's your sense of humor or the way you organize things. Some people just have a presence about them.

It might be the way you sing or play an instrument. Maybe it's the type of songs you write. You might have a special or unique stage show. A special fashion style. Perhaps you appeal to a unique group of fans or followers.

Maybe it's the costumes you design or the sets for theatrical productions. Maybe you write amazing dialogue in your scripts.

Everyone is special in some way. Everyone has a special something they do or say that makes them stand out in some manner. Most people have more than one thing. Spend some time determining what makes you special in a positive way so that you can use it to your advantage.

How to Get Noticed

Catching the eye of people important to your career is another challenge. There are different ways to market yourself, but at this point you need to take some time to try to figure out how to bring yourself and your accomplishments to others. This is the time to brainstorm.

Tip from the Coach

If you don't know what makes you special, take a cue from what others tell you. Listen to those conversations where someone says something in passing like, "You're so funny, I love being around you," or "You always know just what to say to make me feel better," or "You have such a beautiful voice. I love listening to you sing," or "You always are so helpful." Listen to what people say and always take compliments graciously.

The Inside Scoop

Successful people usually have something special about them; something that sets them apart from others. In the late 1970s, rocker Gene Simmons and his group Kiss donned costumes, full makeup, and masks, and made their musical stage show resemble a theatrical performance. While they received accolades for their music, 30 years later, most people remembered them for what set them apart: their costumes, makeup, masks, and stage show.

For example, let's say you're an aspiring actor. How can you bring your talent to the attention of those people who can make a difference to your career? Instead of waiting for performing opportunities to present themselves, actively seek them out. When you find these opportunities and are taking advantage of them, make sure you send out notices to people in the industry. At the very least, you can then put your name in front of them in a positive manner. At best, they might come see you and check out your talent firsthand.

You're going to need to actively market yourself. An effective way for actors to get noticed by agents and casting directors is to make up postcards with your headshot and a brief description of your acting qualifications. Send these out to casting directors and agents as well. And don't just send them out once. Send them out on a regular basis.

Taking part in telethons, not-for-profit charity events, and similar functions also helps get you noticed and may bring you some extra publicity too.

What if you're an aspiring singer? What else can you do to get noticed? See what talent competitions are available locally or nationally. What about television opportunities? How about putting together a showcase?

Perhaps you could put together a demo tape and video. What about appearing in a talent show? Maybe you'll volunteer to be the talent for a fund-raiser. What about finding a way to get on the news? How about sending a brochure with a CD and video to agents? Just keep coming up with ideas and writing them down as you go. You can fine-tune them later.

Are you an aspiring playwright? Offer to give a class in playwriting to a local school. Don't forget to call the media! Get together with a group of actors and offer to put on short vignettes (which of course you write) during lunchtime in your local government office lobby. Don't forget to call the media! Have you won any awards? Honors and awards always set you apart from others and help you to get noticed.

Think about these questions. Can you come up with more? Once you determine the answers, it's easier to move on to the next step of writing your plan.

What Should Your Basic Action Plan Include?

Now that you've done some research and brainstormed some great ideas, you're on your way. Here's what your basic action plan should include.

Career Goals

One of the most important parts of your action plan will be defining your career goals. Are you just starting your career? Are you looking for a new job or career? Are you already in the business and want to climb the career ladder? Are you interested in exploring a different career in theater or the performing arts from the one

you're in now? The sky is the limit if you know what your goals are.

When defining your goals try to make them as specific as possible. For example, instead of writing in your action plan that your goal is to be an actor, refine your goal to be an award-winning Broadway actor. Instead of writing that your goal is to be a singer, refine your goal to be a major recording and performance artist. Instead of defining your goal as to be a publicist, you might define it as being a theatrical press agent for a Broadway play or whatever *your* career goal or aspiration might be.

It's important to include your short-range goals as well as your long-range ones. You might even want to include mid-range plans. That way you'll be able to track your progress, which gives you great inspiration to slowly but surely meet your goals. For example, if you're interested in pursuing a career on the business end of an orchestra, you might set your long-range goal to be the executive director of a major orchestra. Your short-range goals might be first to get an internship at an orchestra and then secure a position in the development office. Your mid-range goals might then be to land a position first as the assistant director of development and then as a director in a midsized orchestra.

Keep in mind that goals are not written in stone and it's okay to be flexible and change them along the way. The idea is that no matter what you want, moving forward is the best way to get somewhere.

What You Need to Reach Your Goals

The next step is to put in writing exactly what you need to reach your goals. Do you need training or more education? Do you need to learn new skills or brush up on old ones? Do you need to move to a different geographic location? Do you need to network more? Do you need to make more contacts?

Your Actions

This is the crux of your action plan. What actions do you need to attain your goals?

- Do you need to take some classes or attend some industry-related workshops?
  - Your actions would be to identify, locate, and take classes and workshops.
- Do you need to find seminars and attend them?
  - Your actions would be to investigate potential seminars to see if they will assist in accomplishing your goals, and if so, attend them.
- Do you need to go to college, get a bachelor's degree, or even a law degree?
  - Your actions would be to go to college and get a degree.
- Do you need to learn how to play your instrument better?
  - Your action would be to take music lessons.
- Do you need to find more ways to network or just network more?
  - Your actions would be to develop opportunities and activities to network and follow through with those activities and opportunities.

Your Timetable

Your timetable is essential to your action plan. In this section you're going to include what you're going to do (your actions) and when you're going to do them. The idea is to make sure you have a deadline for getting things done so your actions don't fall through the cracks. Just saying

---

> ### Tip from the Coach
> Try to be realistic when setting your timetable. Unrealistic time requirements often set the groundwork for making you feel like you failed.

"I have to do this" or "I have to do that" isn't effective.

Designing Your Action Plan

Remember there is no right or wrong way to assemble your action plan. It's what you are comfortable with. You might want yours to look different in some manner from the examples that follow, have different items, or even have things in a different order. That's okay. The whole purpose of action plans is to help you achieve your career goals. Choose the one that works for you.

Let's look at some examples of how you can write your action plan. After reviewing these samples, fill in one of the worksheets to create your own personal action plan. Feel free to change the chart or add in sections to better suit your needs.

> ### The Inside Scoop
> Don't start panicking when you think you are never going to reach your career goals. Just because you estimate that you want to reach your long-range goals within the next five or seven years or whatever you choose, does not mean that you can't get there faster. Your timetable is really just an estimate of the time you want to reach a specific goal.

Example 1

My Basic Action Plan

Career Goals

Long-range goals:
Mid-range goals:
Short-range goals:

My market:

What do I need to reach my goals?

How can I differentiate myself from others?

How can I catch the eye of people important to my career?

What actions can I take to reach my goals?

What actions do I absolutely need to take now?

What's my timetable?
   Short-range goals:
   Mid-range goals:
   Long-range goals:

Actions I've taken: Date completed:

My Personal Action Plan

CAREER GOALS (Long-range):

CAREER GOALS (Short-range):

ACTION TO BE TAKEN	COMMENTS	TIMETABLE/ DEADLINE	DATE ACCOMPLISHED
SHORT RANGE			
LONG RANGE			

Using Action Plans for Specific Jobs

Action plans can be useful in a number of ways. In addition to developing a plan for your career, you might utilize action plans to look for specific jobs. Let's look at an example for someone hoping to succeed as a booking agent.

Use the blank plan provided to keep track of your actions when you find specific jobs you're interested in.

Action Plan Looking for Specific Job

Job title: Booking Agent Trainee

Job description: Make phone calls, learn how to negotiate fees; learn how to write contracts; make sure contracts are signed; look for new business; take phone calls from potential clients.

Company name: Best Talent USA

Contact name: Jeff Post

Secondary contact name: Anita Dobson

Company address: 1214 West 111 St., Some City, NY 11111

Company phone number: (212) 111-1111

Company fax number: (212) 222-2222

Company Web site address: No Web site

Company e-mail: besttalentusa@besttalent.com

Secondary e-mail:

Where I heard about job: Read ad in *Billboard* 3/3

(continues)

Action Plan Looking for Specific Job, continued

Actions taken: Tailored resume and cover letter to job; spoke to references to tell them I was applying for job and make sure I could still use them as references; faxed resume and cover letter.

Actions needed to follow up: Make sure suit and other clothing needed for interview is clean and pressed; review portfolio; make extra copies of my resume; read *Billboard* and other trade information to keep up to date on trends; do research on company to see who their clients are and find out extra information; call if I don't hear back within a week.

Interview time, date, and location: Received call on 3/10; they want me to come in for interview; interview set for 2:00 p.m. on 3/12 with Jeff Post at agency office.

More actions to follow up on: Get directions to building; pick out clothes for interview; try everything on to make sure it looks good; rehearse giving answers to questions most likely to be asked during interview; noticed that company didn't have a Web site; develop a simple sample Web site to show initiative.

Comments: Went to interview; nice office and very nice people working there; I would like the job; Mr. Post seemed impressed that I had put together a sample Web site; he said most people wouldn't take the time to do something like that before they got a job; he also seemed interested in my portfolio; the only thing that bothered me was that I didn't know the specific computer program they used; he said he was conducting interviews for the next week and would get back to me one way or another in a couple of weeks.

Extra actions: Wrote note thanking Mr. Post for interview.

Results: 3/19—Mr. Post called. I didn't get that job. They gave it to someone who had been an intern at the company. He offered me a different job; he said that they had been talking about a Web site for a while and my sample site motivated them to move on the idea. While they are retaining a company to put together a professional Web site, my job would be to coordinate the information included on the site. I would also be the liaison between the agency and their clients, getting information, working on bios, etc.; he still would want me to learn about booking and if I am interested, could start to do a little of that as well. I'm going to meet with him tomorrow to discuss salary and benefits.

Action Plan for Specific Job

Job title:

Job description:

Company name:

Contact name:

Secondary contact name:

Company address

Company phone number:

Company fax number:

Company Web site address:

Company e-mail:

Secondary e-mail:

Where I heard about job:

Actions taken:

Actions needed to follow up:

Interview time, date, and location:

Comments:

Results:

_____

_____

_____

How to Use Your Action Plan

Creating your dream career takes time, patience, and a lot of work. In order for your action plan to be useful, you need to use it. It's important to set aside some time every day to work on your career. During this time you'll be *taking actions.* The number of actions you take, of course, will depend on your situation. If you are currently employed (or you have a day job as many actors and actresses must often have), you may not be able to tackle as many actions as someone who is unemployed and has more time available every day. Keep in mind that some actions may take longer than others.

For example, preparing for auditions often takes time as well as a lot of creative energy, so on days you are getting ready or auditioning you might not be able to accomplish a lot of other things. Putting together your career portfolio will take longer than making a phone call. So if you're working on your portfolio you might not accomplish more than one action in a day.

Try to make a commitment to yourself to take at least one positive action each day toward getting your dream career or becoming more successful in the one you currently have. Do more if you can. Whatever your situation, just make sure you take *some* action every single day.

Keeping a Daily Action Journal

In addition to creating an action plan, you'll find it helpful to keep an action journal recording all the career-related activities and actions you take on a daily basis. Use the journal to write down all the things that you do on a daily basis help you attain your career goals. You then have a record of all the actions you have taken in one place. Like your action plan, your action journal can help you track your progress.

The Inside Scoop
Once you start writing in your daily action journal, you'll be even more motivated to fulfill your career goals.

How do you do this? The sample on page 53 will get you started. This person aspires to a career as an actress. (Names and phone numbers are fabricated.)

With your daily action journal, you can look back and see exactly what you've done, whom you've called, whom you've written to, and what the result was. Additionally you have the names, phone numbers, times, dates, and other information at your fingertips. As an added bonus, as you review your daily action journal, instead of feeling like you're not doing enough, you are often motivated to do more. The next step is to discuss your personal career success book.

Your Personal Career Success Book

What's your personal career success book? It's a folder, scrapbook, notebook, binder, or group of notebooks where you keep all your career information. Eventually, you might have so much that you'll need to put everything in a file drawer or cabinet, and that's okay. That means your career is progressing.

While you will find your personal career success book useful no matter what part of theater or the performing arts you're going into, it will be especially valuable to you if you are tracking your success in the talent and creative areas of the industry.

What can go in your personal success career book? You can keep your action plans, your

Daily Action Journal

Monday, March 8

Read daily papers.
Called Marc Tobin, a casting director I saw doing an interview on local news (212-212-2121). Cold call, not in. His secretary Mary said he would be in on Wednesday.
Surfed Internet looking for stories about casting agents in New York City.
Worked on revamping my professional resume.

Tuesday, March 9

Read daily paper and scanned entertainment section.
Read *Backstage*. Looked to see if there were any open casting calls coming up.
Went to get hair styled for new head shots. (Will stop by tomorrow before head shot appointment.)
Checked clothing I'm going to wear tomorrow for head shots.
Called Ed Young, restaurant and club manager from Takigas. Tentative appointment for next week, Monday at 3 p.m. Confirm on Friday. Wants to discuss the possibility of me playing piano and singing for a few weekends (while I'm waiting for my big break in theater).
Worked on career portfolio.

Wednesday, March 10

Stopped at stylist for hair and makeup for head shots.
Went to photographer for appointment for head shots.
Got a call from Bob Smith, the agent I've been working with (212-111-1111). He set up audition on Monday morning at 1190 Broadway, 6th Floor. I have to stop by and pick up script.
Reviewed my resume.

Thursday, March 11

Picked up script.
Took acting class.
Printed out clean copies of my resume.
Checked on clothing to wear for the audition.

daily action journals, and all of the information you have and you need to get your career to the level you want to reach.

What else can go into your personal career success book? Whether you're pursuing a career on the talent or business end of the industry or anywhere in between, you will probably be sending and receiving a lot of correspondence. It's a good idea to keep copies of all the letters you send out as well as the ones you receive from people in the industry. Don't forget copies of e-mail.

My Daily Action Journal

Date:

Date:

Date:

Date:

Date:

Why do you want to keep correspondence? First of all, it gives you a record of people you wrote to and people who wrote to you. You might also find ways to make use of letters people send you. For example, instead of getting a rejection letter, reading it, crumpling it up, and throwing it in the trash, take the name of the person who signed it, wait a period of time, and see if you can pitch another idea, another song, another job possibility, or anything that might further your career or get you closer to where you want to be.

What else can go in your book? Keep copies of advertisements for jobs that you might want or be interested in now and in the future. If you hope to be a performer, keep copies of information on locations you might perform, clubs, lounges, arenas, concert halls, theaters, and so on. Keep lists in this book of your potential support staff: talent agents, casting agents, managers, attorneys, accountants, publicists, and press agents. Have you seen someone's professional photos that you think are great? Find out who did them and note it in your book. Then you have the information when you need it.

Keep copies of playbills and programs in which you were credited as well. If everything is in one place, you won't have to search for things when you need them.

What else? Lists of media possibilities, names, addresses, phone and fax numbers, and e-mail addresses. Let's say you're watching television and see an interesting interview about something in the performing arts. It might be an interview with an actor, producer, or director. At the time you think you're going to remember exactly what you saw, when you saw it, and who the reporter or producer was. Unfortunately, you will probably forget some of the details. You now have a place to jot down the information in a section of your book. When you need it, you'll know where to look.

Don't forget to clip out interesting interviews, articles, and feature stories. Instead of having them floating all over your house, file them in this book. Want to network a bit? Write the reporter a note saying you enjoyed his or her piece and mentioning why you found it so interesting. Everyone likes to be recognized, even people in the media. You can never tell when you might make a contact or even a friend.

It goes without saying that you should also clip and make copies of all articles, stories, and features that appear in the print media about you. Having all this information together will make it easier later to put together your career portfolio.

What else is going into your personal career success book? Copies of letters of recommendation; notes that producers, directors, talent agents and casting agents have sent you; and even fan mail.

As your career progresses, you will have various resumes, background sheets, bios, and head shots. Keep copies of them in your book as well, even after you've replaced them with new ones. What about networking and contact worksheets? They now have a place too.

We've discussed the importance of determining your markets. This is where you can keep these lists. When you find new possibilities, just jot them down in your book. With your personal career success book, everything will be at your fingertips.

When you go to seminars or workshops and get handouts or take notes, you now know where to keep them so you can refer to them when needed. The same goes for conference and convention material. Keep it in your personal career success book.

You'll find success is easier to come by if you're more organized and have everything you need in one place.

If you're now asking yourself, "Isn't there a lot of work involved in obtaining a career you want?" the answer is a definite yes.

Can't you just leave everything to chance and hope to get what you want? You can, but if your ultimate goal is to succeed in the performing arts, you need to do everything possible to give yourself the best opportunity for success.

Get Ready, Get Set, Go: Preparation

Opportunity Is Knocking:
Are You Ready?

At every seminar and workshop I give on getting what you want, no matter what that might be, I ask the audience the same question. "If opportunity knocks, are you ready to open the door and let it in?"

"If opportunity knocks, I'll get ready," someone always says.

Unfortunately, that's not the way it always works. Sometimes you don't have a chance to prepare. Sometimes you need to be prepared at that very moment or you could lose out on an awesome opportunity. Let's look at a couple of scenarios.

First, imagine you are walking along the beach thinking about your career. "I wish I could be on Broadway," you say out loud, even though no one is there. "I wish I could read for a principal role." You continue planning how success might come your way. As you're walking, the surf washes up and you see something shiny. You reach down to see what it is and pick up what appears to be a small brass lamp. All this while you're still planning your career as you're walking. "I wish I had an audition with a big

Broadway casting agent," you say as you absent-mindedly rub the side of the lamp.

You see a puff of smoke and a genie appears. "Thank you for releasing me," he says. "In return for that, I will grant you your three wishes."

Before you have a chance to ask, "What wishes?" you find yourself in a room on Broadway with a script in your hand in front of one of the biggest casting agents in the world. Evidently, the genie had been listening to you talking to yourself and picked up on your three wishes.

Here's the opportunity you've been wishing for! You're on Broadway with a great script in your hand in front of one of the biggest casting agents in the world. Are you ready? Or is this big break going to pass you by because you're not prepared? Not sure? Read on.

Let's look at another scenario. Now imagine you have a fairy godmother, who comes to you one day and says, "I can get you a one-on-one meeting with the managing director of the biggest symphony orchestra in the world. The only catch is you have to be ready to walk in his office door in half an hour." Would you be ready? Would you miss your big break because you weren't prepared? If your answer is,

"Hmm, I might be ready . . . well, not really," then read on.

Want to think about another one? Let's imagine you're trying to make it as a comedian. You are on your way to a weekend vacation in Las Vegas. You sit down in your seat on the plane and a man sits down next to you. You've seen him before—but where? You search your mind and it comes to you. He is the talent buyer from one of the big Las Vegas casinos. You remember seeing a story about him, with a photo, in one of the trades just last week. Can you take advantage of the opportunity sitting right next to you? Can you be funny just in conversation? Do you have your head shot and professional resume with you? If you had to, could you audition right on the spot?

Or would you let the opportunity pass you by because you were only prepared to go on vacation?

Here's the deal on opportunity. It may knock. As a matter of fact it probably will knock, but if you don't open the door, opportunity won't stand there forever. If you don't answer the door, opportunity, even if it's *your* opportunity, will go visit someone else's door.

While you might not believe in genies, fairy godmothers, or even the concept that you might just be at the right place at the right time, you should believe this: In life and your career, you will run into situations where you need to be ready "now" or miss your chance. When opportunity knocks, you need to be ready to open the door and let it in.

The Inside Scoop

For some reason that we never understood, my grandmother always kept a suitcase packed. "Why?" we always asked her. "You can never tell when you have an opportunity to go someplace," she replied. "If you're ready, you can go. If you're not prepared, you might miss an opportunity."

Evidently she was right. Here's her story.

Many years ago my grandmother worked as a sales associate in a women's clothing store in a well-known resort hotel. The hotel always had the top stars of the day in theater, music, film, and television performing nightclub shows on holiday weekends. One weekend, Judy Garland was doing a show at the hotel. According to the story we were told as children, Judy Garland wanted a few things from the clothing store and called the store to see if someone could bring up a few pieces for her to choose from.

The store was busy and the manager assigned my grandmother the job. She quickly chose some items and brought them up to the star's room. Judy was pleased with my grandmother's choices and after talking to her for a short time, was evidently impressed with her demeanor and attitude.

While signing for the purchases, she said to my grandmother, "I need a nanny for my children. I think you would be the right one for the job. I'm leaving tomorrow morning. If you're interested, I need to know now." Without missing a beat, my grandmother took the job and by the next afternoon was on the road with Judy Garland serving as nanny to her children.

While clearly she didn't give two weeks' notice to her sales job, being at the right place at the right time certainly landed her an interesting job she seemed to love. I don't really remember how long she kept the position. What I do know, however, is that when an opportunity presented itself, my grandmother was ready. Had she not been ready or hesitated, no doubt, someone else would have gotten the job. The moral of the story is when opportunity knocks, you have to be ready to open the door.

How can you do that? Make a commitment to get ready now. It's time to prepare. Ready, set, let's go!

Look Out for Opportunities

Being aware of available opportunities is essential to taking advantage of them. While it's always nice when unexpected opportunities present themselves, you sometimes have to go out looking for them as well.

How many times have you turned on the television or radio or opened the newspaper and seen an opportunity you wished you had known about so *you* could have taken advantage of it? Would you rather open the newspaper and read a feature story profiling up-and-coming performing artists or be the performing artist they are profiling? Would you rather see an advertisement for an evening of entertainment showcasing new acts or be the act being showcased?

Would you rather meet the managing director of a large orchestra who is visiting your campus to work on an internship program or hear from your friend that he or she got the job?

Whether your goal is a hot career in the talent or creative end of theater or the performing arts or a cool career in the business or administrative side of the industry, you want to be the one taking advantage of every available opportunity.

Here's the deal: If you don't know about opportunities, you might miss them. It's important to take some time to look for opportunities that might be of value to you.

Where can you find opportunities? You can find them all over the place. Read through the papers, listen to the radio, look through the trade journals, and watch television. Check out newsletters, music stores, comedy clubs, arts councils, theaters, arts organizations, Web sites, and college campuses.

Schools, universities, and colleges often offer seminars or have programs that might be of interest and are open to the public for a small fee. Contact associations and ask about opportunities. Network, network, and network some more, continuously looking for further opportunities.

What kind of opportunities do you have? What types of opportunities are facing you? Is there a talent competition coming up? Is *American Idol* coming to your part of the country? Have you heard that a new reality show is casting a Broadway show? Is a talent agent looking for new talent?

Are there upcoming comedy showcases? Will internship opportunities at an orchestra, opera, ballet company, or agency be announced soon? Will a trade association conference be hosting a career fair? Is an acclaimed producer speaking at a conference? Is a successful talent agent giving a seminar on tips for making it in the business?

Is there an opening at the orchestra you're working at, in the department you want to work? Did you hear a news story on radio discussing a new performing arts center? These are all potential opportunities. Be on the lookout for them. They can be your keys to success.

Keep track of the opportunities you find and hear about in a notebook or on the Opportunities Worksheet provided on page 59. Above it is a sample to get you started.

Self-Assessment and Taking Inventory

Now let's make sure you're ready for every opportunity. One of the best ways to prepare for anything is by first determining what you

Opportunities Worksheet

Local radio/television stations hosting talent competition. Winner gets appearance on nationwide TV and meeting with major record company executive. Must fill in application and submit tape by 5/10. Competition is during Memorial Day celebration. Judges will be established record company execs, booking agents, DJ, and TV station personalities.

Celebrity softball game in town in July is auditioning people to sing national anthem.

Local portion of national telethon seeking entertainment—will be televised 6/9.

Music television stations holding contest for unsigned talent ends 9/3.

New booking agency, Dome Booking, opening in city.

Daily News is looking for up-and-coming performing artists to profile for feature in newspaper.

Chamber of Commerce is holding large networking event.

Opportunities Worksheet

_____

_____

_____

_____

_____

_____

_____

Tip from the Top

If there is something that you need to do or which can help you in your career, do it now! Don't procrastinate. In other words, don't put off until tomorrow what could have been done today. If you need acting lessons, take them. Don't put it off until "you have time." If you need new head shots, get them taken now! If you need to work on your portfolio or resume, do it now and get it done. Procrastinating can seriously affect your career because it means you didn't get something done which needed to be accomplished. Just the sheer thought about having to get something done takes time and energy. Instead of thinking about it, do it!

want and then seeing what you need to get it. Remembering that you are your own career manager, this might be the time to do a self-assessment.

Your self-assessment involves taking an inventory of what you have to offer and then seeing how you can relate it to what you want to do. Self-assessment involves thinking about yourself and your career goals.

Self-assessment helps you define your strengths and your weaknesses. It helps you define your skills, interests, goals, and passions, giving you the ability to see them at a glance. Your self-assessment can help you develop and write your resume and make it easier to prepare for interviews.

Do you know what you want? Do you know what your strengths and weaknesses are? Can you identify the areas in which you are interested? Can you identify what's important to you in your career?

Answering these questions now can help your career dreams come to fruition quicker. It can help give you the edge others might not have. Doing a self-assessment is a good idea no matter what your career goal.

Strengths and Weaknesses

We all have certain strengths and weaknesses. Strengths are things you do well. They are advantages that most others don't have. You can exploit them to help your career. Weaknesses are things that you can improve. They are things you don't do as well as you could.

What are your strengths and weaknesses? Can you identify them? Why are these questions important? Once you know the answers, you know what you have to work on.

For example, if you don't like speaking in front of groups of people, you might take some public speaking classes or you might force yourself to network and go into situations that could help make you more comfortable around people. If you need better written communication skills, you might take a couple of writing classes to make you a better writer.

Are you a good actor who could be great? Think about taking some acting and drama classes. Does your vocal range need to be extended?

The Inside Scoop

At almost every interview you will go on, you will be asked what your strengths and weaknesses are. Preparing a script ahead of time gives you the edge. When doing this, tailor your answers to the specific position you are going after.

Tip from the Coach

If an agent, human resource director, headhunter, or interviewer asks about your weaknesses, you might say you are a perfectionist but probably don't want to give him or her any information on any of your real weaknesses. As friendly as these people might seem, their job is screening candidates. You don't want to give anyone a reason not to work with you.

Do you need to improve your vocal techniques? Consider taking some vocal lessons.

Do your songwriting skills need some help? A songwriting workshop might help get you on track. Do your playwriting skills need some tweaking? A class or seminar on script writing might be what you need.

Take some time now to define your strengths and weaknesses. Then jot them down in a notebook or use the Strengths and Weaknesses Worksheet on page 62. Be honest and realistic. Here are a couple of sample worksheets to help you get started. One was filled in by someone interested in the business end of the industry, and the other by someone pursuing a career in the talent area.

Once you know some of your strengths and weaknesses, it's time to focus on your personal inventory. Your combination of skills, talents, and personality traits are what help to determine your marketability.

Strengths and Weaknesses Worksheet—Business

My strengths:
I have a lot of energy.
I can get along with almost everyone.
I can follow instructions.
I'm a team player yet can work on my own.
I'm organized.
I am good at teaching others.
I know how to create Web sites.

My weaknesses:
I'm a perfectionist.
I don't like speaking in front of groups of people.
I need better written communication skills.
I'm not good with numbers.

What's important in my career?
Working in an executive position at a major orchestra in development area; living and working in a culturally active city. I want to be the top person in my field. I want to eventually become the managing director of a top orchestra.

Strengths and Weaknesses Worksheet—Talent

My strengths:
I am a good actor.
I have a great voice.
I can dance.
I get along with others.
I'm organized.
I have a degree in theater.

My weaknesses:
I'm a perfectionist.
I don't live in New York City.
While I'm not shy on stage, I'm not great at networking.
I have a difficult time being on time for things.

What's important in my career?
Acting and singing are both important to me. I want a career in musical theater. While I would love to be on Broadway, I would be happy finding a way to earn a good living acting and singing until I get there.

Strengths and Weaknesses Worksheet

My strengths:

_____

_____

My weaknesses:

_____

_____

What's important in my career?

_____

_____

_____

Tip from the Coach

A good way to deal with an interviewer asking you how you will deal with a specific weakness that they identify is by saying you are actively trying to change it into a strength. For example, if an interviewer discovers that you dislike speaking in public, you might say you are working on turning that into a strength by taking a public speaking class. Telling an interviewer you are working on your shortcomings helps him or her form a much better picture of you.

What Are Your Skills?

Skills are acquired things that you have learned to do well. They are part of your selling tools. Keep in mind that there are a variety of relevant skills. There are job-related skills that you use at your present job. Transferable skills are ones that you used on one job and that you can transfer to another. Life skills are ones you use in everyday living such as problem solving, time management, decision making, and dealing with people. Hobby or leisure time skills are related to activities you do during your spare time for enjoyment. These might or might not be pertinent to your career. There are also technical skills connected to the use of machinery. Many of these types of skills overlap.

Tip from the Top

Keep in mind that some skills also need talent. For example, songwriting is a skill. It can be learned. To be a great songwriter, however, you generally need songwriting talent. Similarly, learning to play an instrument is a skill. The talent is how you play it.

Most people don't realize just how many skills they have. They aren't aware of the specialized knowledge they possess. Are you one of them?

While it's often difficult to put your skills down on paper, it's essential so you can see what they are and where you can use them in your career. Your skills, along with your talents and personality traits, make you unique. They can set you apart from other job applicants, actors, singers, musicians, dancers, comedians, playwrights, composers and songwriters, and help you land the career of your dreams.

Once you've given some thought to your skills, it's time to start putting them down on paper. You can either use the worksheet or a page in a notebook. Begin with the skills you know you have. What are you good at? What can you do? What have you done? Include everything you can think of from basic skills on up, and then think of the things people have told you you're good at.

Don't get caught up thinking that "everyone can do that" and so a particular skill of yours is not special. *All* your skills are special.

Review these skill examples to help get you started. Then fill in your own Skills Worksheet.

- computer proficiency
- public speaking
- time management
- analytical skills
- organizational skills
- writing skills
- listening skills
- verbal communications
- management
- selling
- problem solving
- language skills
- leadership
- math skills

(continues)

Skills Worksheet

_____

_____

_____

_____

_____

_____

_____

_____

_____

_____

_____

_____

_____

_____

_____

_____

_____

◎ decision-making skills
◎ negotiating skills
◎ money management
◎ word processing skills
◎ computer repair
◎ teaching
◎ customer service
◎ cooking
◎ Web design
◎ singing
◎ songwriting
◎ playwriting
◎ acting
◎ playing an instrument
◎ interior decorating
◎ instrument repair

Your Special Talents

You are born with your talents. They aren't acquired like skills, but they may be refined and perfected. Many people are reluctant to admit what their talents are, but if you don't identify and use them, you'll be wasting them.

What are your talents? You probably already know what some of them are. What are you not only good at, but better at than most people? What can you do with ease? What has been your passion for as long as you can remember? These will be your talents.

Are you a great actor or actress? Can you bring a character to life on stage? Are you a great singer? Are you a talented musician who can seemingly make an instrument sing? A prolific songwriter? Are you a talented writer? A talented dancer? Can you tell stories and jokes in such a manner that those listening just can't stop themselves from laughing?

Does your talent fall in the science area? How about math? What about art? Do you have an "ear" for being able to choose just the right song? Can you *see* raw talent? Can you look at a new performing artist and just *know* that with a little training and work, he or she can be great?

Think about it for a bit and then jot your talents in your notebook or in the Talents Worksheet. Here is an example to get you started.

My Talents Worksheet—Actor

I can bring characters to life. I am a good actor.

I am multilingual and can speak with a variety of dialects. (English, Australian, Irish, Scottish, and Spanish)

I am funny and can deliver comedy as well as dramatic works.

I am a talented singer. I have a wide vocal range.

I can dance. (tap, jazz, and ballet)

I have the ability to make people around me feel good about themselves.

Talents Worksheet

_____

_____

_____

_____

_____

Your Personality Traits

We all have different personality traits. The combination of these traits is what sets us apart from others. Certain personality traits can help you move ahead whether you're interested in a career in the talent end or the business end of the music industry. Let's look at what some of them are.

- ability to get along well with others
- adaptable
- ambitious
- analytical
- assertive
- charismatic
- clever
- compassionate
- competitive
- conscientious
- creative
- dependable
- efficient
- energetic
- enterprising
- enthusiastic
- flexible
- friendly
- hard worker
- helpful
- honest
- imaginative
- innovative
- inquisitive
- insightful
- observant
- optimistic
- outgoing
- passionate
- personable
- persuasive
- positive
- practical
- problem solver
- reliable
- resourceful
- self-confident
- self-starter
- sociable
- successful
- team player
- understanding

Personality Traits Worksheet

_____

_____

_____

_____

_____

_____

_____

_____

_____

What are your special personality traits? What helps make you unique? Think about it, and then jot them down in your notebook or on the Personality Traits Worksheet.

Special Accomplishments

What special accomplishments have you achieved? Special accomplishments help distinguish you. They make you unique and often will give you an edge over others.

Have you won any awards? Were you awarded a scholarship? Did you write a song that won an award, even on a local level? Were you asked to sing the national anthem at a special event?

Have you won a talent competition? Did you get a four-star review for your role in a theatrical production?

Were you the chairperson of a special event? Have you won a community service award? Were you nominated for an award even if you didn't win? Has an article about you appeared in a regional or national magazine or newspaper?

All these things are examples of some of the special accomplishments you may have experienced. Once you identify your accomplishments, write them down in your notebook or on your Special Accomplishments Worksheet.

Special Accomplishments Worksheet

_____

_____

_____

_____

_____

_____

_____

_____

_____

_____

_____

_____

_____

_____

Education and Training

Education and training are important to the success of your career, whether it be in theater or any of the other performing arts. A college background can't guarantee you a job in the performing arts, but it often helps prepare you for life, whether it be on stage or in the workplace. If your goal is a career on the business end of the industry or arts administration, most positions will either require or prefer you to have a college background. A college education will also be helpful as you learn your craft, hone skills, learn about the business, and make important contacts if your dream is a career in the talent end of the industry.

If your goal is a career in music, a music conservatory might help develop your talent and refine your skills. Professional acting schools are often the choice of those who are Broadway bound. These schools train actors and actresses in a variety of areas including acting, singing, and dancing.

Keep in mind that education may encompass other training opportunities. This may include classes, courses, seminars, programs, and learning from your peers.

What type of education and training do you already possess? What type of education and training do you need to get to the career of your dreams? What type of education will help you get where you want to go?

The Inside Scoop

At the beginning of your acting career when you don't have a lot of professional experience, casting agents will often look at your resume to see what type of training you have gone through.

Would drama or acting classes help you reach your career goal? Is there are special acting coach who will give you the edge? How about private vocal lessons? What about music lessons? Dance classes? Would some classes in stand-up comedy or comedy writing help move your career forward?

Is a college degree what you're missing to give you the edge over other applicants seeking jobs in the business end of the industry or arts administration? How about some workshops or seminars? What about attending some conferences?

Now is the time to determine what education or training you have and what you need so that you can go after it. On page 70 is a sample to get you started.

Tip from the Coach

Courses, seminars, and workshops are great ways to meet and network with industry insiders. Actively seek them out.

Words from the Wise

Before investing time and money, be sure to check out schools you are considering. If you aren't familiar with a school, contact the Better Business Bureau to verify there haven't been any complaints. You might also check with the National Association of Schools of Theatre (http://nast.arts-accredit. org) to see if the school of your choice is accredited.

Education and Training Worksheet

What education and training do I have?
Associate's degree with a major in business
Two semesters away from bachelor's degree in arts administration
Private music lessons

What education or training do I need to reach my goals?
Finish college to get my bachelor's degree
Seminars and workshops in arts administration

What classes, seminars, and workshops have I taken that are useful to my career aspirations?

Arts administration workshop
Performing arts overview
Entertainment publicity

Fund-raising workshops
Grant writing workshops

What classes, seminars, workshops, courses, and other steps can I take to help my career?
Take electives in bookkeeping.
Attend publicity workshops.
Find additional arts administration workshops.
Look for internship at orchestras, operas, ballet, or theater companies.

Fill in the blank Education and Training Worksheet with your information so you know what you need to further your career and meet your goals.

Location, Location, Location: Where Do You Want to Be?

Location is an important factor in your career. Where do you have to live if you want to work in theater? What about the other performing arts? Do you have to live in New York City? What about other culturally active cities? Let's discuss a few areas of the performing arts and your best bets for location.

While it's possible to make a living in other areas, New York City is the best place to be for a top career in theater. If you want to work on Broadway, off Broadway, or even off-off Broadway, you're going to have to live in (or close to) New York City.

New York City is the theater capital of the world. It's where it's happening if you want to work in legitimate theater. It's where it's hap-

Words from a Pro

If you're interested in a career in legitimate theater, training in an accredited professional acting school in New York City often gives you opportunities you might not get elsewhere.

Education and Training Worksheet

What education and training do I have?

_____

_____

What education or training do I need to reach my goals?

_____

_____

What classes, seminars, and workshops have I taken which are useful to my career aspirations?

_____

_____

_____

What classes, seminars, workshops, courses, and other steps can I take to help my career?

_____

_____

_____

_____

pening if you want to make it in theater. It's where you can win a Tony!

"I want to work in theater, but I _don't_ live in New York," you say. "Now what?"

Before you panic, remember the key word here is _best_. It is not the only place. Is New York City the only city to work in theater? Absolutely not! While it might be your dream to work on

⭐ **The Inside Scoop**

If you're an aspiring performing artist, one advantage of not going directly to New York City or the other major markets is that it is usually easier to break in and get your foot in the door by starting off in a smaller area than one of the very large competitive cities. Whether you're hoping to work as an actor, singer, dancer, musician, comedian, or any other performing artist, if you don't have a lot of experience, you will generally have a better chance of landing a job in a smaller area. Once you're in, you will have the opportunity to learn the ropes, gain experience, hone your craft, and move onward and upward if that's your dream.

Smaller cities and other areas offer opportunities in regional, stock, and dinner theaters. Touring productions present even more opportunities throughout the country.

What's the best place to live if you want to work in symphonies, ballet companies, or operas? Once again, large culturally active cities such as New York City, Los Angeles, Atlanta, Washington, D.C., Boston, and Philadelphia will offer the greatest number of possibilities.

If you want to work as a comedian or other similar performing artist, your best bet is to be headquartered in (or close to) an area that has a lot of opportunities. Will the biggest cities be the best? Not always. If you're just starting out you might find it easier to locate gigs in smaller areas. That way you can work on your show, iron out any problems, and perfect your performance.

Where's the best place to live if you want to work in the music industry? While it's possible to make it living in other regions, New York City, Los Angeles, and Nashville are the best places to be for a top career in the music or recording industry. Why? These are the music

the Great White Way, there is an array of other locations where you can have a career in theater. Los Angeles, Washington, D.C., Boston, Philadelphia, Seattle, Chicago, Atlanta, and Las Vegas as well as other large, culturally active cities all offer opportunities.

Location Worksheet

Type of area I reside in now:

_____

Location of job or career choice I want:

_____

Other possible locations:

_____

Reviewing Your Past

Let's look at your past. What have you done which can help you succeed in your career in the performing arts?

"I really haven't done anything that is remotely related," you might say.

I'm betting you have.

Make a list of all the jobs you have had and the general functions you were responsible for when you held them. Look at this information and see what functions or skills you can transfer to your career in the performing arts. Did you have a summer job at the ticket booth at your local movie theater? Have you volunteered and helped a not-for-profit organization execute a special event? Have you worked in the record department of a major retailer? Have you taught music or dance? Have you worked at a local music club in any capacity? What about a community theater? What about your job at the concession stand at the local movie theater? Have you interned at an arts organization?

"None of my past jobs have anything to do with the performing arts," you say. That's okay. Many skills are transferable.

Have you held a job as a reporter for a local newspaper? That shows that you know how to develop and write an article or news story and can do it in a timely fashion. These skills can easily be transferred if you are interested in a career as an entertainment journalist or publicist.

Have you worked as a bookkeeper? What about a job in the bookkeeping department of an orchestra, opera, or ballet company? With some education and certification you might be able to fulfill your goals of working as an accountant in arts administration.

Are you a schoolteacher and wish you could be involved with the entertainment industry? Your talents, skills, and education might get you into a

---

> ### ★ The Inside Scoop
>
> Unless you land a standing engagement at a club or other venue, as a comedian you're going to have to be prepared to travel to work on a regular basis. If you are going to drive to get where you're going, make sure you have a good, reliable vehicle to get where you're going on the time, every time. Conversely, if you are going to have to fly to most of your engagements, it's imperative to live in an area convenient to a good airport that services most of the major airlines. That way you can get out on a moment's notice if an unexpected gig presents itself.

capitals. These are the cities where the headquarters for most of the major recording labels in the United States are located. This is where it's happening in music.

No matter what career area you want to pursue in the performing arts, in deciding where you want to be headquartered, remember that it is helpful to be where it's happening. You have more opportunities to meet the people you need to meet who will help you get to the top level of your career. You will also have more opportunities to make important contacts necessary to your career success.

There's also something to be said about being at the right place at the right time. What does that mean? Let's say you happen to hear about an open casting call in New York City for a new production. If you live locally, you can grab your head shots, your resume, and go. If you live in New Hampshire, by the time you get to New York City, the opportunity might be gone.

As we'll discuss throughout this book, success comes from a combination of a number of things including talent, luck, perseverance, and being at the right place at the right time.

position teaching the children of recording stars when they're on the road, or child actors performing in television shows or film or on stage.

The idea is to use your existing talents, skills, and accomplishments to get your foot in the door. Once in, you can find ways to move up the ladder so you can achieve the career of your dreams. When going over your list of past positions include full- and part-time positions. Look at the entire picture, including not only your jobs but your accomplishments and see what they might tell about you.

"Like what?" you ask.

Did you graduate from high school in three years instead of four? That illustrates that you're driven and can accomplish your goals. Were you the chairperson for a not-for-profit charity event? That illustrates that you take initiative, work well with people, can delegate, and organize well. Do you sing in your church choir? Have you volunteered to handle the choir's music? This shows that you can sing and that you have the dedication to attend rehearsals. Handling the music illustrates your organizational skills.

Now that you have some ideas, think about what you've done and see how you can relate it to your dream career.

Using Your Past to Create Your Future

When reviewing past jobs and volunteer activities, see how they can be used to help you get what you want in the performing arts. Answer the following questions:

◎ What parts of each job accomplishment or volunteer activity did you love?
◎ What parts made you happy?
◎ What parts gave you joy?
◎ What parts of your previous jobs excited you?

◎ What skills did you learn while on those jobs?
◎ What skills can be transferred to your career in the performing arts?
◎ What accomplishments can help your career in the performing arts industry?

Jot down your answers in your notebook or use the Using Your Past to Create Your Future worksheet provided.

The more ways you can find to use past accomplishments and experience to move closer to success in your career in the performing arts, the better you will be. Look outside the box to find ways to transfer your skills and use jobs and activities as stepping-stones to get where you're going.

Passions and Goals

Once you know what you have, it's easier to determine what you need to get what you want. You've made a lot of progress by working on your self-assessment, but you have a few more things to do. At this point, you need to focus on exactly what you want to do.

In what area of the performing arts do you want to be involved? Do you want to be an actor, singer, songwriter, dancer, or musician? Do you want to be a comedian, juggler, or mime? Do you like working with numbers, public speaking, or organizing things? Is selling your passion? What about teaching? Do you want to create intricate costumes or elaborate sets? Do you want to choose just the right actor or actress for the part?

Do you want to be a member of an orchestra or a rock group? Do you want to be a pop singer or opera singer? Do you want to travel? Do you want to entertain or work behind the scenes?

Do you want to work on the business end of the industry? How about administration? What

Using Your Past to Create Your Future

Past Job/ Volunteer Activity/ Accomplishment	Parts of Job/ Volunteer Activity/ Accomplishment which I Enjoyed	Skills I Learned and Can Transfer to Career in the Performing Arts

about the talent or creative side of the performing arts? It's all up to you.

What are your passions? You can be the most talented singer in the world, but if you don't have a passion for singing, it's a bad career choice. You owe it to yourself to have a career that you love, that you're passionate about, and that you deserve. Take the time now to make sure that you get it by going after your passions. Believe it or not, passion in many cases can override talent.

What does that mean? It means that while talent is important, the desire to do something you're passionate about can make it happen.

There are thousands of people in all aspects of the performing arts who are less talented than others, yet they've made it big. They've succeeded where their more talented counterparts have not. What's the difference? They have more passion for what they want, they have drive, they have determination, and they never give up on their goals. If *you* have that passion, you can reach your goals too.

Whether your career choice is in the talent or creative area of the performing arts, on the business or administrative side of the industry, or anywhere in between, you've taken another step toward preparing for success.

5

JOB SEARCH STRATEGIES

Using a Job to Create a Career

Unfortunately you don't just go out and *get* a career. You generally have to create one. This is especially true in the performing arts whether you want to work in the business or administrative end of the industry or in the talent area. How can you create your dream career? You have to take each job you get along the way and make it *work* for you. Developing the ultimate career requires a lot of things, including sweat, stamina, and creativity. Think of every job as a rung on the career ladder, every assignment within that job as a stepping-stone. Completing the puzzle takes lots of pieces and lots of work, but it will be worth it.

Except for a lucky few or those with specialized skills, breaking into the performing arts often requires starting at low-level, low-paying, or even volunteer positions. But every job helps to sharpen your skills and adds another line to your resume. Every situation is an opportunity to network, learn, and most of all to get noticed.

Of course, if you know that your ultimate goal is a career in theater or any of the other performing arts, it's much easier to see how each job you do can get you a little closer. And this doesn't just apply to the business or admin-

istrative end of the industry. For performing artists, every gig or engagement, no matter how small, gives you another experience, hones your skills, helps you gain confidence in front of an audience, and gives you the opportunity to be discovered. Every job can lead you to the career you've been dreaming about.

One of the things you should know is that while most anyone can get a *job*, not everyone ends up with a career. The difference between a job and a career is that a job is just a means to an end. It's something you do to get things done and to earn a living. Your career, on the other hand, is a series of related jobs you build using your skills, talents, and passions. It's a progressive path of achievement.

When you were a child, perhaps your parents dangled the proverbial carrot in front of you, tempting you to eat your dinner so that you could have chocolate ice cream and cake for dessert. Whether dinner was food you liked,

---

⭐ **Tip from the Coach**

It may take some time to get where you want to in your career. Try to make your journey as exciting as your destination.

---

didn't particularly care for, or a combination, you probably ate it most of the time to get to what you wanted—dessert. In this case, your dessert will be ultimate success in your career in the performing arts.

Use every experience, every job, and every opportunity for the ultimate goal of filling your life with excitement and passion while getting paid. Will there be things you don't enjoy doing and jobs you wish you didn't have along the way? Perhaps, but there will also be things you love doing and jobs you look back on and remember with joy.

Moving Into the Performing Arts: Changing Careers

Are you currently working in another industry but really want to be in some segment of the performing arts? If so, you're not alone. Many people have dreamed about a career in theater, dance, music, singing, comedy, or one of the other performing arts and for a variety of reasons, ended up doing something else. If this is you, read on.

Perhaps at the time you needed a job. Possibly it looked too difficult to obtain a career in theater or the performing arts. Maybe you just didn't know how to go about it. Maybe you weren't ready. Maybe people around you told you that you were pipe dreaming. Maybe you were scared. Or maybe someone offered you a job in a different industry and you took it for security. There might be hundreds of reasons why you wanted a career in theater or the performing arts, but you didn't pursue it at the time. The question is, do you want to be there now?

"Well," you say, "I do, but . . ."

Before you go through your list of *buts,* ask yourself these questions: Do you want to give up your dream? Do you want to live your life saying, "I wish I had," but never trying? Wouldn't

> ### ⭐ Tip from the Coach
> Are you living someone else's dream? You can't change your past, but you can change your future. If your dream is to work in an aspect of the performing arts, go for it. Things might not change overnight, but the first step you take toward your new career will get you closer to your dream. Every day you put it off is one more day you're wasting doing something you don't love. You deserve more. You deserve the best.

you rather find a way to do what you want than never really be happy with what you're doing? Wouldn't it be great to look at others who are doing what they want and know that *you* are one of them? Here's the good news. You can! You just have to make the decision to do it.

How can you move into the performing arts from a different industry? How can you change your career path? Let's begin with the business end of the industry. First take stock of what you have and what you don't have. Learn how to transfer skills. That means going over your skills and finding ways you can use them in the career of your choice.

Do you have strong writing skills? Consider seeking a position at an orchestra, opera, or ballet company in the public relations department. Think about working in the publications department. How about a job in a theatrical, music industry, or entertainment-oriented public relations or publicity firm? What about looking for a job as an entertainment reporter for a newspaper, magazine, or even one of the trade journals?

Are your skills in number crunching? What about seeking a position in an orchestra, opera, ballet, or theatrical company's accounting department? What about working with a CPA who handles clients in the entertainment industry? What about going on the road with a theatrical touring company, a major recording act, or other performing artists to handle their finances on tour?

Do you have office skills? Are you a good manager? Do you have good organizational skills? Consider a job as an administrative assistant at an arts council, ballet, orchestra, opera, or theater company. What about a position at a record label, with a booking agent, talent agent, or other performing arts industry business? One of the exciting things about these types of positions is that you get to learn the ropes and often have a great chance of moving up the career ladder.

Do you have information technology (IT) skills? Are you a webmaster? Do you have other computer skills? Today, most entertainment companies, agencies, and businesses have a Web site even if they have no IT department. What about doing Web sites for individual performing artists?

Are your skills in marketing? Are you working in marketing in another industry? Consider a position in the marketing department at an orchestra, opera, ballet, or theater company. What about a position in a management firm helping to market its performing artists? How about a marketing position at a club, arena, or other venue?

Are your skills in sales? Lucky you! The possibilities are endless. Every orchestra, opera, ballet, theater, arena, club, and venue needs salespeople. What about a position in a booking agency? What about a position with a talent or literary agent? A great deal of the work involved in booking artists or their work is selling.

"Wait a minute," you say. "What if I don't want to work in the area where my skills are? What if I want to be something like a top exec in arts administration? What if I want to be a talent agent? What then?"

Use your skills and your talents to get your foot in the door. Once in, you have a better opportunity to move into the area you want.

Should you quit your present job to go after your dream? And if so, when should you do it? Generally, you are much more employable if you are employed. You don't have that desperate "I need a job" look. You don't have the worries about financially supporting yourself and your family if you have one. You don't have to take the wrong job because you've been out of work so long that *anything* looks good.

It's best to work on starting your dream career while you have a job to support yourself. Ideally you'll be able to leave one job directly for another much more to your liking.

You should focus on exactly what you want to do, set your goals, prepare your action plan, and start taking actions now. You're going to have to begin moving toward your goals every day. This is a job in itself, but a job that can lead to the career of your dreams.

Now let's talk about the talent end of the industry. To survive financially, many aspiring performing artists hold down day jobs to earn a living and make ends meet until they have their big break.

Whether you're working as a waitperson secretary, administrative assistant, sales associate, or you hold an administrative or managerial position, whether you work full time, part time, or as a temp, your goal should be to make enough money to support yourself until you make it in the performing arts.

The question many ask is, "When do I quit my day job?" No one can answer this for you, but try to be realistic. You don't want to be in the position where you can't do what you want

The Inside Scoop

A number of years ago, a man raised his hand at one of our seminars. "I'm 40 years old," he said. "I always wanted a career in the performing arts, but I've always had a family to support. I just can't give up my job to go after my dream."

"What are you doing now?" I asked him.

"I work for a newspaper. I'm a reporter," he told me.

"What do you want to do?" I asked. "If you could do anything, without worrying about supporting your family or about any obstacles stopping you, what would it be?"

"I would absolutely love to work around a symphony. I love going. I love the music. I just love the energy," he said excitedly. "It's not that I don't like what I'm doing now, because I do, but I'm so envious of people who get to work around orchestras. They're so lucky."

"What type of reporter are you?" I asked.

"I'm a business reporter," he replied.

"Okay," I said. "Here's an idea. Why don't you talk to your editor and see if he or she might be interested in a feature story on working in an orchestra. Come up with an angle. If you live close to a symphony, it might be an interesting story."

"Do you think he might let me?" he asked.

"If you pitch it right, he just might," I told him. "When you're doing research for the story, make contacts—as many as you can. After the story comes out, call the people who you think might be useful in helping you achieve your dream, thank them for their help with the story, and tell them about your dream. See if anyone has any ideas."

"I'm going to give it a try," he said. "I'll let you know what happens."

A few months later a florist delivered me a beautiful floral arrangement. Attached was a note that said, "Thanks for your advice. Guess what? I got a great job at an orchestra . . . just like I dreamed of. I'll call you with details."

Later that day, the man called to share his good news. Evidently he had talked his editor into letting him do the story. While doing research for the article, he went to one of the orchestra's fund-raising events and had the opportunity to meet a number of the board of directors, the managing director, and human resources manager. The next morning, he met with the public relations director who brought him around to interview other orchestra employees.

When he met many of the people at the orchestra, the first thing he told them was that they were living his dream. He mentioned that he had always wanted to work in an orchestra in some capacity and how excited he was to hear about their jobs.

Unbeknownst to him, the orchestra was looking for a director of publications and correspondence. While they didn't know the reporter was looking for a new job, they were impressed with his attitude and enthusiasm and knew his writing style from stories and articles in the paper. Before the article even came out, the orchestra administration asked the man if he would be interested in the job. And because they asked *him,* he was in a better bargaining position for salary and benefits.

Could he have gotten the job if he wasn't doing the feature story? He might have, but the position hadn't even been advertised. Additionally, while members of the orchestra administration probably had read his stories in the newspaper prior to meeting him, he was just one of many reporters. No one really knew anything about him, or knew that his passion was to work in an orchestral setting. What he had done, in essence, was networked his way to a job.

because you don't have any funds. To have the best shot at what you want to do, you need to be as financially stable as possible.

Before you quit your day job, you need to ask yourself a few questions.

◎ Are you getting paying roles or engagements on a consistent basis?
◎ Are your fees increasing?
◎ Are you earning more money as a performing artist than you are in your day job?
◎ Are you turning down engagements or roles because of your job?
◎ Do you have a nest egg put away in case of emergencies?
◎ Can you support yourself on the monies you're earning from your performing arts career?

Once you answer these questions, you'll know what you have to do. If you can't support yourself on what you're earning as a performing artist, keep your day job until things change.

This doesn't mean you shouldn't work toward your goals. Continue searching out ways to make your performing arts career more lucrative. Later chapters discuss some ways to do this.

"But I don't have time to do everything," you say.

You're going to have to make time. It's amazing how you can expand your time when you need to. Remember your action plan? It's imperative that you carve time out of your day to perform some of those actions.

If you think you don't have the time, look at your day a little closer. What can you eliminate doing? Will getting up a half an hour early give you more time to work on your career? How about cutting out an hour of TV or computer time during the day? Even if you can only afford

to take time in 15-minute increments, you usually can find an hour to put into your career.

Finding the Job You Want

Perseverance is essential to your success in the performing arts no matter what you want to do, what area of the industry you want to enter, and what career level you want to achieve. It doesn't matter whether you want to be an actor, singer, dancer, musician, comedian, or any other performing artist. It doesn't matter if you want a career in the talent end of the industry or the business or administrative area.

Do you want to know why most people don't find their perfect job in theater or the other performing arts? It's because they gave up looking *before* they found it.

Difficult as it might be to realize at this point, remember that your job, your great career, is out there waiting for you. You just have to locate it. How do you find that elusive position you want in the performing arts?

For the most part, jobs are located in two areas: the open job market and the hidden job market. What's the difference? The open job market is composed of jobs that are advertised and announced to the public. The hidden job market is composed of jobs not advertised or announced to the public.

Where can you find the largest number of jobs—the hidden job market or the open job market? A lot depends exactly on what you want to do in the industry, but be aware that there are a great many jobs in all areas of the performing arts that just aren't advertised. Why? There are a few reasons, but basically because positions in the performing arts are often so coveted, putting an ad in the classified section of the newspaper might mean that there could be hundreds of responses, if not more.

"But isn't that what employers want?" you ask. "Someone to *fill* their job openings?"

Of course employers want job openings filled, but they don't want to have to go through hundreds of resumes to get to that point. It is much easier to try to find qualified applicants in other ways and that is where the hidden job market comes in.

This doesn't mean, however, that you shouldn't look into the open market. The smart thing to do to is utilize every avenue to find your job. Let's discuss the open job market and then we'll go on to talk about the hidden job market in more detail.

The Open Job Market

When you think of looking for a job where do you start? Most people head straight for the classifieds. Let's go over some ways to increase your chances of success in locating job openings this way.

The Sunday newspapers usually have the largest collection of help wanted ads. Start by focusing on those. You can never tell when a company will advertise job openings, so you might also want to browse through the classified section on a daily basis if possible. Will you find a job in theater, the performing arts, or arts administration advertised in your local hometown newspaper? That depends on what type of job you're seeking and where you live. If you live in a small town and you're looking for a position at a major orchestra, probably not. If you're looking for a position at an arts council or at a local dinner theater your chances are better. If you are looking for employment in large, culturally active cities, check out newspapers from those areas. If you don't live in the area, many larger bookstores and libraries often carry Sunday newspapers from metropolitan

Words from the Wise

If you are going to use an employment agency to help you find a job, be sure to check before you sign any contracts to see who pays the fee—you or the company. There is nothing wrong with paying a fee. You simply want to be aware ahead of time and know what the fee will be.

cities in the country. You can also usually order short-term subscriptions for most papers. One of the easiest ways to view the classified sections of newspapers from around the country is by going online to the newspapers' Web sites.

Many major entertainment-based companies including large orchestras, operas, ballet companies, record labels, booking agencies, and music publishers also use boxed or display classified ads. These are large ads that may advertise more than one job and usually have a company name and/or logo. There are also employment agencies specializing in the music industry that may advertise openings in the employment agency area of the classifieds. These will usually be located in newspapers in the music capitals.

The Trades, Industry Publications, Newsletters, and Web Sites

Where else are jobs advertised? Trade journals are often a good source. Trades are periodicals geared toward a specific industry. Every industry has trade magazines and newspapers, and the performing arts is no exception.

Variety, for example, is filled with information on news in all aspects of the entertainment industry. *Backstage* and *Playbill* focus on news in the theatrical world. *Billboard* is chock full of information on the music business, trends, and the music charts.

⭐ The Inside Scoop

If you aspire to work as an actor, singer, dancer, musician, or any other performing artist or creative talent, it's essential that you remember your ultimate goal. A number of years ago I met a woman who worked for the conference management company that hired me to speak. While we were talking, she happened to mention that she had moved to New York City to be a singer-actress. I asked her how her career was going.

"That depends which career you're talking about," she said. "My career here (with the conference management company) is going great. I got a promotion. I'm making a lot of money. And, while I know I should be happy, I'm not."

"What about your singing and acting career?" I asked.

"Oh that," she said. "Not too well. I'm so busy with my day job, I don't have any time to devote to singing and acting. I moved to be close to where everything is happening. I wanted to be available for auditions. I wanted to be near the record companies and the clubs. I wanted to be near Broadway. I'm now close to all those things and I'm so busy doing this, that my career goals are almost secondary."

"What are you going to do?" I asked.

"You tell me," she said. "Do you have any ideas to get me back on track?"

"Your boss knows you want to be a singer," I replied. "Most of the conferences you're in charge of are part of trade shows. Most of them I've been to open with someone singing the national anthem. Your next few shows are in Las Vegas and then you have a couple in Atlantic City. Why don't you start by asking your boss if they'll let you open the trade show by singing the national anthem? I bet he'll let you."

"He's a pretty cool boss," she said. "I'm going to ask him. They video all of the show openings. Maybe if he lets me do it, he'll also let me use my appearance as part of my press kit," she continued excitedly.

The woman was one of the company's prized employees who had endeared herself to everyone. Before the day was over she had asked her boss and after checking the idea with the top brass, they decided to give it a try. She called me to tell me the good news. "What else should I do?" she asked.

"Make sure you take some time every day to work on your career," I said. "When you get back to New York, try to find some auditions, seek out some opportunities, and network. Remember why you moved to New York in the first place and what your goal is."

About nine months later she called to tell me things were going much better with her acting and singing career. I knew she had already sung at a couple of trade show openings. She also found a way to telecommute so she could do a good portion of her job at home, which gave her the flexibility to go on auditions and work on her true career goals. She also landed a few voice-over commercials, appeared in a short-lived off-Broadway production, and was called in for a second audition for a supporting role in a Broadway musical.

She said while she didn't get the role, just after that opportunity fell through, she landed a really good part in one of the Broadway-style shows in Las Vegas. The casting director had heard her while singing the national anthem at the trade show.

How can you use the trades to your advantage? Read them faithfully. If you don't want to invest in a subscription, go to your local or college library to see if they subscribe. Television and radio stations often subscribe to *Billboard* or *Broadcasting*. Orchestras subscribe to *Symphony*. Theater companies may subscribe to *Backstage* or *Playbill*. Many of the trades also have online versions of their publication. Browse through the help-wanted ads in the classified section every week to see if your dream job is there.

Newsletters related to the various areas of the performing arts might offer other possibilities for job openings. What about career Web sites such as Monster.com, Hotjobs.com, and other employment sites? Don't forget company Web sites. Orchestras, operas, and ballet companies, record labels, booking agencies, entertainment industry publicity, and public relations firms, music publishers, venues, clubs, theaters and other performing arts businesses generally host Web sites. Many of these sites have specific sections listing career opportunities at their company. It's worth checking out.

Are you already working in the industry and wanting to move up the career ladder? Do you, for example, have a job with an orchestra or theatrical company and want to move up a rung on the career ladder? Many companies post their employment listings in the human resources department or in employee newsletters. What if you don't have a job there already and are interested in finding out about internal postings? This is where networking comes into play. A contact at the company can keep you informed.

If you're still in college or have graduated from a school that had programs in arts administration, music business, or theater, for example, check with the college placement office. In some cases, companies searching to fill specific positions may go to colleges and universities where they had internship programs.

The Hidden Job Market

Let's talk about the hidden job market. Many people think that their job search begins and ends with the classified ads. If they get the Sunday paper and their dream job isn't in there, they give up and wait until the next Sunday. I am bet-

ting that once you have made the decision to have a career in theater or the performing arts, you're not going to let something small like not finding a job opening in the classifieds stop you. So what are you going to do?

While there may be job openings in your field that are in the classifieds, it's essential to realize that many jobs are not advertised at all. Why? In addition to not wanting to be bombarded and inundated by tons of resumes and phone calls, for example, some employers may not want someone in another company to know that they are looking for a new marketing director or a new director of publicity until they hire one. They may not want the person who currently holds the job to know that he or she is about to be let go. Whatever the reason, once you're aware that all jobs aren't advertised you can go about finding them in a different manner.

Why do you want to find jobs in the hidden job market? The main reason is that you will have a better shot at getting the job. Why? To begin with, there is a lot less competition. Because positions aren't being actively advertised, there aren't hundreds of people sending in their resumes trying to get the jobs. Not everyone knows how to find the hidden job market, nor do they want to take the extra time to find it, so you also have an edge over other job applicants. Many applicants in the hidden job market also often come recommended by someone who knew about the opening. This means that you are starting off with one foot in the door.

While there are entry-level jobs to be found in the hidden job market, there are also a good number of high-level jobs. This can be valuable when you're trying to move up the career ladder.

How does the hidden job market work? When a company needs to fill a position, instead of placing an ad, they quietly look for the perfect candidate. How do they find candidates without advertising?

◎ Employees may be promoted from within the company.
◎ An employee working in the company may recommend a candidate for the position.
◎ Someone who knows about an opening may tell their friends, relatives, or coworkers who then apply for the job.
◎ People may have filled in applications or sent resumes and cover letters to the company asking that they be kept on file. When an opening exists, the human resources department might review the resumes and call one of the applicants.
◎ Suitable candidates may place cold calls at just the right time.
◎ People may have networked and caught the eye of those who need to fill the jobs.

Networking in Theater and the Performing Arts

Often, it's not just what you know but who you know. Contacts are key in *every* area of the performing arts. Networking is therefore going to be an important part of succeeding. It's so important that it can often make you or break you.

How so, you ask?

You may be a more talented actor or actress than those appearing on Broadway, but unless you have a chance to audition for roles, it will be difficult to find an agent or showcase your talent.

You might be a great singer, but if you don't get the right people to hear you, the furthest you might get in your career is singing in the shower. You can be the most talented singer in the world, but if you can't get the right people to hear you, it's going to be difficult to find a manager, an agent, and a record label.

The importance of networking is not limited just to the talent area of the industry. Networking is just as important on the business end. The fact of the matter is that without the power of networking it is often difficult to get your foot in the door.

Earlier chapters have touched on networking, and because of its importance to your success, it will be discussed further throughout the book. Networking isn't just something you do at the beginning of your career. It's something you're going to have to continue doing for as long as you work.

How do you network? Basically, you put yourself into situations where you can meet people and introduce yourself. Chapter 7 discusses more about the basics of networking. However, right now you're going to have to learn to get comfortable walking up to people, extending your hand, and introducing yourself. Make sure you ask for their card and give them your card as well.

Every situation can ultimately be an opportunity to network, but some are more effective than others. Look for seminars, workshops, and classes that professionals in the various performing arts and arts management might

---

★ Voice of Experience

You never want to be in a position where someone remembers that they met you and remembers that you would be perfect for a job, yet they have no idea how to get in touch with you. Don't be stingy with your business cards. Give them out freely.

attend. Why would an industry professional be at a workshop or seminar? There are many reasons. They might want to network just like you, or they might want to learn something new, or they might be teaching or facilitating the workshop.

Where else might professionals who work in the performing arts be? What about theaters, clubs, concert halls, or other venues? How do you get to the right people? Call the theater, hall, or venue manager or assistant manager. Tell him or her about your career aspirations and ask if he or she would be willing to give you the names of a couple of industry people whom you might call.

"Why would anyone want to help me?" you ask.

Most people like to help others. It makes them feel good. Don't expect everyone to go out of their way for you, but if you find one or two helpful people, you may wind up with some useful contacts.

Where else can you network? A lot of that depends on what segment of the performing arts you are trying to target. Want to network with people in theater? Attend theatrical events. Want to network with people in the music industry? Then attend concerts. Want to network with professionals in the dance field? Attend ballets and other dance performances.

The Inside Scoop

It's great to network with those at the top, but a good and often more practical strategy is to try networking with their assistants and support team. The people at the top might not always remember you; those a step or two down the line usually will.

Tip from the Coach

Remember that networking is a two-way street. If you want people to help you, it's important to reciprocate. When you see something you can do for someone else's career, don't wait for them to ask for help. Step in, do it, and do it graciously.

"But how do I get through to the industry professionals?" you ask.

You're going to have to be creative. For example, opening night galas are generally full of industry professionals.

"I can't afford to go to an opening night gala," you say.

Get creative. Volunteer to be a host or hostess. Offer to help serve. See if you can cover the event for the newspaper. Think outside of the box.

Trade Shows, Conferences, and Conventions

Trade shows, conferences, and conventions geared toward the various areas of the performing arts are a treasure trove for making contacts. Those who attend are going for a specific reason. Most are industry professionals. By attending a good trade show, you probably will find businesses within the performing arts industry that you might not even have known existed, and you'll meet more people as well.

A trade show and conference can dramatically increase the contacts in your network very quickly. You will have the opportunity to meet literally hundreds of people in the industry.

Most trade shows and conferences also have an educational track that is chock full of seminars, workshops, and keynote presentations.

> ### ★ Tip from the Top
> When networking at an event, don't just zero in on the people you think are the important industry insiders and ignore the rest. Try to meet as many people as you can and always be pleasant and polite to everyone. You never can tell who knows who and who might be a great contact later.

Some have certification programs in various areas. More important, many shows now incorporate career fairs where you have the opportunity to meet people from companies with job openings to fill. When you go to any of these events it's essential to introduce yourself, spend time talking to people, and let them know you are in the market for a job.

The Right Place at the Right Time

Have you ever looked down while you were walking and seen money sitting on the ground? It could have been there for a while, but no one else happened to look down. You just happened to be in the right place at the right time.

It can happen any time. Sometimes you hear about an interesting job opening from an unlikely source.

You might be visiting your favorite aunt in the hospital and her roommate turns out to be a casting agent who was in town on vacation. While hiking she tore a ligament in her knee and was hospitalized. Over the course of the day she had mentioned to your aunt that she hoped she was going to be released the following morning because her assistant had recently quit and she needed to fill the position. Your aunt knew that you were trying to get a job in some aspect of

theater, mentioned it to her roommate, and told her all about you. You walked into the hospital room and were practically interviewed on the spot. Before the week was up, you got a call from the woman asking if you would be interested in the job. Think it can't happen? It can and it does. It's just a matter of being at the right place at the right time.

It happens in the performing arts in both the business and talent areas of the industry. If you are at the right place at the right time, it can happen to you too.

How many people in the performing arts have you seen interviewed on television, heard on radio, or read about in an article who told stories of their success saying something to the effect of, "I was just in the right place at the right time." Perhaps the "right" person may have been sitting in the audience when they were performing on stage. Perhaps they sat next to a talent agent on the airplane. There is no question that being in the right place at the right time can help. The question is, however, what is the right place and the right time and how do you recognize it?

The simple answer is, it's almost impossible to know what the right place and right time is. You can, however, stack the deck in your favor. How? While you never know what the right place or the right time to be someplace is, you can put yourself in situations where you can network. Networking with people outside of the industry can be just as effective and just as important as networking with industry professionals.

The larger your network, the more opportunities you will have to find the job you want. The more people who know what you have to offer and what you want to do, the better. Who do you deal with every day? Who do these people know and deal with? Any of these people in your network and your extended network may know about your dream career in theater or the other performing arts.

If you aren't employed and don't have to worry about a current boss or supervisor hearing about your aspirations, then spread the news about your job search. Don't keep it a secret. The more people who know you're looking to be in the industry, the more people who potentially can let you know when and where there is a job possibility.

If I haven't stressed it enough, if at all possible do not keep your career aspirations to yourself. Share them with the world.

Cold Calls

What exactly is a cold call? In relation to your career, a cold call is an unsolicited contact in person, by phone, letter, or e-mail with someone you don't know in hopes of obtaining some information, an interview, or a job. It is a proactive strategy.

Let's focus on the cold calls you make by phone. Many find this form of contact too intimidating to try. Why? Not only are you calling and trying to sell yourself to someone who may be busy and doesn't want to be bothered, but you are also afraid of rejection. None of us like rejection. We fear that we will get on the phone, try to talk to someone, and they will not take our call, hang up on us, or say no to our requests.

The majority of telemarketing calls made to homes everyday are cold calls. In those cases the people on the other end of the phone aren't trying to get a job or an interview. Instead they are attempting to sell something such as a product or a service. When you get those calls, the first thing on your mind is usually how to get off the phone. The last thing you want to do is buy anything from someone on the other end. But the fact of the matter is that people do buy things from telemarketers if they want what they're selling.

Your job in making cold calls is to make your call compelling enough that the person on the other end responds positively. Why would you even bother making a cold call to someone? It's simply another job search strategy and it's one that not everyone attempts, which gives you an edge over others.

How do you make a cold call? Identify who you want to call, put together a script to make it easier for you, and then make your call. Keep track of the calls you make. You may think you'll remember who said what and those you didn't reach, but after a couple of calls, it gets confusing. Keep track of people you call with the Cold Call Tracking Worksheet on page 88.

Who do you call? That depends on who you're trying to reach. If you want to pursue a career as a booking agent, you might call booking agency owners directly.

> **You:** Hi, Ms. Domier. This is David Gere. I'm not sure you're the right person to speak to, but I was hoping I could tell you what I was looking for and perhaps you could point me in the right direction. Are you in the middle of something now or would it be better if I call back later?

★ Voice of Experience

You will find it easier to make cold calls if you not only create a script but practice it as well. To be successful in cold calling, you need to sound professional, friendly, and confident.

Cold Call Tracking Worksheet

Company	Phone Number	Name of Contact	Date Called	Follow-up Activities	Results

Ms. Domier: Are you trying to book a show?

You: No, I'm actually looking for a job. I was wondering if you knew of any opportunities for agent trainees. I don't have a lot of experience in the entertainment industry, but I'm great at sales. I'm working in sales now and I have a 75 percent conversion rate.

Ms. Domier: Seventy-five percent conversion. That's pretty impressive. What are you selling?

You: Internet advertising for a radio station. I would really like to come in to talk to you. Would it be possible for me to make an appointment when you have some time? I understand that you might not have a position but you might know someone or might be able to give me some advice.

Ms. Domier: I'm pretty busy for the next couple of weeks.

You: I understand. Would it be an imposition if I called you in a few weeks to try to set up a meeting? I'm flexible in my time. I could fit into your schedule.

Ms. Domier: Why don't you come in next Tuesday? I'll probably have some time then. I'm going to put you on with Anna, my secretary, and she'll set up an appointment.

You: Thanks for your time. I look forward to meeting with you.

Ms. Domier: See you then. Hold for Anna please.

It's not that difficult once you get someone on the phone.

"But what if they say no?" you ask.

So they say no. Don't take it personally. Just go on to your next call and use your previous call as practice.

Where do you find people to call? Browse company Web sites for names. Look for arts councils. Read trade journals. Read the newspaper. Look for magazine articles and feature stories. Watch television and listen to the radio. Go through the yellow pages. You can get names from almost anyplace. Is there an orchestra you're interested in? What about an opera company? How about a ballet company? What about a talent agent, a booking agent, or a management company? How about an entertainment industry publicity firm? What about an entertainment magazine or a newspaper's entertainment editor? Call up. Take a chance. It may pay off.

Depending on where you're calling and the size of the company, in many cases when you start your conversation during a cold call, the person you're speaking to will direct you to the human resources (HR) department. If this is the case, ask who you should speak to in HR. Try to get a name. Then, thank the person who gave you the information and call the HR department asking for the name of the person you were given. Being referred by someone else in the company will often get you through. Try something like this:

> **You:** Good afternoon. Would Mike Robbins be in, please?
>
> **Secretary:** Who's calling?
>
> **You:** This is Ernest Rowe. Mr. Adams suggested I call him.

Believe it or not, the more calls you make, the more you will increase your chances of success in getting potential interviews.

If you're really uncomfortable making the calls, or you can't get through to the people

> ⭐ **Tip from the Coach**
>
> Expect rejection when making cold calls. Some people may not want to talk to you. Rejection is a lot easier to deal with when you decide ahead of time it isn't personally directed toward you.

you're trying to reach by phone, consider writing letters. It takes more time than a phone call, but it is another proactive method for you to get through to someone.

While these techniques are very effective when trying to get through to someone in the business or administration area of the performing arts, they are equally as effective when attempting to reach through to casting agents, talent agents, literary agents, booking agents, and managers. Don't be afraid to use the cold-calling technique to find new places to send your head shots and resume, to meet with people who can help your career move forward, or even to find auditions.

Creating Your Career

Do you want one more really good reason to find the hidden job market in the performing arts? If you're creative and savvy enough, you might even be able to *create* a position for yourself even if you are only on the first or second rung of the career ladder. What does that mean? Here are a few examples.

Let's say you're working as a receptionist at an arts council. It comes to your attention that people often call asking about training opportunities to get into theater and the performing arts. Through research, you realize that there is no one source for locating training and educational opportunities in the performing arts. You talk to

your supervisor about the possibility of putting together a booklet of these opportunities and he or she agrees. Within a few months you complete the project. You then suggest that you put together the information for an electronic database. You are enjoying your new responsibilities and research other special projects. Before long, you talk to your supervisor about the possibility of creating a new position coordinating special projects.

Here's another example. Let's say you're working as an administrative assistant at a record label. In the course of your job, you get an idea. Wouldn't it be great to have a newsletter about new artists that goes out a couple of times a week via e-mail to fans. That way fans could request the artist's music videos be played on music television and CDs be played on radio. You do a prototype and bring it to your supervisor. He or she may speak to the publicity department. While there was no position planned for this job, they ask you if you would be interested in taking over this project. Voila! You've created your own position and you've moved up the ladder.

What if you don't yet have a job? Is it still possible to create a position? If you are creative, have some initiative, and are assertive enough to push your idea, you can. Come up with something that you could do for the company that you want to work for which isn't being done now or that you could do better. Do you have any ideas? What about being a concierge for a major talent agency's big acts? What about being a media trainer, coaching performing artists in dealing with the press so they can be effective when doing interviews? What about putting together media events for touring artists?

Get creative. Come up with an idea, develop it fully, put it on paper so you can see any problems, and fine-tune it. Then call up the company that you want to work with, lay out the idea, and sell them on it. You've just created your own job!

Don't think that you can only create your own job in the business or arts administration end of the performing arts. If you're creative enough you can even come up with ways to create a role for yourself in the talent end of the industry.

Need an example? We were covering this subject at a seminar a few years ago. A man raised his hand.

"I work in customer service at a large hotel," he said. "I want to be a comedian. It's not so much that I want the fame. I just want to perform. Do you have any ideas?"

"What do you do at the hotel?" I asked.

"I'm one of the people you talk to when you have been waiting in line for a half an hour to check in and you're just not happy," he replied.

"Do you like to tell jokes, or build on stories?" I asked. "Is your show relatively clean? By that I mean, could you do snippets of a comedy show and not offend anyone?"

"Yeah, I could do that," he said. "But where?"

"Why don't you go to your supervisor and suggest that you have an idea to make days that they have an especially heavy check-in better for the guests. Suggest that while guests are in line, you walk around and entertain them. A joke

here, a story there. Ask if he would be willing to try it once or twice to see how it works out."

"I'm going to give it a try," he said.

A few months after that, I received a phone call. The man had spoken to his supervisor who agreed to try the idea. It worked so well that the man was given a raise and a new title. The guests loved it. A few more months passed and I heard from the man again to update me on his career. Evidently, he had been on duty one busy Friday afternoon, mingling with guests. Two of the guests in line were in a rush and slightly agitated because checking in was taking so long. The man went over and started talking to the two gentlemen, putting a humorous spin on the situation. Soon the two were laughing. One of the guests mentioned to the man that he was very funny and perhaps he should look into stand-up as a career instead of what he was doing. "That's my dream," he replied. He spent the rest of the night pleased that someone had recognized his talent.

That might have been the end of the story, but it turns out that those two guests were the manager and tour manager for a recording act who coincidentally had been looking for an opening act for their new tour. To make a long story short, after a number of auditions and interviews, a deal was struck and the man was hired to open for the act.

If you put your fear aside and think outside of the box, the same could happen for you.

6

Tools for Success

Every trade has its own set of tools that help the tradesperson achieve success. Without these tools, their jobs would be more difficult, if not impossible, to accomplish.

The performing arts are no exception. Whether your career choice is on the business end of the industry or performing arts administration, talent, creative, or somewhere in between, there are certain tools that can help you achieve success faster as well.

These include things like your resume, business and networking cards, brochures, career portfolio, professional reference sheets, press kits, quote sheets, bios, head shots, and Web sites.

This chapter will get you started putting together these tools. Some of these tools are specifically for those in the business and administrative end of the industry. Several are generally just needed by those in the talent end of the industry. Others can be useful to everyone.

Let's get started!

Your Resume as a Selling Tool

Whether utilizing publicity, ads in newspapers or magazines, television or radio commercials, billboards, banners or the Web, or a variety of additional marketing vehicles, there is virtually

no successful company which does not advertise or market their products or services in some manner.

Why do they do this? The main reason is to make sure others are aware of their products or services so they can then find ways to entice potential customers to buy or use those products or services.

What does this have to do with you and your career? When trying to succeed, no matter what area of theater or the performing arts you're interested in pursuing, it is a good idea to look at yourself as a *product*.

What that means in a broad sense is that you will be marketing yourself so people know you exist: so they begin to differentiate you from others, so they see you in a better light. How can you entice potential employers to hire you? How can you help potential managers or agents or others in the industry to know you exist?

The answer is simple. Start by making your resume a selling tool! Make it your own personal printed marketing piece. Everyone sends out resumes. The trick is making yours so powerful that it will grab the attention of potential employers.

Resumes are important whether you're interested in a job in arts administration and the business end of the industry or the talent side of the industry. Let's focus first on the business end of the industry and then we'll move on to the talent side.

Does your resume do a great job of selling your credentials? Does it showcase your skills, personality traits, and special talents? Is your resume the one that is going to impress the employers or human resources directors who can call you in for that all-important interview and ultimately land you the job in arts administration you're after? Is it going to land you the job in the performing arts you've been dreaming about?

If an employer doesn't know you, their first impression of you might very well be your resume. This makes your resume a crucial part of

Tip from the Top

Keep updated copies of your resume on CD, DVD, diskette, or a flash drive. You can never tell when your computer hard drive will die just when someone tells you about a great opportunity or you see an advertisement for the perfect job. If your resume is on a CD or other media, you simply need to just put it in another computer, tailor your resume for that particular job, and send it off.

Words from the Wise

If you're using different resumes, make sure you know which one you send to which company. Keep a copy of the resume you use for a specific job with a copy of the cover letter you send. Do it every time. Otherwise when sending out numerous resumes and letters it's very easy to get confused.

getting an interview that might ultimately lead to your dream job.

A strong resume illustrates that you have the experience and qualifications to fill a potential employer's needs. How can you do this? To begin with, learn to tailor your resume to the job you're pursuing. One of the biggest mistakes people make in job hunting is to create just one resume and then use it every single time they apply for a position, no matter what the job.

If this is what you've been doing, it's time to break the habit. Start by crafting your main resume. Then, don't be afraid to edit it to fit the needs of each specific job opening or opportunity.

Always keep a copy of each resume you develop on your computer and make sure you note the date it was done and its main focus. If you don't have your own computer, keep your resume on a CD, DVD, diskette, or a flash drive so you always have access to it without having to type it all over again.

How can you make your resume a better marketing tool? Present it in a clear, concise manner, highlighting your best assets. Organize things in an order that makes it easy for someone just glancing at your resume to see the points that sell you the best and then want to take a second look.

The decision about the sequence of items in your resume should be based on what is

> **Tip from the Top**
>
> When replying to a job advertisement, use words from the advertisement in both your resume and your cover letter. It makes you look like more of a fit with the company's expectations.

most impressive in relation to the position you are pursuing. Do you have a lot of experience in not-for-profit theaters, orchestras, or opera companies? Put that information first. Are your accomplishments extraordinary? If so, highlight those first. Do you have little experience, but you just graduated cum laude with a degree in arts administration? Then perhaps your education should be where your resume should start.

Sometimes it helps when creating your own resume to imagine that you just received it in the mail. What would make you glance at it and say, "Wow," and keep on reading? Or would you glance at it and hope that there is a more interesting one coming in?

One of the most important things to remember is that there really is no right or wrong type of resume. The right one for you will end up being the one that ultimately gets you the position you want. There are so many ways to prepare your resume that it is often difficult to choose one. My advice is to craft several different ones, put them away overnight and then look at them the next day. Which one looks best to you? That probably will be the style you want to use.

Here are some tips that might help:

◎ Tailor every resume for every position.
◎ Make sure you check for incorrect word usage. No matter what position you're pursuing, most employers prefer to have someone who has a command of the English language. Check to make sure

you haven't inadvertently used the word *their* for *there*, *to* for *too* or *two*, *effect* for *affect*, *you're* for *your*, *it's* for *its*, and so on. Don't rely solely on your computer's spell and grammar checker. Carefully go over your work yourself as well.

◎ Every time you edit your resume or make a change, check carefully for errors. It is very easy to miss a double word, a misspelled word, or a wrong tense. Have a friend or family member look over your resume. It is often difficult to see mistakes in your own work.

◎ Tempting as it is to use different colored inks when preparing your resume, don't. Use only black ink.

◎ Use a high-quality paper of at least 40-pound weight for printing your resumes. Paper with texture often *feels* different, so it stands out. While you can use white, beige, or cream colored papers, soft light colors such as light blue, salmon pink, gray, or light green will help your resume stand out from the hundreds of white and beige ones.

◎ Make sure your resume layout looks attractive. You can have the greatest content in the world, but if your resume just doesn't look right, people may not actually read it.

   ▫ You know the saying, "You can't judge a book by its cover?" Well, you really can't, but if you don't know anything about the book or its contents you just might not pick it up unless the cover looks interesting.

◎ When sending your resume and cover letter, instead of using a standard number 10 business envelope and folding your resume, use a large manila envelope. That way you won't have to

---

> ### ★ Words from the Wise
> Whatever color paper you use for your resume and cover letters, make sure it photocopies well. Some colored papers photocopy dark or look messy.

---

fold your resume and your information gets there looking clean, crisp, and flat.

◎ Don't use odd fonts or typefaces. Why? In many large companies, resumes are scanned by machine. Certain fonts don't scan well. What should you use? Helvetica, Times, Arial, and Courier work well.

◎ Similarly, many fonts don't translate well when e-mailing. What looks great on the resume on your computer may end up looking like gibberish at the recipient's end, and you probably will never know. Once again, use Helvetica, Times, Arial, or Courier.

◎ When preparing your resume make your name larger and bolder than the rest of your resume. For example, if your resume is done in 12-point type, use 14-, 16-, or 18-point type for your name. Your name will stand out from those on other resumes.

◎ Remember to utilize white space. Margins should be at least one inch on each side as well as on the top and bottom of each page. White space also helps draw the reader's attention to information.

Redefining Your Resume

You probably already have a resume in some form. How has it been working? Is it getting you the interviews you want? If it is, great. If not, you might want to consider redefining it.

You want your resume to stand out. You want it to illustrate that you have been successful in your accomplishments. You want potential employers to look at your resume and say to themselves, "That's who I want working here!"

How do you do that? Make your resume compelling. Demonstrate through your resume that you believe in yourself because if you don't believe in you, no one else will. Show that you have the ability to solve problems and bring fresh ideas to the table.

First decide how you want to present yourself. What type of resume is best for you? There are a couple of basic types of resumes. The chronological resume lists your jobs and accomplishments beginning with the most current and going backwards. Functional resumes, which may also be referred to as skills-based resumes, emphasize your accomplishments and abilities. One of the good things about this type of resume is that it allows you to lay it out in a manner that spotlights your key areas, whether they be your qualifications, skills, or employment history.

What's the best type of resume for you? That depends on a number of factors including where you are in your career. If you are just entering the job market and you haven't held down a lot of jobs, but you have relevant experience through internships and/or volunteer activities, you might want to use the functional type. If, on the other hand, you have held a number of jobs in the field and climbed the ladder each time you moved, you might want to use the chronological variety. You can also sometimes combine elements from both types. This is called a combination resume. As I noted earlier, there is no one right way. You have to look at the whole picture and make a decision.

Use common sense. Make your best assets prominent on your resume. Do you have a lot of experience? Are your accomplishments above

> ### ★ Voice of Experience
> Your resume is your place to toot your own horn. If you don't, no one will know what you have accomplished.

the bar? Did you graduate cum laude with a degree in arts administration or music business management? Determine what would grab your eye and find a way to focus on that first.

What Should Your Resume Contain?

What should you have in your resume? Some components are required and some are optional. Let's look at some of them.

What do you definitely need? Your name, address, phone number, and e-mail address. What else? Your education, professional or work experience, accomplishments, and professional memberships. What might else might you want to put in your resume? Your career objective, a summary of skills, and a career summary.

What shouldn't you put in your resume? Your age, marital status, any health problems, current or past salaries, and whether or not you have children. What else shouldn't you put down? Any weakness you have or think you have.

Career Summary

Let's discuss your career summary. While a career summary isn't a required component, it often is helpful when an employer gets a huge number of resumes and gives each a short glance. A career summary is a short professional biography—no longer than 12 sentences—that tells your professional story. You can do it in a number of ways. Here's an example:

Bachelor's degree with a major in arts administration and a minor in communications. Proven ability to deal with media on the local, regional, and national level. Fully knowledgeable in all aspects of public relations, publicity, advertising, and marketing. Accomplished entrepreneur in a variety of areas including product merchandising. Increased merchandising revenues for four artists by 45 percent. Assisted in season-opening events for major orchestra. Fluent in English, French, Spanish, and German. Energetic, passionate, and articulate team player with a good sense of humor and the goal of making a success out of every opportunity.

A potential employer looking at this might think, "This Larry Evans has a degree in arts administration, so he at least has an understanding and background in the arts. He also has managed his own business in merchandising and increased revenues so he has a business sense. The ability to speak more than one language is always a plus. It looks like he has an understanding of marketing, publicity, promotion, and the like, and on top of that he looks successful. Why don't I give him a chance to tell me more? I think I want to bring him in for an interview."

"What if I'm just out of college and have no experience?" you ask. "What would my career summary look like?"

In situations like this you have to look toward experience and jobs you held prior to graduating. How about this:

Recent graduate of State University with a major in arts administration and a minor in business with a GPA of 4.0. Intern in rotating departments at major orchestra. Proven ability to handle various tasks quickly, effectively, and efficiently. Ability to successfully bring a project to fruition on time and under budget. Member of college campus activities board, assisting in the booking of all college entertainment events as well as handling artist rider fulfillment on days of events. Handled publicity for college theater club productions.

If you prefer, you can use a bulleted list to do your career summary:

◎ Recent graduate of State University with a major in arts administration and a minor in business; GPA of 4.0
◎ Intern at Philadelphia Orchestra
◎ Member of college campus activities board, assisting in the booking of all college entertainment events
◎ Publicist for college theater club productions

Career Objective

Do you need a career objective in your resume? It isn't always necessary, but in certain cases it helps. For example, if you are just starting out in your career, having a career objective or a specific goal illustrates that you have some direction—that you know where you want to go in your career.

Tip from the Top
Many people sabotage themselves by giving more information than is required on their resume. When preparing your resume, always stop to think, "Will this help or hinder my career?"

When replying to a job opening, make sure the career objective on your resume is as close to the job you are applying for as possible. For example, if you are applying for a job as a publications assistant at a ballet company, you might make your career objective, "To work in the publications department of a ballet company in a position where I can fully utilize my creativity and writing skills."

If, on the other hand, you are sending your resume to a company "cold" or not for a specific job opening, don't limit yourself unnecessarily by stating a specific career objective. If you use a career objective in this type of situation, make sure it is general.

In many instances, you might send copies of your resume with a cover letter to companies you want to work for who aren't actively looking to fill a job in hopes of garnering an interview. If your resume indicates, for example, that your sole goal is to work in a company's publications department, you might be overlooked for a position in the marketing or public relations department. Your career goal in this situation instead might be, "To work at an orchestra, opera, ballet, or other arts management company in a position where my people skills can be combined with my love and understanding of the performing arts and my degree in marketing and public relations." Remember, you want the person reviewing your resume to think of all the possible places you might fit in the organization.

Education

Where should you put education on your resume? If you recently have graduated from college, especially if you have a degree in something related to the performing arts industry, put it toward the top. If you graduated a number of years ago, put your education toward the end of your resume. Unless you recently graduated, it's not necessary to put the year you graduated. Just indicate the college or university you graduated from and your major.

If you went to college but didn't graduate, simply write that you attended or took coursework toward a degree. Will anyone question you on it? That's hard to say. Someone might. If questioned, simply say something like, "I attended college and then unfortunately found it necessary to go to work full time. I plan on getting my degree as soon as possible. I only have nine credits left to go, so it will be an easy goal to achieve."

In addition to your college education, don't forget to include any relevant noncredit courses, seminars, and workshops you have attended such as public speaking, writing, grant writing, communications, or teamwork.

Professional and Work Experience

List your work experience in this section of your resume. What jobs have you had? Where did you work? What did you do? What were your accomplishments?

How far back do you go? That once again depends where you are in your career. Don't go back to your job as a babysitter when you were 15, but you want to show your work history.

In addition to your full-time jobs in or out of the performing arts, include any part-time work that relates to the industry or illustrates transferable job skills, accomplishments, or achievements.

Skills and Personality Traits

There's an old advertising adage which says something to the effect of, "Don't sell the steak, sell the sizzle." When selling yourself through your resume, do the same. Make your skills and personality traits sizzle! Do this by using descriptive language and key phrases.

Need some help? Here are a few words and phrases to get you started:

- creative
- dedicated
- hard working
- highly motivated
- energetic
- self-starter
- fully knowledgeable
- strong work ethic
- team player
- problem solver

Accomplishments and Achievements

What have you accomplished in your career in or out of the performing arts industry? Have you increased sales? Have you increased attendance? Coordinated the opening of an entertainment event? Written a weekly entertainment column? Won an industry award? Done the publicity for a theatrical production? Written a large innovative grant? Your achievements inform potential employers not only about what you have done but also about what you might do for them.

Sit down and think about it for a while. What are you most proud of in your career? What have you done that has made a difference or had a positive impact on the company for which you worked? If you are new to the workforce, what did you do in school? What about in a volunteer capacity?

Just as you made your skills and personality traits sizzle with words, you want to do the same thing with your accomplishments and achievements. Put yourself in the position of a human resources director or the owner of a company for a moment. You get two resumes. Under the accomplishments section one says, "Worked on executing concert for charity." The other says, "Planned, coordinated, and successfully executed charity concert from inception through fruition, generating $35,000 profit for Green County Arts Council" Which resume would catch your eye?

You can help your accomplishments and achievements sizzle by adding action verbs to your accomplishments. Words such as *achieved, administered, applied, accomplished, assisted,* and *strengthened* are helpful.

When drafting your resume include any honors you have received whether or not they have anything to do with the performing arts industry. These honors help set you apart from other candidates. Did one of your newspaper articles win a journalism award? Did a review in the newspaper say you were the highlight of a theatrical production?

Were you honored with the "Volunteer of The Year" award at a local hospital? Did you receive a community service award from your local civic group? While these have absolutely nothing to do with the performing arts industry, they illustrate that you are a hard worker and good at what you do.

Community Service and Volunteer Activities

If you perform community service or volunteer activities on a regular basis, include it on your resume. These illustrate to potential employers that you "do a little extra." Additionally, you can never predict when the person reviewing your resume might be a member of the organization with which you volunteer. An unexpected connection like that helps you stand out. Additionally, many performing arts industry organizations are not-for-profits. Illustrating that you are involved in the not-for-profit world may be a plus to potential employers.

Words from a Pro

If you are instructed to send references with your resume, attach them on a separate sheet of paper.

References

The goal for your resume is to have it help you obtain an interview. If you list your references on your resume, be aware that someone may check them to help them decide if they should interview you. You don't really want people giving their opinions about you *until* you have the chance to sell yourself, so it usually isn't a good idea to list your references on your resume. Instead, include a line on your resume stating that "references are available upon request."

Your Resume Writing Style

How important is writing style in your resume? Very important. Aside from conveying your message, your writing style helps to illustrate that you have written communication skills.

When preparing your resume write clearly and concisely and do not use the pronoun "I" to describe your accomplishments. Instead of writing "I developed key PR campaigns for entertainment industry clients" or "I got clients over 1,000 appearances and mentions in major media," try "Developed key PR campaigns for entertainment industry clients resulting in over 1,000 major media appearances, interviews, and mentions in a two-month period." Note the inclusion of a time period. It's good to be specific about your achievements.

Instead of "I've designed costumes for many stage shows," try "Designed and constructed costumes from period to modern for more than 25 theatrical productions."

⭐ Tip from the Coach

Unless you are doing a theatrical resume, don't worry if you can't get your resume on one or two pages. While most career specialists insist a resume should only be one or two pages at most, I strongly disagree. You don't want to overwhelm a potential employer with a 10-page book, but if your resume needs to be three or four pages to get your pertinent information in, that's okay. Keep in mind, though, that lengthy resumes like these are generally used by high-level professionals with many years' experience and work history to fill the additional pages. If your resume is longer than normal, you should use a brief career summary at the beginning so a hiring manager can quickly see what your major accomplishments are. If they then want to take their time to look through the rest of the resume, your information will be there.

One thing you should *never* do is lie on your resume. Don't lie about your education. Don't lie about experience. Don't lie about places you've worked. Don't lie about what you've acted in or where you have performed. *Do not lie!* The performing arts community is close knit. Once someone knows you have lied, that is what they will remember about you and they may pass on that information to others.

"Oh, no one is going to find out," you might say.

Someone might find out by chance, deduce the truth based on their industry knowledge, or hear the facts from a coworker or industry colleague. When the truth comes out it can end up blowing up in your face.

"By that time, I'll be doing such a good job, no one will fire me," you say.

That's the best-case scenario, and there's a chance that could happen, but think about this.

Once someone lies to you, do you ever trust them again? Probably not, and no one will trust you or anything you say. That will hurt your chances of climbing the career ladder. The worst-case scenario is that you will be fired, left without references, lose some of your contacts, and make it much more difficult to find your next job.

Believe it or not, whether you're interested in working in the talent or creative end of the performing arts, the business or administrative segment, or anywhere in between, the people who are doing the hiring know everyone has to start someplace. If you don't have the experience, impress them with other parts of your resume and your cover letter.

If you have the experience and you are trying to advance your career, this is the time to redefine your resume. Add action verbs. Add your accomplishments. Make your new resume shine. Create a marketing piece that will make someone say, "We need to interview this person. Look at everything he's done."

Resumes for Actors: Theatrical Resumes

If you are an actor, your resume will be different from the traditional resume you probably are accustomed to seeing. Exactly what is a professional theatrical resume? It's a one-page compilation of your theatrical and acting experiences including your stage roles, television and film roles, and any commercials you might have under your belt. It will also include your education and training.

"What's the difference between a theatrical resume and a traditional resume?" you ask. A number of things; most notably, on a traditional resume you generally don't include your physical description. On your professional theatrical resume you do.

> ### ★ Words from the Wise
>
> For safety reasons, it is not a good idea to put your home address on theatrical resumes, which often have your photo attached. To get around this, use a PO box instead.

People who hire you to appear in theatrical productions, commercials, television or movies *need* to know what you look like. Casting directors, producers, and directors generally have an image in their mind of what they want the actor or actress they are casting to look like. Knowing ahead of time makes this process easier.

"But I'm including a head shot. Can't they use that?" you ask.

They'll use that as well, but you still need to create your resume in the professional format agents, producers, and directors expect.

The purpose of the theatrical resume is to help casting directors and agents learn more about you so they can determine if you should be cast in one of their roles. This resume, together with your head shot, is your introduction to these important people. The more professional you make it look, the better your chances are of landing an audition, which can lead to a role.

Your theatrical resume should be one page. Before you say, "Can't it be longer?" the answer is no. You are going to be attaching your head shot to the other side of your resume.

What should you include?

◎ Your professional or stage name. This is the name you are known as professionally in the performing arts industry.
  ▫ Make sure your name is prominent on the page. (You might want to have your name in a larger, bolder type.)

◎ Any union affiliations you have such as Actors' Equity (AEA), SAG, AFTRA, AGMA, AFM, etc.
◎ Contact information. You want the people who are going to hire you have a way to get in touch with you.
  ▫ Phone number. Include the phone number where a casting director can reach you. You might want to also include your cell phone number to make sure you are easily reachable.
  ▫ If an agency is either representing you or sending you on an audition, supply the agency's phone number.
  ▫ Your e-mail address.
  ▫ Your Web site address.
◎ Your height, weight, hair color, and eye color.
◎ Your acting experience. You will want to include the name of the production, the type of part you played, and the role.
  ▫ If you have worked in various genres of the performing arts, subdivide your experience.
    ◇ Stage
    ◇ Film
    ◇ Television
    ◇ Commercials
    ◇ Voice-overs
    ◇ Miscellaneous (Theme parks, cruise ships, hotels, trade shows, clubs, etc.)
◎ Acting studies, education, additional training, etc. Include where you studied and with whom.
  ▫ Acting
  ▫ Vocal
  ▫ Dance
  ▫ Comedy

(continues)

Dean Bush

AEA, SAG, AFTRA

Statistics:

Hair: Brown
Eyes: Blue
Height: 6'0"
Weight: 185

Contact:

Phone: (212) 111-1111
E-mail:deanbush@bestinternet.com
Web site: http://www.deanbush.com
Representation: Cap Theatrical
Phone: (212) 222-3333

Theater	Role	Theater Company
My Town Blues	Jess (supporting)	Circle Star Theatre Company, NYC
Fiddler on the Roof	Teve (lead)	New Theater Touring Company, Miami
Treasure Hunting	Steve	Angel Theater Company, Philadelphia
Out the Window	The Policeman	Jeffries Theater Company, Philadelphia
42nd Street	Julian Marsh	NBT Theater, Minneapolis
The Lamp Post	Todd (lead)	Columbia University Theater, NYC
Goodnight Tomorrow	Bing (lead)	Columbia University Theater, NYC

Film

Convoy Emergency	George Johnson	Best Films, Director, Shaun Pirot
The River Man	Dick Zaan	BNG Films, Director, Bobbie Biloxi

Television

Beverly Hills Hotel	Bill Reynolds	Carol Notting, Producer/LRK Network
The Bank Family	Gene Thompson	Beverly Jones, Producer/ TBC Network

Commercials

West Shopping Center
Coffee Shop Stop

Voice-Over

Bright-White Toothpaste	Announcer	Brian Edie, Director
Top Shop Groceries	Announcer	Gino Park, Director

Education & Training

Bachelor of Arts in Theater Arts	Columbia University, New York, NY
Circle In The Square Theatre School	New York, NY
Acting: Bill Blitzer	The Bill Blitzer Studio, 2 Year Program
Shakespeare:	British American Drama Academy
Stage Combat:	Richard Black, Will Bullock
Cold Reading:	Art Phillips, Joan East
Voice:	Ari Johnson, Jane Gray

Special Skills

Dance: ballet, tap, jazz; Dialects: Scottish, English, Irish, Yiddish, French; Fluent in French; juggler, skilled magician and illusionist.

> ### ⭐ The Inside Scoop
>
> Instead of just making your resume an outline of your accomplishments, make it a powerful marketing tool.

◎ Special skills. This is where you add in special skills that may set you apart from another actor. Are you fluent in other languages? Can you speak different dialects? Can you juggle?

◎ Awards and honors.

Okay, you now have an idea of what is going to go into your resume if you are an actor or actress. Now it's time to begin developing yours. The sample on page 102 will help you get started.

One of the mistakes that many people make when preparing their professional theatrical resume is that they keep adding accomplishments without deleting any of the earlier or less important ones. While it's very tempting to do this, it's not the best idea because your theatrical resume can only be one page.

Update your resume when necessary, listing your newest or most important roles and accomplishments and deleting the older ones. You can always have a special sheet listing all your roles and accomplishments available upon request.

The Picture Worth a Thousand Words: Head Shots

They say that a picture is worth a thousand words. This is especially true if you are an actor because head shots are essential to your career. Good head shots can help you get roles. Bad ones have the potential of holding back your career.

As an actor or actress, your head shot is one of the most important marketing tools you have. It is your calling card. It is often the first impression you make to talent agents, managers, directors, and casting agents.

Make sure head shots are great! They can not only get you in the door, but help you obtain the acting role of your dreams.

While your resume gives casting agents and directors an explanation of your accomplishments and what you have done, your head shot gives them the visual necessary to determine if you have the *look* they are seeking to fill a role.

The best advice I can give you regarding your head shots is to get them done professionally by someone in the industry who knows what they are doing and with whom you feel comfortable.

What you're looking for are headshot photographers. Find a number of photographers who work with actors and actresses or at least other people in the performing arts and entertainment industry and ask to see *their* portfolio. Don't be shy. This is your career on the line.

Where do you find photographers? If you live in one of the entertainment capitals such as New York or Los Angeles, the yellow pages are a good resource for finding photographers. Advertisements in the trades such as *Backstage* or *Variety* are good sources as well. Your best bet, however, is word of mouth. Ask other actors where they get their photos done. Check with your agent or manager if you already have one. See who they recommend.

"Can't I get a friend to take my head shots for me?" you ask. Unless your friend is a professional photographer, he or she probably doesn't have the necessary tools. Generally head shots are done against a neutral background and with special lighting. To do that, you usually need to be in a studio. Additionally, professional photographers who specialize in the theatrical industry have the expertise and knowledge to guide you on poses, clothing, background, etc.

Good head shots are costly, but a necessary expense in your career as an actor or actress. Prices can range dramatically from approximately $100 to $1,000 or more, and that is just for the photo session.

Just because a photographer is more expensive does not always mean that he or she is better. As I noted previously, make sure you *like* the photographer's work and then deal with price.

Most photographers will ask you to sign a contract. This is not a bad thing, so don't panic. The contract is an agreement between the photographer and you stating what the photo shoot will cost, when payment is due, who gets the negatives or originals, and any extras that you have agreed upon. These might include a variety of things including retouching or hairstyling and makeup sessions before the shoot. Some photographers will facilitate the reproduction of your photos and include this in the price. In other cases, they may recommend a reproduction house to make copies of your photo.

Make sure you read the contract carefully and understand everything before you sign it. If you don't understand something or are not happy with any of the terms or conditions, ask ahead of time.

At our theater and performing arts seminars, attendees always have a lot of questions about their head shots. What does the perfect head shot look like? Should they be black and white or color? What size should they be?

> ### ⭐ Tip from the Coach
> Your head shots are not set in stone. As your career progresses, your appearance changes, or your agent feels you should project a different look, you will need to update and get new photos.

What should you wear in your shoot? How glamorous should they be? And the list goes on.

Let's address some of those questions. To begin with, there is no one "right" way or perfect way to do a head shot. Basically, your head shot will be an 8-by-10 glossy photograph of you from your chest up. What you want to end up with is a photo that not only looks like you, but helps your personality shine through; a photo which catches the eye of casting directors, agents and directors.

In the past head shots were done almost exclusively in black and white. Today many head shots are also done in color. You are going to have to decide which you prefer. Your photographer can help guide you.

While you want to look your best, you also want to make sure that the photograph looks like you. You want the casting director to look at you and your head shot and know it's the same person.

Choose your clothing for the shoot based on the image you are trying to portray to casting directors and agents. If you are using a photographer who is experienced in head shots, talk to him or her to get advice on the type of clothing to bring to the shoot and the best colors to wear. Get advice on hair and makeup. Many photographers provide hairstylist and/or professional

⭐ The Inside Scoop

Proof sheets are sheets that are printed with the pictures the photographer has taken in thumbnail size.

makeup artist services to clients. These are all things you should consider.

After the photo shoot you'll have some decisions to make. The photographer (or a developer) will give you a proof sheet of all the photographs taken during your session. If the photographer has taken the photos with a digital camera instead of film, you might even be able to look at the pictures on your computer.

Once you get the proof sheets, you have to choose the one that you like the best for your head shot. You probably will want to show the proof sheets to friends, family, and your manager and agent to get their opinion on which picture they like best.

In some cases, after you've chosen your favorite, you may decide that you would like to re-touch it a bit. While it's fine to air-brush out small imperfections, don't go overboard. You want your head shot to look like you, not the way you wish you looked. Once you're happy with your photo, you're ready to have it reproduced.

Depending on the deal you made with the photographer, he or she may handle this task for you or may recommend a reproduction company. If you're just starting out in your career, start off with between 100 and 250 copies. That way, if you decide that you need (or want) a different head shot, you won't have thousands of useless ones laying around. If you want to keep your head shot and find you need more, you can have more made. If you're already established, you

probably have a better sense of how many head shots you use in a given time and might want to make 500 or more.

Don't forget that you need to have your name printed on the bottom of each photograph so that the people you are giving it to know who you are in case your photo gets separated from your resume.

Various people in the industry have different views whether to put your contact number on your head shots. Most feel that because your head shot goes with your resume (which has your contact information) it isn't necessary. Another factor to consider is that if you have representation, they are going to want their contact information on your photos.

What do you do with your head shots? Attach them to your resume. The most common method is to place the blank back side of the photo to the blank backside of your resume and staple both pieces together.

Many actors additionally print their head-shots on postcards with key parts of their resume. They then send regular mailings to agents, casting directors, and other important people in the industry. The idea is if you constantly keep your information in front of people who are doing the hiring, when they need someone to fill a role who fits your description, they'll hopefully think of you.

What About References?

References are another of your selling tools. References are the individuals who will vouch for your skills, ethics, and work history when a potential employer calls. A good reference can set you apart from the crowd and give you the edge over other applicants. A bad one can seriously hinder your career goals.

It's always a good idea to bring the names, addresses, and phone numbers of the people you are using for references with you when you apply for a job or when you are going on an interview. If you're asked to list them on an employment application, you'll be prepared.

Who should you use for references? To begin with, you'll need professional references. These are people you've worked with or know you on a professional level. They might be current or former supervisors or bosses, the director of a not-for-profit organization you've worked with, internship program coordinators, a former professor, and so on.

Do your references have to be from the performing arts genre? If you have references in the industry, it can't hurt. What you are looking for, however, are people whom you can count on to help sell you to potential employers. Those will be your best references.

Always ask people if they are willing to be a reference before you use them. Only use people you are absolutely positive will say good things about you. Additionally, try to find people who are articulate and professional.

Who would be a bad reference? A boss who fired you, a supervisor you didn't get along with, or anyone you had any kind of problem with whatsoever. Do not use these people for references even if they tell you that they'll give you a good one. They might keep their word, but they might not, and you won't know until it's too late.

You might be asked to list references on an employment application, but it's a good idea to prepare a printed sheet of your professional references that you can leave with the interviewer. This sheet will contain your list of three to five references including their names, positions, and contact information. As with your resume, make sure it is printed on high-quality paper.

Here's an example to get you started:

Professional Reference Sheet for Tony Blast

Mr. Tom White
President
Mid Town Theater
121 Broadway
Anytown, NY 11111
(212) 333-3333
twhite@midtowntheater.com

Ms. Debbie Holbrook
Intern Coordinator
TRG Symphony
303 4th Avenue
Anytown, NY 11111
(212) 333-4444
dholbrook@trg.org

Mr. Scott Carter
Theater Critic
Daily Record
491 Fifth Avenue South
Cityville, NY 12222
(111) 444-4444
scarter@dailyrecord.com

Personal References

In addition to professional references, you might also be asked to provide personal references. These are friends, family members, or others who know you. You probably won't need to print out a reference sheet for your personal references, but make sure you have all their contact information in case you need it quickly.

As with professional references, make sure the people you are using know you are listing them as references. Give them a call when you're going on an interview to let them know someone might be contacting them. Ask them to let you know if they get a call.

Letters of Recommendation

As you go through your career, it's a good idea to get letters of recommendation from people who have been impressed with your work. Along with references, these help give potential employers a better sense of your worth. How do you get a letter of recommendation? You usually simply have to ask. For example, let's say you are close to completing an internship.

Say to your supervisor, "I've enjoyed my time here. Would it be possible to get a letter of recommendation from you for my files?"

Most people will be glad to provide this. In some cases, people might even ask you to write it yourself for them to sign. Don't forego these opportunities even if you feel embarrassed about blowing your own horn. The easiest way to do it is by trying to imagine you aren't writing about yourself. In that way you can be honest and write a great letter. Give it to the person and say, "Here's the letter we discussed. Let me know if you want anything changed or if you aren't comfortable with any piece of it." Nine times out of 10, the person will sign the letter as is.

Who should you ask for letters of recommendation? If you are still in school or close to graduating, ask professors with whom you have developed a good relationship. Don't forget internship coordinators or supervisors, former and current employers, executive directors of not-for-profit, civic, or charity organizations you have volunteered with, and so on.

Your letters of recommendation will become another powerful marketing tool in your quest to career success in the performing arts. What do you do with them? Begin by photocopying each letter you get on high-quality white paper,

making sure you get clean copies. Once that's done, you can make them part of your career portfolio, send them with your resume when applying for a position, or bring them with you to interviews.

Creating Captivating Cover Letters

Unless instructed otherwise by a potential employer or in an advertisement, always send your resume with a cover letter. Why? Mainly because if your resume grabs the eye of someone in the position to interview you, he or she often looks at the cover letter to evaluate your written communications skills as well as to get a sense of your personal side. If your letter is good, it might just get you the phone call you've been waiting for. On the other hand, a poorly written letter might just keep you from getting that call.

What can make your letter stand out? Try to make sure your letter is directed to the person to whom you are sending it instead of "Hiring Manager," "To Whom It May Concern," or "Sir or Madam."

"But the name of the person isn't in the ad," you say. "How do I know what it is?"

You might not always be able to get the correct name, but at least do some research. You might, for example, call the company and ask the name of the person to which responses are directed.

If you are sending your resume to a company cold, it's even more important to send it to a specific person. It gives you a better shot at someone not only reviewing it but taking action on it.

It's okay to call the company and say to the receptionist or secretary, "Hi, I was wondering if you could give me some information? I'm trying to send my resume to someone at your company and I'm not sure to whom I should address it. Could you please give me the name of the human resources director?"

If he or she won't give it to you for some reason, say thank you and hang up. For various reasons, in some companies, receptionists may not give out names easily.

How do you get around this? Wait until lunch time or around 5:15 p.m. when the person you spoke to might be at lunch or done working, call back, and say something to the effect of, "Hi, I was wondering if you could please give me the spelling of your booking director's name?"

If the person on the other end of the line asks you to be more specific about the name simply say, "Let's see, I think it was Brownson or something like that. It sounded like Brown something."

Don't worry about sounding stupid on the phone. The person at the other end doesn't know you. This system usually works. Believe it or not, most companies have someone working there whose name sounds like Brown or Smith.

The person on the phone may say to you, "No, we don't have a Brownson. What department are you looking for?" When you say booking, he or she will probably say, "Oh, that's not Brownson, it's John Campbell. Is that who you're looking for?"

Then all you have to say is, "You know what, you're right, sorry, I was looking at the wrong notes. So that's C-A-M-P-B-E-L-L?"

Voila. You have the name. Is it a lot of effort? It's a little effort, but if it gets you the name of someone you need and ultimately helps get you an interview, isn't it worth it?

You sometimes can get names from the Internet. Perhaps the company Web site lists the names of their key people. Key names for large companies may also often be located on Hoovers.com, an online database of information about businesses, but this is a paid service. Do what you can to get the names you need. It can make a big difference when you direct your letters to someone specific within the company.

What else can help your letters stand out? Make them grab the attention of the reader. How? Develop creative cover letters.

Take some time and think about it. What would make you keep reading? Of course, there will be situations where you might be better off sending the traditional, "In response to your ad" letter. But what about trying out a couple of other ideas?

Take a look at the following sample cover letter. Would this letter grab your attention? Would it make you keep reading? Chances are it would. After grabbing the reader's attention, it quickly offers some of the applicant's skills, talents, and achievements. Would you bring in Richard Douglas for an interview? I think most employers would.

RICHARD DOUGLAS
411 Avenue K
Different Town, NY 22222
Phone: 111-222-3333
rdouglas@moreinternet.com

Ms. Dee Nelson
Human Resources Manager
Gold City Orchestra
PO Box 1222
Gold City, NY 11111

Dear Ms. Nelson:

CONGRATULATIONS!

I'm pleased to inform you that you have just received the resume that can end your search for the Gold City Orchestra new marketing director. In order to claim your "prize," please review my resume and call as soon as possible to arrange an interview. I can guarantee you'll be pleased you did!

As the assistant marketing manager for a 1,000-seat facility, I helped coordinate the marketing activities of the facility for a year before being promoted to the position of full-fledged marketing manager. During my two-year tenure in this position I have developed a number of creative, innovative events to bring people in during "off" times as well as for major concert, dance, theater, and entertainment events. Through these extra events, the bottom-line revenue has increased dramatically and attendance has jumped 200 percent. In this position I have also worked with other large corporate businesses developing sponsorship opportunities for facility events, saving monies for the facility while generating large amounts of media attention for both entities.

While I love what I do now, my dream and passion has been a career in marketing at a major orchestra. When I saw this opportunity I was even more excited because I have not only been a season ticket holder of your symphony since graduation, but a supporter at many of your special events.

I welcome the challenge and opportunity to work with the Gold City Symphony and believe my experience, skills, talents, and passion would be an asset to your organization.

I look forward to hearing from you.

Sincerely yours,
Richard Douglas

Now check out some other creative cover letters.

CARNIE PHILLIPS
322 D Avenue
Different Town, NY 33333
Phone: 999-999-9999
cphillips@moreinternet.com

Mr. Phil Wilson
Promotion Manager
BLZ Records
912 Broadway
Anytown, NY 11111

Dear Mr. Wilson:
ARE YOU LOOKING FOR YOUR LABEL'S NEXT NUMBER-ONE RECORD?

While I can't guarantee a number-one record, I can promise you I'll be your label's number-one promotion staffer…if you give me a chance.

I'm an enthusiastic, pleasantly aggressive individual with a bachelor's degree in marketing. While still in school, I worked at Tower Records moving up from a sales associate to a third key management position in two years.

In college I began working as a part-time receptionist at WMAX radio. Within two months I was promoted to the position of administrative assistant in the traffic department. Six months after that, I moved into the promotion department working as an assistant. Upon college graduation, I was offered my current position of assistant station promotion director.

While I enjoy my job and have been getting excellent employment reviews, my career goal is to work at a major record label. I believe with my love for music, ability to sell and knowledge of both music and radio industries, I have the skills and talents to be an asset to your label in the promotion department.

I have enclosed my resume for your review and would very much appreciate the opportunity to meet with you to discuss opportunities at your label. In the event that you have no current openings, I was hoping you could still take a few minutes to speak to me to give me some ideas.

Thanks for your consideration. If I don't hear from you within a couple of weeks, I'll give you a call.

I look forward to hearing from you.

Sincerely yours,
Carnie Phillips

AARON COOPER
404 West Avenue
Different Town, NY 33333
Phone: 111-111-1111
acooper@moreinternet.com

Mr. Lewis Ackerly
Human Resources Director
State Street Theatre Company
411 State Street
Anytown, NY 11111

Dear Mr. Ackerly:

IS YOUR THEATER IN NEED OF FUNDS?

Thousands of dollars can be yours with just one call...

to me!!!

I was excited to learn about your opening for a Director of Fund-Raising and Development for the State Street Theatre. How lucky for me that just as I moved back into the area, the perfect job became available.

I have recently graduated from King University with a major in arts administration and a minor in theater arts. Before you pass by my resume for lack of experience, I urge you to read on. I'm sure you will agree that what I lack in professional experience in fund-raising, I more than make up for in my volunteer activities.

While still in college, I volunteered to work on fund-raising for a large not-for-profit theater in the area. I began by assisting in the coordination of a number of fund-raising events. I soon was helping develop and implement additional fund-raising events and activities for the theater, helping to raise over $800,000. After researching and writing a number of grants I was also able to secure three large grants totaling close to $1 million, which the theater desperately needed.

I'm sure your theater is like every other not-for-profit theater, orchestra, opera, and ballet company depending on grants, donations, sponsorships, and bequests for a large part of your funding. While, of course, I can't guarantee the exact amount I can help you raise for the theater, I can promise you that I will work tirelessly, using every avenue possible to secure funds.

I strongly believe that all the performing arts are important to a good quality of life and theater holds a special place in my heart. While I have acted in a number of theatrical productions in school and even received a couple of really good reviews for my performances, I realize that my true gift and passion is not acting on stage. Instead, it is raising funds, developing and implementing programs, and cultivating potential donors to sustain performing arts programs.

I'm an enthusiastic, creative, motivated team player who can also work effectively on my own. I am focused and goal oriented. If you give me

the chance, I'll be your theater's number-one cheerleader. I believe with my love for theater, and proven ability to secure funds, I have the skills and talents to be an asset to your theater.

I have enclosed my resume, copies of news stories on grants and fund-raising programs I was involved with, as well as a brief outline of a number of ideas I developed for fund-raising and development for the State Street Theater.

I would very much appreciate the opportunity to meet with you to discuss this exciting opportunity.

Thanks for your consideration. I look forward to hearing from you.

Sincerely yours,
Aaron Cooper

More Selling Tools—Business and Networking Cards

The best way to succeed at things is to do everything possible to stack the deck in your favor. Most people use a resume to sell themselves. As we just discussed, done right, your resume can be a great selling tool. It can get you in the door for an interview. But putting all your eggs in one basket is never a good idea. What else can you do to help sell yourself? What other tools can you use?

Business cards are small but powerful tools that can positively affect your career if used correctly. We've discussed the importance of busi-

---

⭐ Tip from the Coach

Business cards are networking cards. You give them to people you meet so they not only remember you and what you do, but how to contact you if necessary. These are important whether you are seeking to succeed in the business and administrative segment of the performing arts or the talent and creative area.

ness cards throughout the book. Let's look at them more closely.

Whatever level you're at in your career, whatever area of the industry you're interested in pursuing, business cards can help you progress. If you don't have a job yet, business cards are essential. At this point, they may also be known as networking cards because that is what they are going to help you do. If you already have a job, business cards can help you climb the ladder to success. Get your business cards printed and get them printed now!

Why are cards so important? Mainly because they help people not only remember you, but find you. Networking is so essential to your success in the industry that once you go through all the trouble of doing it, if someone doesn't remember who you are or how they can contact you, it's almost useless.

How many times have you met someone during the day or at a party and then gone your separate ways? A couple days later, something will come up where you wish you could remember the person's name or you remember their name, but have no idea how to get a hold of them. How bad would you feel if you found out that you met someone, told him or her that

> ### The Inside Scoop
>
> Don't try to save money making business cards on your computer. They never really end up looking professional and will not project the professional image you want.

you were looking for a job in the industry, they ran into someone else who was looking for someone with your skills and talents, and they didn't know how to get a hold of you? Business cards could have helped solve that problem.

When was the last time you ran into someone successful who didn't have business cards? They boost your prestige and make you *feel* more successful. If you feel more successful, you'll *be* more successful. And cards are not just for those interested in the business end of the industry. If you are an actor, dancer, singer, comedian, musician, in a group, a songwriter, or other performing artist, business cards are just as important.

What's your next step? Start by determining what you want your business cards to look like. You might want to go to a print shop or an office supply store such as Staples or Office Max to look at samples, or you can create your own style.

Samples of Business and Networking Cards

Ernest Davis

Career Goal: Position in performing arts administration utilizing degree in performing arts administration

PO Box 1500   Phone: 111-222-1111
Anytown, NY 11111   Cell: 888-999-0000
        Ernest@moreinternet.com

Samples of Business and Networking Cards, continued

420 Edwards Avenue
Anytown, NY 11111

IVY BETULA

Excellent verbal and written communication skills
Accomplished entertainment publicist
Marketing skills

Phone: 111-111-1111
Cell: 888-999-0000
Ivy@moreinternet.com

---

420 National Avenue   Phone: 222-111-1111
Anytown, NY 11111   Cell: 111-999-0000
E-mail: jodi@moreinternet.com

Jodi Frand

Graduate of State University – Communications Major
Intern – Middletown State Ballet Company
Summer Job – Administrative Assistant,
Woodbridge Symphony Orchestra
Excellent verbal and written communications skills
Sales skills
Detail oriented

Topper
Country/Pop

You won't be able to stay in your seats
Mark Toomy–Lead Singer

PO Box 140   Phone: 444-444-4444
Anytown, NY 11111   Cell: 999-999-9999
Mark@topperband.com   www.topperband.com

Samples of Business and Networking Cards, continued

Amy Gilford

Actress

SAG/AFTRA/AEA

PO Box 9090
Anytown, NY 11111
E-mail: amygilford@gilford.com

Phone: 111-222-3333
Cell: 111-999-9999
www.gilford.com

Johnny Tyler

Dancer

Modern, Jazz, Ballet, Tap

PO Box 1240
Anytown, NY 11111
E-mail: jtyler@Internet.com

Phone: 111-444-5555
Cell: 111-888-9999
www.johnnytylerdance.com

JEANNE WEAVER

Costume Designer
Theatrical Costume Design
Tony Award Nominee

PO Box 333
Anytown, NY 11111
E-mail: jeanneweaver@Internet.com

Phone: 222-333-4444
Cell: 222-444-4444
www.jeanneweaver.com

What should your cards say? At the minimum, include your name, address (or PO Box), e-mail, and phone number (both home and cell if you have one). It's a good idea to add in your job or your career goal or objective. You might even briefly describe your talents, skills, or traits. Your business card is your selling piece, so think about what you want to sell.

At every career-oriented seminar I give when we get to the section on business cards, someone always raises their hand and says something to the effect of "I don't have a job yet. What kind of cards do I make up? What would they say? 'Unemployed but wants to be an actor? Unemployed but wants to work in the performing arts? Unemployed but wants to work in the music industry?'"

So before you think it or say it, the answer is no; you definitely don't put the word *unemployed* on your card. You will put your name, contact information, and career goals on your business card, and then use them to *become* employed in your career of choice.

Remember that cards are small, and that limits the number of words that can fit so the card looks attractive and can be read easily. If you want more room, you might use a double-sided card (front and back) or a double-sized card that is folded over, in effect giving you four times as much space. I've seen both used successfully. The double-sized card can be very effective for a mini-resume.

You have a lot of decisions on how you want your business cards to look. What kind of card stock do you want? Do you want your card smooth or textured; flat or shiny? What about color? Do you want white, beige, or a colored card? Do you want flat print or raised print? What fonts or type faces do you want to use? Do

you want graphics? How do you want to have the information laid out? Do you want it straight or on an angle? The decisions are yours. It just depends what you like and what you think will sell you the best.

Order at least 1,000 cards. What are you going to do with 1,000 cards? You're going to give them to everyone. While everyone might not keep your resume, most people in all aspects of business keep cards, and those in the performing arts are no exception.

Brochures Can Tell Your Story

While you're always going to need a resume, consider developing your own brochure, too. A brochure can tell your story and help you sell yourself. The various segments of the performing arts are creative industries and sometimes something out of the ordinary can help grab the attention of someone important.

What's a brochure? Basically it is a selling piece that gives information about a product, place, event, or person, among other things. In this situation, the brochure is going to be about you. While your resume tells your full story, your brochure is going to illustrate your key points.

Why do you need one? A brochure can make you stand out from other job seekers, songwriters, singers, musicians, or groups.

What should a brochure contain? While it depends to a great extent whether you're pursu-

---

★ Tip from the Coach

Look at other people's business cards (both in the performing arts industry and out) to try to find a style you like. Then fit your information into that style.

ing a career in the talent and creative segment of the performing arts or the business and administrative end, there are some basic things you should include.

Definitely your name and contact information. Then add your selling points. Maybe those are your skills. Perhaps they are your talents or accomplishments. What about something unique or special that you do? Definitely try to illustrate what *you* can do for a company and what benefits they will obtain by hiring you. A brief bio is often helpful to illustrate your credentials and credibility. What about three or four quotes from some of your letters of recommendation. For example:

◎ "One of the best interns we ever had participate in our internship program." Pat Anderson, New City Orchestra

◎ "A real team player who motivates the team." Phil Sagget, Tri-State Council of the Arts

What about quotes from reviews in the media on one of your performances?

◎ "Kate Brown made Portia come alive in *The Merchant of Venice*. A truly exceptional performance." Larry Cooper, *Midtown News*.

◎ "Scott Albert could have kept the audience laughing for a week. A must-see when you're in Las Vegas." Ginny Jones, *Las Vegas Entertainment*.

⭐ Tip from the Coach

You are going to use your brochure in addition to your resume, not in place of it.

◎ "Toni Star is the most innovative costume designer of the century." Dennis Barnes, *LA Entertainment Today*.

Keep your wording simple. Make it clear, concise, and interesting.

What should your brochure look like? The possibilities are endless. Brochures can be simple or elaborate. Your brochure can be designed in different sizes, papers, folds, inks, and colors. You can use photographs, drawings, illustrations, or other graphics.

If you have graphic design ability and talent, lay out your brochure yourself. If you don't, ask a friend or family member who is talented in that area or use a software program for designing brochures.

If you want to design your brochure, but want it printed professionally, consider bringing your camera-ready brochure to a professional print shop. Camera-ready means your document is ready to be printed, and any consumer print shop should be able to help guide you through the steps needed to prepare your work for them. In addition to print shops, you might consider office supply stores like Staples and Office Max that do printing.

If you don't feel comfortable designing your own brochure, you can ask a printer in your area if there is an artist on staff. Professional design and printing of a brochure can get expensive. Is it worth it? Only you can decide, but if it helps get your career started or makes the one you have more successful, probably the answer is yes.

Can brochures be effective? I certainly think so. Not only do I know a great number of people who have used them successfully, I personally used one when I was breaking into the music business and have continued using them ever since. Here's my story.

At the time I was sending out a lot of resumes and making a lot of calls in an attempt to obtain interviews. I had learned a lot about marketing and noticed that many companies used brochures. My father, who was a marketing professional, suggested that a brochure might just be what I needed. By that time I had realized that if I wanted to *sell* myself, I might need to market myself a little more aggressively than I was doing, so I decided to try the brochure idea.

We designed a brochure that was printed on an 11-by-17-inch piece of paper folded in half, giving me four pages to tell my story. We artistically mounted a head shot on the front page and printed it in hot pink ink. The inside was crafted with carefully selected words indicating my accomplishments, skills, talents, and the areas in which I could help a company who hired me. The brochures were professionally printed and I sent them to various record labels, music instrument manufacturers, music publishers, music industry publicity companies, artist managers, and so on. I started getting calls from some of the people who received the brochure, obtained a number of interviews, and even landed a couple of job offers. None of them, however, interested me.

Five years after I sent out my first brochure, I received a call from a major record company who told me that at the time they first received my brochure they didn't need anyone with my skills or talents, but they thought the brochure was so original that they kept it on file. Five years passed, and they needed an individual with my skills, so someone remembered my brochure, pulled it out, and called me. By that time I was already on the road with another group and couldn't take the job, but it was nice to be called.

What is really interesting, however, is that companies and people I originally sent that first brochure years ago still remember it. They can describe it perfectly and many of them still have it in their files.

When creating your brochure, make sure it represents the image you want to portray. Try to make it as unique and eye catching as possible. You can never tell how long someone is going to keep it.

Your Career Portfolio: Have Experience, Will Travel

People in creative careers have always used portfolios to illustrate what they have done and can accomplish. You can do the same.

What exactly is a career portfolio? Basically, it's a portfolio or book that contains your career information and illustrates your best work. Your portfolio is a visual representation of your potential. Why do you need one? Because your career portfolio can help you get the positions you want in the performing arts.

What would you believe more—something someone told you or something you saw with your own eyes? If you're like most people, you would believe something you saw. And that's what a good career portfolio can do for you. It can provide actual illustrations of what you've done and what you can do.

For example, you might tell a potential employer that you can write dynamic press releases. Can you really? If you have samples in your portfolio, you can pull out a couple and show your work.

What would be more impressive to you—looking over someone's resume and reading that they won the salesperson of the month award, or actually seeing a copy of the award certificate? Reading that an actor received a standing ovation for his performance, or seeing a copy of the article and picture in the newspaper?

Have there been articles or feature stories about you that appeared in the media?

Copies of all these documents can be part of your career portfolio. Often, if you have buzz around you, potential employers as well as potential personal managers, talent agents, and booking agents will feel you will be a commodity to the company.

Your portfolio is not only going to be useful when you're first obtaining a job. It will be useful in advancement throughout your career. As time goes on, omit some of your earlier documents and replace them with more current ones. Having an organized system to present your achievements and successes is also helpful when going through employment reviews, or asking for a promotion or a raise. It also is very effective in illustrating what you've done if you're trying to move up the ladder at a different company.

Your portfolio is portable. You can bring it with you when you go on interviews so you can

> ### ⭐ Tip from the Top
> When compiling your portfolio be careful not to use any confidential work or documents from a company even if you were the one who wrote the report or the letter. A potential employer might be concerned about how you will deal with their confidential issues if you aren't keeping other confidences.

show it to potential employers. You can make copies of things in your portfolio to give to potential employers or have everything at hand when you want to answer an ad or send out cold letters.

How do you build a detailed portfolio illustrating your skills, talents, experiences, and accomplishments? What goes into it? You want your portfolio to document your work-related talents and accomplishments. These are the assets that you will be selling to your potential employers. Let's look at some of the things you might want to include.

- your profile
- resume
- bio
- reference sheets
- skill and abilities
- degrees, licenses, and certifications
- experience sheet
- summary of accomplishments
- professional associations
- professional development activities (conferences, seminars, and workshops attended, as well as any other professional development activities)
- awards and honors
- volunteer activities and community service

◎ supporting documents

◎ samples of work

◎ newspaper, magazine, and other articles and/or feature stories about you

◎ articles you have written and published

◎ reports you've done

◎ letters or notes people have written to tell you what a good job you've done

◎ photos of you accepting an award or at an event you worked on

◎ photos of events you were involved in

◎ news stories or feature articles generated by your execution of a project (For example, if you did the publicity for a theatrical production and the paper did a feature story on the play or one or more of the actors.)

This list is just to get you started. Your portfolio can contain anything that will help illustrate your skills, talents, and accomplishments.

Those in the talent end of the industry can effectively use a career portfolio, too. In these situations, your target market might be talent agents, booking agents, casting agents, or managers. It might be club owners or other people who could potentially need your services. If you're a songwriter or composer your portfolio audience might be playwrights, film or television producers, record company executives, singers or groups, or music publishers looking for new material. You might include items like some of the following:

◎ reference sheets (from industry people you've worked with or performed for)

◎ skill sheet (singer, songwriter, ability to read and write music)

◎ experience sheet

◎ summary of accomplishments (Danced at halftime show at Superbowl, sang national anthem at National Basketball Association [NBA] game, went on tour with three top recording acts, featured role in touring company of *Grease*, wrote song for local literacy fund-raising dinner dance, etc.)

◎ supporting documents

◎ samples of work

◎ newspaper, magazine, or other articles and/or feature stories done on you/your act

◎ audio or videos of radio interviews, television interviews, and so on

◎ audio recordings of songs you've written or your performances

◎ videos of performances

◎ head shots

◎ photographs of you at performances or events where you have performed

◎ press releases

If you're in the talent end of the performing arts as an actor, actress, musician, dancer, singer, comedian, magician, etc., your portfolio will be much like a press kit. That's okay. You can use the portfolio in conjunction with your press kit or in situations where a press kit isn't needed.

While you can compile your portfolio in a variety of booklets, binders, or other formats, make sure whatever you choose is clean, neat, and professional looking. Depending on your contents, a large three-ring binder is often a good choice. Your information should also be well organized. Many find using dividers or tabs helpful.

Press Kits Tell the Story

If you have already achieved a level of success, you might have a publicist, press agent or public relations counselor handling your publicity and press relations. In some instances, even if you're just starting out your agent or manager may take care of this for you. If you are not in this posi-

> ⭐ **Tip from the Top**
>
> Make good-quality copies of key items in your portfolio to leave with interviewers or potential employers, agents, etc. Visit an office supply store to find some professional looking presentation folders to hold all the supporting documents you bring to an interview.

tion yet, or even if you are and you want to stay on top of your publicity, read on.

Press kits might be called media kits, promo kits, or press packs. Whatever they're called, if you're in the talent area of the industry, you're going to need one. A well-designed and well-conceived press kit can be an effective marketing and selling tool for anyone in the talent end of the performing arts. It's another key element in your success if you are an actor, dancer, musician, singer, comedian, or any other talent in the industry. You might also find a press kit useful if you are a songwriter, composer, playwright, lighting designer, sound designer, costume designer, scenic designer, etc.

What's a press kit? Your press kit is a sales pitch. Done right, it's a chance to shine, to set yourself apart, and to get noticed.

Physically, it's a binder or folder that contains background material, promotional material, photos, and publicity to help market and publicize your act. Press kits are handy to give to anyone who needs information about you as a performing artist or creative talent. This includes:

◎ the media
◎ reporters
◎ editors
◎ journalists
◎ TV and radio producers
◎ talent coordinators
◎ column planters
◎ entertainment buyers
◎ producers
◎ club owners
◎ promoters
◎ booking agents
◎ theatrical contacts
◎ entertainment industry contacts
◎ music industry contacts
◎ record company executives
◎ music publishers
◎ producers
◎ entertainment attorneys
◎ radio and television contacts
◎ station music directors
◎ station program directors
◎ disc jockeys
◎ casting agents
◎ others in the performing arts and entertainment industry

How do you put together a press kit? Depending on where you are in your career and your financial resources, you can retain a publicist or publicity firm to handle the task, or you might want to try your hand at putting together a press kit yourself.

What goes into a press kit? There are a variety of documents. You don't have to use each one every time. Tailor your press kit to the person to whom it's being sent. Here's a list to get you started.

◎ biography (bio)
◎ fact sheet (one-page sheet giving key information)
◎ press releases
◎ professional photos
◎ press clippings

- reprints of articles and feature stories
- reviews
- testimonials
- preview video
- CD, demo tape
- business cards
- quote sheets
- song list

Now that you have all the components of your press kit, what should you do with them? You have a few choices. You can put your information in attractive presentation folders or have a graphic artist design a press kit folder for you. It's important to remember that a press kit which can grab the right people's attention is worth its weight in gold because that ultimately is your goal. There are some areas where you just can't skimp; putting together your press kit is one of them.

Don't send anything out that doesn't look totally professional or it stands the chance of getting tossed into a "look at it some day" pile or even worse—the trash. You want people to look at your press kit the moment they receive it. Use the best designed presentation folder you can afford. When you make copies and reprints make sure they are clean and crisp.

Photos for your press kit should be done by a professional. These pictures not only show who you are, but they will be the ones used in publicity and in the print media. Glossy black and whites are best for reproduction in newspapers. Once you get the photos you want to use, you can get them duplicated inexpensively. Make sure you have your name (or the name of the act) and contact information printed on the photos. (Right now we're talking about photos for your press kit, *not* the head shots you're going to use with your professional theatrical resume.)

★ Words from the Wise

When compiling your press kit, make sure that your contact information (or that of your agent, manager, or other representative) is on each and every piece of your kit. If you have a Web site, add that to each piece as well.

Videos are also a helpful marketing tool for those in the performing arts. Whether you're a musician, dancer, comedian, actor or actress, or any other performing artist videos can illustrate your talents. There are a couple different types you should know about depending on which area of the performing arts you're pursuing.

You might, for example, have a professional video producer shoot part of one of your live shows or performances and then splice it attractively to make a great 10- or 15-minute preview video. Here's another idea that is usually a lot less expensive if you can make it work. If you perform at an event and the television news comes to cover it, all you have to do is speak to the producer or someone at the station and ask if you can buy the raw footage. Ask if you can have the rights to it or if you can use the footage for promotional purposes if you give them credit. Then just get the footage spliced into a five- or ten-minute tape and get it duplicated. Generally when television covers news, they film for a while, and then they edit what they have filmed for broadcast.

How can you get into a situation like this? One way is by volunteering to provide the entertainment to a major not-for-profit event in your community that is usually covered by the media. While this shouldn't be your motivating reason for doing something nice, it is a great benefit. Another way is to offer to perform at a televised telethon. A third method is to take part in televised talent competitions. While you won't usually get a 10-minute tape, you generally can at least get a video of your performance.

Professional music videos, of the sort you see on music television, are expensive to produce. If you can afford this and you're professionally ready for it, that's great, but if what you're trying to do is show agents, promoters, club owners, or other entertainment buyers what your act is like, consider a lower-priced alternative. If you don't have a professional-looking video, don't use one at all.

Quote Sheets

If you are lucky enough to have industry professionals make positive comments about you either verbally or in writing, you can use these by adding quote sheets to your press kits. Sometimes people make these comments on their own. A theater critic may, for example, review the production you're in and give your performance a glowing review in the morning paper.

In some cases you may also want to solicit comments to use in quote sheets. Who do you ask? Industry professionals who know and like your work. Put the quotes on a sheet under a heading like "Here's What They're Saying About (your name)." Don't overwhelm people. Just choose a few selected quotes with the person's name and title. For example: "Amazing vocals," . . . Jim McMann, *Music Today.* "An astounding performance the audience won't soon forget," . . . Delia Walters, *Theater Roundup.* "Robert Branch makes his violin sing," . . . Jane Poland, *City News.*

Here's a sample to give you an idea.

Here's What They're Saying about (Your Name)

" _____quote_____
_____,". . . name and title of person to whom quote is attributed.

" _____quote_____
_____,". . . name and title of to whom quote is attributed.

" _____quote_____
_____,". . . name and title of to whom quote is attributed.

" _____quote_____
_____,". . . name and title of to whom quote is attributed.

" _____quote_____
_____,". . . name and title of to whom quote is attributed.

CDs

If you have already recorded a CD, include it. If you don't have a commercial CD and you're sending your press kit to agents, managers, record labels, club owners, promoters, or others, make sure you use a good-quality, professionally duplicated demo tape, cassette, or CD showcasing your best work. Your demo should contain no more than three songs. Graphically pleasing labels should include your name (or the name of the act), the contents of the tape, and contact information.

DVDs

Have you appeared in a commercial? Have you had roles on television shows? What about appearances in movies? Even if your parts are small, get clips, compile them on a DVD, and add it to your press kit and career portfolio. Make sure you include a label and directory of the contents of the DVD.

More About Your Press Kit

Build a press kit that makes you stand out from others and you will be that much closer to getting noticed. It's a good idea to send a cover letter with your press kit introducing yourself. When doing so, if at all possible, personalize your letter. As suggested with any cover letter, you stand a better chance of a good response if you send correspondence to a specific person and not just to News Editor, Director, Booking Agent, etc.

Every Talent Needs a Bio

Whether you are an actor, singer, dancer, musician, comedian, magician, juggler, solo artist or part of a group, songwriter, composer, playwright, or any other creative talent in the entertainment industry, you are going to need a bio or biography. As in other marketing pieces, you have the option of retaining a professional publicist or publicity firm to write your bio or you can write it yourself. Whether it's for your press kit, your career portfolio, your Web site, or any other opportunity that comes your way, a good bio can effectively tell your story.

Your bio will illustrate the following:

◎ Who you (or your act) are
◎ What you do
◎ Why you (or your act) are special
◎ Your history in the performing arts

Remember, your bio isn't a resume. It doesn't have to be a book. It's going to be a one- to two-page story about you as a performing or creative artist. The more interesting you can make it, the better. Be creative when developing your bio, but as in your resume, don't lie. It will make you lose all credibility.

To write an effective bio, you are going to have to take some time to think about what is important. Try to start off with an interesting fact or two that grabs the attention of the reader, and then go on to give some information on the act.

Here are a few examples of the first paragraph performing artists in various areas might use for their bios.

ROBIN MYERS

If all of Robin Myers's fans stood side by side, they would circle the world many times over. Robin is a dynamic, energetic, and charismatic singer, songwriter, and entertainer who took the world by storm five years ago. She has been going strong ever since.

JACKIE BRAND

The first comedy set Jackie Brand remembers performing was when she was seven years old and jumped on the living room table with a flashlight as a microphone to tell jokes at her parent's party. Brand has been performing as a comedienne ever since.

LINCOLN TUNNEL

If you like R&B vocals, you'll love Lincoln Tunnel. The group is a five-member R&B vocal act that has generated a fan base from their home city of Detroit to Philadelphia, New York City, Atlanta, Los Angeles, and everywhere in between.

Keep in mind that these are just samples. Your bio can be similar or totally different. Take some time working on it. When it's done, it is a good idea to give it to friends, family, and others to review. Get their comments and make corrections if necessary.

Print your bio on high-quality paper. It should be graphically pleasing to the eye and easy to read. As in all other pieces of your press kit, make sure your contact information is prominent.

It's www. . . . Your Personal Web Address

If you're on the talent end of the industry, sooner or later you're going to need a Web site. Why? Because the Internet is where it's at today. Your competition probably has a Web site, which means that you need one too! It's yet another of the key tools for your success and a marketing tool you really can't do without.

What can a Web site do for you? It can present you and your talent to the world. Your bio, photos, appearances, news, and more are right there with a simple click of the mouse. Whether you're trying to obtain bookings, appearances and engagements, garner roles, looking for a manager, an agent or letting people know what you're doing, a Web site can help. Your Web site can also help you build a fan base. This can be very helpful in your road to success.

Whether you develop the site yourself or have a professional do it for you, make sure you have a recognizable domain name. You want to be able to say, "Check me out at www.myname. com." You want to make it easy to remember and easy for people to find you.

Your Web site can be simple or elaborate as long as it showcases you in a professional manner and accurately portrays your image.

Whether you're pursuing a career in the business or arts administration area or talent or creative end of theater or one of the other performing arts, competition is keen. Get the edge over others who want the same success as you do by using every tool you can.

7

GETTING YOUR FOOT IN THE DOOR

While there is no sure way to become successful in your career, it is clear that in order to succeed in any capacity, the one thing you generally need is to at least get your foot in the proverbial door. Getting your foot in the door can mean the difference between success and failure.

Once in, you have a chance to sell yourself, sell your talent, and sell your products and services. The problem is that sometimes the hardest part *is* getting your foot in the door. Whether you simply walk in off the street to see someone or call to make an appointment, you often are faced with the same situation. You need to get past the receptionist, the secretary, or whoever the "gatekeeper" happens to be between you and the person with whom you want to speak.

Are you trying to get through to a casting director? What about a talent, booking or literary agent? Are you trying to set up a meeting with a potential manager? What about trying to get through to a director or producer? How about a record company exec? What about the director of a large orchestra, opera, or ballet? It doesn't matter whom you are trying to get through to. As a rule, there generally will be someone who will be between you and them.

We have already discussed the rejection often encountered by those in a quest for success in the performing arts. We've also discussed why rejection should not be taken personally. However, to feel rejected when you didn't even get the chance to really be rejected because you couldn't get through to someone is quite another thing. It's not personal, but the secretary, receptionist, assistant, and even the person you're trying to reach often think of you and most other unsolicited callers as unwanted intruders who waste their time. It doesn't really matter whether you're perfect for the role, trying to sell something, get a job, or anything else. Unless these people can see what you can do for *them,* it's going to be hard to get through.

No matter what segment of the performing arts you are currently working or aspire to work, in reality you are trying to sell something. You might be trying to sell your acting, your music, your songs, comedy, or dancing. You might be trying to sell your screenplay, libretto, or vocal talent. You might be trying to sell yourself when trying to get a job.

Whatever you're selling, the trick in getting through to the people you need to talk to is to try not to let them know exactly what you want. I am in no way telling you to lie or even stretch the truth. What I'm telling you to do is find a way to change their perception of you. Be creative.

Theater and all the performing arts are very competitive industries. Everyone wants to talk to the talent agents, directors, producers, casting directors, orchestra directors, club owners, potential managers, and booking agents. Similarly, everyone wants to talk to the A&R directors, record company presidents, and industry human resources directors. Whether you want a career in the creative or talent area or to work in the business or administrative end of the industry, you need to get past the gatekeeper so you can get your foot in the door. Before you rush in and find the door locked, let's look at some possible keys to help you get in.

Getting Through on the Phone

Let's start with the phone. If your goal is to talk to a specific person or make an appointment, it's important to know that many high-level business people don't answer their own phone. Instead, they rely on secretaries, receptionists, or assistants to handle this task. And that's not even counting the dreaded voice mail.

You can always try the straightforward approach. Just call and ask to speak to the person you are looking for. If that works, you have your foot in the door. If not, it's time to get creative.

Let's look at a couple of scenarios and how they might play out.

Scenario 1

Secretary: Good afternoon, Perfect Talent.

You: Hello, this is Rob Cooper. May I please speak to Mr. Nagin?

Secretary: Does he know what this is in reference to?

You: No, I'm looking for a job and would like to see if I could set up an interview.

Secretary: I'm sorry, Mr. Nagin isn't looking to fill any positions at this time. Thank you for calling.

You: Thanks. Good-bye.

With that said, you're done. Is there something you could have said differently that might have lead to a better ending? Let's look at another scenario.

Scenario 2

Secretary: Good afternoon, Perfect Talent.

You: Is Mr. Nagin in?

Secretary: Who's calling?

You: Rob Cooper.

Secretary: May I ask what this is in reference to?

You: Yes, I was trying to set up an informational interview. Would Mr. Nagin be the person who handles this or would it be someone else at your company?

[Asking the question in this manner means that you stand a chance at the gatekeeper giving you a specific name that you can call if Mr. Nagin is the wrong person.]

Secretary: Informational interview for what purpose?

You: I was interested in some information on a career at a talent agency. Would Mr. Nagin be the right person to speak to?

[Make sure you are pleasant. This helps the person answering the phone want to help you.]

Secretary: No, he doesn't handle that. You need to speak to Kyra King in personnel. Would you like me to switch you?

[What you are really doing is helping her, get you off the phone even if it means she is dumping you on someone else.]

You: Yes that would be great. What was your name?

[Try to make sure you get the name. In this manner, when you get transferred, the person answering at the other end, will be more apt to help you.]

Secretary: Ann Kennedy.

You: Thanks for your help. I really appreciate it.

Secretary: I'll switch you now.

Kyra King: Kyra King, may I help you?

You: Hi Ms. King. Ann Kennedy in Mr. Nagin's office suggested you might be the right person for me to speak to. I'm interested in setting up an informational interview regarding the possibility of working with your company.

At this point, she probably will either say, "Sorry, we have no openings," ask you some additional questions, or set up an appointment. If she says, "Sorry, we have no openings at this time," say something like: "I understand. Would it be possible for me to send my resume for you to review and keep on file?" If this is the case, make sure you ask to whose name your information should be directed as well as getting the exact addresses and her extension.

If she starts to question you about what type of job you are looking for make sure you have an answer prepared. Never say: "Oh, I don't care; any job would be fine" or "I just want to work in a record company to get to meet famous people."

Instead, have a definitive answer. For example: "I'm interested in talent development. I

Tip from the Top
Remember that skills are transferable. If you've done publicity for a hospital, a bank, or any other type of business, you can usually do publicity in the performing arts. If you've worked effectively in sales in another industry, you generally can transfer your skills to working in sales in the performing arts.

have a degree in arts administration with a minor in theater arts. When I was still in school I worked as an intern at a talent agency in Los Angeles in the film industry. Now that I've moved back to New York, I'm really interested in working with an agency which handles artists in the theatrical segment of the industry."

Have your calendar in front of you so that at this point, if she wants to set up an interview, you can make every effort to go with the time and date she suggests.

Scenario 3
Sometimes mentioning that you're looking for a job is not a good idea. Often, those already working in the performing arts, may not be that open about helping those on the outside.

Receptionist: Good afternoon, Perfect Talent.

You: Hi, my name is Rob Cooper. I'm working on a project involving careers in theater and the performing arts and was told your company was one of the best ones to talk to. Do you know who in your company I might speak to?

[Here is where it can get a little tricky. If you are very lucky, he or she will just put you through to someone in publicity, public relations, or human resources. If you're not so lucky, he or she will ask you questions.]

Receptionist: What type of project?

You need to be ready with a plausible answer. What you say, will, of course, depend on your situation. If you are in college, you can always say you are working on a project for school. If not, you can say you are doing research on career opportunities in theater or the performing arts. If you have writing skills, you might contact a local newspaper or magazine to see if they are interested in an article on careers in the performing arts. If you can't find someone to write for, you can always write a story on "spec." This means that if you write a story, you can send it in to an editor on speculation. They might take it and they might not. Don't think about money at this point. Your goal here is to get the "right people" to speak to you and get an appointment.

One of the interesting things about writing an article (whether on spec or on assignment) is that you can ask people questions and they will usually talk to you. They won't be looking at you like you're looking for a job. You have changed their perception about why you're talking to them. One of the most important bonuses of interviewing people about a career in the performing arts is that you are making invaluable contacts. While it might be tempting, remember to use this opportunity to ask questions and network. Do not try to sell yourself at this point. After you write the article, you might call up one of the people you interviewed and say something like, "You made the performing arts sound so interesting, I'd like to explore a career in the industry. Would it be possible to come in for an interview or to fill in an application?

This particular scenario works if you're trying to get through to agents, directors, casting people, or managers as well. Just remember that if you *say* you're working on a story, you better really be working on a story. If you're not, your credibility could be shot.

Scenario 4

Receptionist: Good afternoon, Central Broadway Casting.

You: Hi, my name is Rob Cooper. I'm not sure exactly who to speak to. I'm working on an article on the theatrical casting process and how it works. We're trying to follow a couple of productions from inception to fruition. Do you know who in your company I might speak to?

Receptionist: What type of article?

[Once again, it's imperative to be ready with a plausible answer. What you say, will of course, depend on your situation.]

You: I'm doing research for an article on theatrical productions with a focus on how casting directors choose talent as well as the whole casting process for the *Daily Tribune.*

Try not to go into too much detail unless you're asked. Also remember that when you speak to people and do your interviews, don't focus on the fact that you're an actor or actress trying to get into the business. Ask questions, be enthusiastic, act professionally and write a great article. After that, it will be easier to place a call and make contact with the important people you want to get in touch with.

"But what if I can't find a newspaper or magazine to write for," you ask? "I live in a large city. No one is going to hire an unknown writer."

While writing an article for the *New York Times*, *Los Angeles Times*, *Philadelphia Enquirer*, or a major magazine would be great, large, well-known publications are not your only option. Be sure to check out smaller or lesser-known publications. Many of these are hungry for interesting articles. Often, you just need to ask.

You might also consider doing an article for a Web site. Search for sites that might be interested in the subject you want to write about. Then contact them and make your pitch.

"But I really don't like writing," you say. "What else can I do?"

If you don't like writing or writing is not your forte, consider doing a short piece for a radio show or television show. Once again, it doesn't have to be a network. A local station will be fine.

Remember that if you're interested in something, there are usually other people who are interested in the same thing. Call up station or program managers, new directors, or anyone else you can think of and pitch your idea. The concept is the same. You want to find creative ways to get your foot in the door. In doing so you can make contact with people who can help you in your career and do it in a way which helps set you apart from the others.

What can you do if none of these scenarios work? The receptionist may not be very eager to help. He or she may have instructions on "not letting anyone through." It may be his or her job to block unsolicited callers and visitors from the boss. What can you do?

Here are a few ideas that might help. See if you can come up with some others.

◎ Try placing your call before regular business hours. Many executives and others in the industry you might want to talk to come in before the secretary or receptionist is scheduled to work.

◎ Try placing your calls after traditional business hours when the secretary probably has left. Executives, agents, directors and producers or others you want to reach generally don't punch a time clock and often work late. They also may be doing business with those on the other coast. More importantly, even if people utilize voice mail, they may pick up the phone themselves after hours in case their family is calling.

◎ Lunch hours are also a good time to attempt to get through to people. This is a little tricky. The executive may use voice mail during the lunch hour period or he or she may go out to lunch themselves. On the other hand, you might get lucky.

◎ Sometimes others in the office fill in for a receptionist and aren't sure what the procedure is or who everyone is. While you might not get through on the first shot, you might use this type of opportunity to get information. For example, you might ask for the person you want to speak to and when the

---

★ ## Voice of Experience

Make sure you get the correct spelling of the name of everyone who helps you. Send a short note, thanking them for their help immediately. This is not only good manners, but helps people remember who you are in a positive way.

Words from the Wise

If you finally get through to someone you've been trying to reach, if he or she sounds frazzled, make sure you ask if it's a good time. Say something to the effect of, "You sound like you're in the middle of something. Would it be better if I call back at a more convenient time?" Try to make sure you're the person doing the call back if at all possible.

substitute tells you he or she isn't in and asks if you want to leave a message, say something like, "I'm moving around a lot today. I'll try to call later. Is Mr. Brown ever in the office after 6:00 p.m.?" If the answer is yes, ask if you can have his direct extension in case the switchboard is closed.

Remember these three Ps to help you get through to people. You want to be:

◎ pleasant
◎ persistent
◎ positive

Always be pleasant. Aside from it being general good manners to be nice to others, being pleasant to gatekeepers is essential. Gatekeepers talk to their bosses and can let them know if you were annoying or obnoxious. When someone tells you their boss "never takes unsolicited calls or accepts unsolicited tunes" tell them you understand.

Then ask what they suggest. Acknowledge objections, but try to come up with a solution.

Be persistent. Not getting through on the first try doesn't mean you shouldn't try again. Don't be annoying, don't be pushy, but don't give up. And be positive. People like to help positive people.

Persistence and the Guilt Factor

Don't forget the guilt factor. If you consistently place calls to an individual and each time his secretary tells you he is busy, unavailable, or will call you back and he doesn't, what should you do? Should you give up? Well, that's up to you. Be aware that persistence often pays off.

In many cases, after a number of calls, you and the secretary will have built up a relationship of sorts. As long as you have been pleasant, he or she may feel guilty that you are such a nice person and his or her boss isn't calling you back. In these cases, the secretary may give you a tip on how to get through, tell you to send something in writing, or ask the boss to speak to you.

Voice mail is another obstacle you might have to deal with. This system is often more difficult to bypass than a human gatekeeper. Many people don't even bother answering their phone, instead letting their voice mail pick up the calls and then checking their messages when convenient.

Decide ahead of time what you're going to do if you get someone's voice mail. Try calling once to see what the person's message is. It might, for example, let you know that the person you're calling is out of town until Monday. What this will tell you is that if you are calling

Voice of Experience

While persistence can work, don't be annoying. Calling more than once a day or, in most cases, even more than once a week (unless you are given specific instructions by the secretary to do so) will put you on the annoying list.

someone on a cold call, you should probably not call until Wednesday because they probably will be busy when they get back in town.

If the message says something to the effect of "I'm out of town, if you need to speak to me today, please call my cell phone" and then provides a phone number, don't. You don't *need* to speak to him or her; you *want* to. You are cold-calling a person who doesn't know you to ask for something. It is not generally a good idea to bother them outside the office.

If you call a few times and keep getting the voice mail, you're going to have to make your move. Leave a message something like this.

> **You:** Hi, this is Andy Wells. My phone number is (123) 456-7890. I'd appreciate if you could give me a call at your convenience. I'll look forward to hearing from you. Have a great day.

If you don't hear back within a few days, try again.

> **You:** Hi, Ms. Brown. This is Andy Wells. My number is (123) 456-7890. I'm a comedian and wanted to explore the possibility of your agency representing me. I have a video and press kit that I'd like you to see. I look forward to hearing from you. Thanks.

You might not hear from Ms. Brown herself, but one of her assistants might call you. What do you do if you don't get a call back? Call again. How many times should you call? That's hard to say. Remember that the person on the other end may start feeling guilty that he or she is not calling you back and place that call.

Be prepared. When you get a call back, have your ducks in a row and be ready to sell yourself. Practice ahead of time if need be and leave notes near your phone.

I suggest when making any of these calls that you block your phone number, so that no one knows who is calling.

Getting Them to Call You

While persistence and patience in calling and trying to get past the receptionist is usually necessary, you may need something else, too. You want something to set you apart, so the busy executive, human resources director, casting agent, director, manager, producer, etc. not only want to see you, but remember you. You want them to give you a chance to sell yourself.

What can you do? Once again, creativity to the rescue! The performing arts personify creativity, so you have a lot more latitude than you might in more straight-laced industries.

Your goal is to get the attention of the important person who can give you a chance to sell yourself. Once you have their attention, it's up to you to convince them that they should work with you.

Let's look at some ideas that either I have personally used to get someone's attention or that others have told me worked in their quest to get a foot in the door. Use these ideas as a beginning, but then, try to develop some more of your own.

My Personal Number-One Technique for Getting Someone to Call You

I am going to share my number one technique for getting someone to call you. I have used this technique successfully over the years in many different situations.

I first tried this when I wanted to get a job in the music industry. Unfortunately, at that time, there was no book to help. There was no career coach. There was no one who really wanted to help.

I had tried all the traditional methods. I had tried calling. Most of the time, I couldn't get past the gatekeeper. When I did, no one called me back. I had tried sending out resumes. As I had just graduated from college, I had no "real" experience. I didn't know anyone and didn't even know anyone who knew anyone who could help. I needed a break. Here's what I came up with.

When I was younger my parents used to take raw eggs, blow out the contents, and then decorate the shells. As I was trying to come up with some way to get people to call me back, I remembered those eggs. Before too long, I found a method to get people to call me back. Here's how it works.

Get a box of eggs. Extra-large or jumbo work well. While either white or brown eggs can be used, because of the coloration differences in brown eggs, start with white ones. Wash the raw eggs carefully with warm water. Dry the eggs. Hold one egg in your hand and using a large needle or pin, punch a small hole in the top of the egg. The top is the narrower end. Then, carefully punch a slightly larger hole in the other end of the egg. You might need to take the needle or pin and move it around in the hole to make it larger. Keep any pieces of shell that break off.

Now, take a straw and place it on the top hole of the egg. Holding the egg over a bowl, blow into the straw, blowing the contents of the egg out. This may take a couple of tries. Because of concerns with salmonella, don't put your mouth directly on the egg. Keep in mind that the bigger you have made the hole, the eas-

ier it will be to blow the contents out of the egg. However, you want the egg to look as "whole" as possible when you're done. The bigger the hole, the harder this is to accomplish.

After blowing the contents out of the egg, carefully rinse out the shell, letting warm water run through it. Get the egg as clean as possible. Shake the excess water out of the egg and leave it to dry thoroughly. Depending on the temperature and humidity when you are preparing the eggs it might take a couple of days.

Do at least three eggs at one time in case one breaks or cracks at the next step. Keep a few extra eggs around for when you want to get someone's attention fast and don't have time to prepare new ones.

Next, go to your computer and type the words, "Getting the attention of a busy person is not easy. Now that I have yours, could you please take a moment to review my resume." You can customize the message to suit your purposes by including the name of the recipient if you have it or specifying your background sheet or demo recording if that's what you want them to consider. Then type your name and phone number.

Use a small font to keep the message to a line or two. Neatly cut out the strip of paper with your message. Roll the strip around a toothpick. Carefully, insert the toothpick with the strip of paper into the larger of the holes in the egg. Wiggle the toothpick around and slowly take the toothpick out of the egg. The strip of paper should now be in the shell.

Visit your local craft store and pick up a package of small moveable eyes, miniature plastic or felt shaped feet, and white glue. Glue the miniature feet to the bottom of the egg, covering the hole. Make sure you use the glue sparingly so none goes on your message. Now, glue on two of the moving eyes making the egg look like a face.

Go back to your computer and type the following words: "BREAK OPEN THIS EGG FOR AN IMPORTANT MESSAGE." Print out the line and cut it into a strip. You might want to use bright-colored paper. Glue the strip to the bottom of the feet of the egg.

Now you're ready. Take the egg and place it in a small box that you have padded with cotton, bubble wrap, or foam. These eggs are very fragile, and you don't want the egg to break in transit! Wrap the egg-filled box in attractive wrapping paper and then bubble wrap to assure it won't move around. Put your resume (or background sheet) and a short cover letter in an envelope. Put it on the bottom of a sturdy mailing box. Put the egg box over it.

Make sure you use clean boxes and pack the egg as carefully as possible. Address the box. Make sure you include your return name and address, and then either mail, Fedex, UPS, or hand deliver it to the office of the person you are trying to reach. Even if that person has a secretary opening his or her mail, the chances are good that the "gift" will be opened personally. In the event that a secretary opens the package, he or she will probably bring the egg into the boss to open.

So now the recipient has the egg in front of them. He or she will probably break it open, see the message, and glance at your resume. Here's the good news. By the time the person breaks open the egg, he or she won't even notice the hole on the bottom and usually has no idea how you got the message in there. Generally people who have seen this think it is so neat they want to know how you did it, and call you to ask.

Once you have them on the phone, your job is to get an interview. You want to get into their office and meet with them. When you get that call, tell the recipient, you would be glad to

show them how you did it; it's kind of complicated. Offer to show them how it is done and ask when they would like you to come in.

Voila, you have an appointment. Now all you have to do is sell yourself.

Are you trying to get the attention of a theatrical agent? Is your letter sitting in a pile of hundreds of others asking permission to send a demo? Can't get a record company executive to listen to your demo? Are you having difficulties getting a booking agent to call you back? Do you want your resume to stick out amongst the hundreds that come in?

While I love the egg idea and have used it successfully to secure appointments, obtain callbacks, and to get noticed throughout my career, there are a myriad of other ideas that work too. You might want to try a couple of these.

Have you ever considered using these simple items to help you succeed? If you haven't, perhaps now is the time.

- ◎ fortune cookies
- ◎ chocolate chip cookies
- ◎ candy bars
- ◎ mugs
- ◎ roses

Fortune Cookies

Almost no one can resist cracking open a fortune cookie to see what the "message" says. This can be good news for your career in the performing arts.

Some fortune cookie companies make cookies similar to the ones you get in Chinese restaurants but with personalized messages inside. What could you say? That depends on what you are looking for. How about something like, "He or she who watches Jimmy Heart's preview video will have good luck." Then list your contact number. If, on the other hand, you're interested in having a human resources director at a record company review your resume and call your back, you might use a message like, "Human Resources Director who interviews Sean Block will have good luck for the rest of the day. Sean's lucky number: 111-222-3333."

Whatever message you choose, remember that you generally need to make all the messages the same or it gets very expensive to have the cookies made. You also need to either print cards on your computer or have cards printed professionally that read something to the effect of, "Getting the attention of a busy person is not easy. Now that I have yours, could you please take a moment to review my resume?" (or whatever action you want them to take). Make sure your name and phone number are on the card.

Put a couple of cookies with the card and your resume, press kit, demo, or other material in a clean, attractive mailing box and address it neatly. Make sure you address the box to someone specific. For example, don't address it to H.R. Department, Major Orchestra. Instead address it to Ms. Nancy Green, Human Resources Director, Major Orchestra.

While you might have heard of sending fortune cookies to get attention before, here's the twist. Send the same package of cookies, the card, and whatever else you sent (your demo, resume, or press kit) every day for two weeks. Every day, after the first day, also include a note that says, "Cookies for [Name of person] for Day 2," "Cookies for [Name of Person] for Day 3," and so on. At the end of the two-week period, stop. By now your recipient will probably have called you. If not, he or she will at least be expecting the cookies. If you don't hear from your recipient, feel free to call the office, identify yourself as the fortune cookie king or queen, and ask for an appointment.

> ### ★ Words from the Wise
> Make sure cookies are individually wrapped and factory sealed. Otherwise, some people may just toss them.

This idea can be expensive, but if it gets you in the door and you can sell yourself, your idea, your music, or your song, it will more than pay for itself.

Another great idea which can really grab the attention of busy executives is finding a company that makes gigantic fortune cookies with personalized messages. These cookies are often covered in chocolate, brightly colored sprinkles, or other goodies and almost command people to see who sent them. Send these cookies with the same types of messages and supporting material as the others. The only difference is that if you choose to send the gigantic cookies, you only need to send one. If you don't get a call within the first week, feel free to call the recipient yourself.

Chocolate Chip Cookies

Chocolate chip cookies are a favorite of most people. Why not use that to your advantage? Go to the cookie kiosk at your local mall and order a gigantic pizza-sized cookie personalized with a few words asking for what you would like done. For example:

◎ "Please Review My Resume". . . John Jackson
◎ "You're Invited To Opening Night". . . Chris Lawson
◎ "I am perfect for the role of Thomas". . . Larry Ing
◎ "Please Listen To Our Demo". . . The Diamond Crush

◎ "Please Call Me For An Interview". . .
  Joan Block
◎ "You're Invited To Our Showcase". . .
  The Miracle Makers

Keep your message short. You want the recipient to read it, not get overwhelmed. Generally, the cookies come boxed. Tape a copy of your resume, your head shot or whatever you are sending to the inside of the box. If it is a demo or preview video put it in an envelope, and tape it inside the top cover.

Write a short cover letter to your recipient stating that you hope he or she enjoys the cookie while reviewing your resume and head shot, watching your preview video, listening to your demo, etc. Put this in an envelope with another copy of your resume, your demo, or other material. On the outside of the box, neatly tape a card with the message we discussed previously, stating, "Getting the attention of a busy person is not easy. Now that I have yours, would you please take a moment to review my resume?" Or ask them to listen to your demo, give you a call, or whatever you are hoping they will do. Make sure your name and phone number are on the card.

If the cookie company has a mail or delivery service, use it. Otherwise, mail or deliver the cookie yourself. You should get a call within a few days.

Candy Bars

There have been a number of studies that tout chocolate as a food that makes people happy.

The Inside Scoop

To avoid potential problems with people who have allergies, do not send any food with nuts as an ingredient.

Voice of Experience

Do not try to save money by making the cookies (or any other food product) yourself. In today's world, many people won't eat food if they don't know where it came from or that it was prepared by a commercial eatery.

Keeping this in mind, you might want to use chocolate to grab someone's attention and move them to call you. Most people love chocolate and are happy to see it magically appear in their office. There are a number of different ways you can use chocolate to help your career.

◎ Buy a large, good-quality chocolate bar. Carefully fold your resume, a copy of your head shot and/or a letter stating what you would like accomplished and slip it into the wrapping of the chocolate bar.
◎ Buy a large, high-quality chocolate bar. Wrap the chocolate bar with your resume or the letter stating what you would like accomplished.
◎ There are companies that create personalized wrappings for chocolate bars. Use one to deliver your message.
◎ Create a wrapping on your computer, but if you do this, make sure you leave the original wrapping intact and cover it.

Whatever method you choose, put the candy bar in an attractive box, and attach the card with the same message, "Getting the attention of a busy person is never easy. Now that I have yours, could you please take a moment to (what ever you want done)?" or review your resume or media kit or whatever you are asking. Add a cover letter and send it off.

Mugs

When was the last time you threw out a mug? Probably not for a while. How about using this idea to catch the attention of a potential employer, booking agent, record company executive, or manager? Depending on your career aspirations, have mugs printed with replicas of your business card, key points of your resume, or background sheet along with your name and phone number, the name of your act and songs on your demo, the name of your act and places you have appeared along with your name and phone number, or even snippets of articles from the newspaper where your act has been mentioned along with your name and phone number.

Add in a small packet of gourmet or flavored coffee and perhaps an individually wrapped biscotti or cookie and, of course, the card with the message that states, "Getting the attention of a busy person is never easy. Now that I have yours, could you please take a moment to check out my resume and head shot?" or whatever else you are requesting. Put the mug, a short cover letter, and your resume, head shot, background sheet, press kit, demo, or other material in a box and mail or deliver to your recipient.

Roses

A pricey but effective way to get your recipient's attention is to have a dozen roses delivered to his or her office. No matter how many things you have tried with no response, there are very few people who will not place a thank you call when they receive a dozen roses. Talk to the florist ahead of time to make sure that the roses are fragrant. Send the roses to your recipient with a card that simply says something to the effect of "While you're enjoying the roses, please take a moment to review my resume and head shot sent under separate cover." Sign it "Sincerely hoping for an audi-

tion" or "Sincerely hoping for an interview," depending on what you sent and include your name and phone number.

It is imperative to send your information so it arrives on the same day or at the latest the next day, so the roses you sent are still fresh in the recipient's mind.

It's Who You Know

Breaking into the performing arts industry can be difficult, no matter what the genre. Competition in both the talent end and the business area is keen. There are thousands of talented people who never make it; thousands of people who are trained in theater arts, acting, or the other performing arts, yet never get past the door. Knowing someone who can get you in the door will most certainly help.

Before you say, "Me? I don't know anyone," stop and think. Are you sure? Might you know someone, anyone, even on a peripheral basis who might be able to give you a recommendation, make a call, or would be willing lend his or her name?

What about your mother's aunt's husband's friend's neighbor's boss? Sure, it might be a stretch. But think hard. Who can you think of who might know someone who might be able to help? This is not the time to be shy. Call up your aunt. Explain what you're trying to do with your career. Then ask if she would be willing to talk to her husband's friend about talking to their neighbor about using their name to make an appointment with the neighbor's boss.

What if you don't have a relative who has a contact down the line? What about your local arts council? Do they have any professional programs scheduled? If so, there might be someone you might make contact with who could be helpful in your career. Whether it's an agent, actor, actress, singer, dancer, tour manager, or anyone else in the industry, it's worth a shot. What about a local radio station? Do they have reps come in from record companies? How about your newspaper? Is there someone on staff who writes about theater or other performing arts? Might he or she have some contact with anyone else who could potentially help you in your career?

Don't forget about school drama coaches and theater arts professors as well as community theater directors and casting agents. All of these people might be a treasure trove of contacts. Sometimes all you need to do is ask.

The trick here is to think outside the box. If you can find someone who knows someone who is willing to help you to get your foot in the door, then all you will have to do is sell yourself. If someone does agree to lend their name, make a call or help you in any manner, it's important to write thank-you notes immediately. These notes should be written whether or not you actually get an interview or set up a meeting.

If you do go on to an interview or meeting or speak to the person someone suggested, it's also a good idea to either call or write another note letting your contact know what happened.

Meeting the Right People

You think and think and you can't come up with anyone you know with a connection to anyone at all in the aspect of the performing arts in which you're interested. What can you do? Sometimes you have to find your own contacts. You need to meet the right people. But how can you do this? The best way to meet the right people in the performing arts is to be around people in the performing arts.

What area of the performing arts are you interested in pursuing? In which area do you want to succeed? Is it theater, classical music, opera, ballet, comedy, the music industry, or something else? Whatever area it is, there are industry-specific organizations, associations, and unions.

Consider joining those associated with your area of the performing arts. Many of these organizations offer career guidance and support. They also may offer seminars, workshops, and other types of educational symposiums. Best of all, many have periodic meetings and annual conventions and conferences. All of these are treasure troves of possibilities to meet people within the industry. Some of them may be industry experts or insiders. Others may be just like you: people trying to get in and succeed.

Workshops and seminars are great because not only can you make important contacts, but you can learn something valuable about the industry. Most of these events have question and answer periods built into the program. Take advantage of these. Stand up and ask a good question. Make yourself visible. Some seminars and workshops have break-out sessions to encourage people to get to know one another. Use these to your advantage as well. Walk around and talk to people. Don't be afraid to walk up to someone you don't know and start talking. Network, network, network!

After the session has ended, walk up, shake the moderator's hand and tell him or her how much you enjoyed the session. This gives you the opportunity to ask for his or her business

---

⭐ **Words from a Pro**

Don't just blend in with everyone else at a seminar or workshop. Make yourself visible and memorable in a positive way. Ask questions and participate when possible. Smile and be pleasant and positive.

card. When you get home, send a short note stating that you were at the session he or she moderated, and just wanted to mention again how much you enjoyed it. You might also ask, depending on the person's position, if it would be possible to set up an informational interview (or send head shots, a resume etc.) or if he or she could suggest who you might call for that. If you don't hear back within a week, feel free to call up, identify yourself, and ask again.

One of the best ways to meet people in the industry is to attend industry or organization annual conventions and conferences. These events offer many opportunities you might not normally have to network and meet industry insiders.

There is usually a charge to attend these conventions. Fee structures may vary. (Many industry trade organizations offer special convention entry fees for students. Make sure you ask ahead of time.) Sometimes there is one price for general admission to all events and entry to the trade show floor. Other times, there may be one price for entry just to the trade show floor and another price if you also want to take part in seminars and other events.

Are they worth it? Absolutely! If you want to meet people in the industry, these gatherings are the place to do it.

How do you find these events? Trade journals and association Web sites usually post information about their conventions or offer a calendar of industry events.

If you are making the investment to go to a convention, conference, seminar or workshop, take full advantage of the opportunity. As we've discussed throughout this book, network, network, network! Some events to take part in or attend at conventions and conferences might include

The Inside Scoop

Many industry organization conference managers have begun having mini career fairs at these events to help industry people who have been downsized. Check out Web sites of association conferences ahead of time.

◎ opening events
◎ keynote presentations
◎ educational seminars and workshops
◎ certification programs
◎ break sessions
◎ breakfast, lunch, and/or dinner events
◎ cocktail parties
◎ trade show exhibit areas
◎ career fairs

More Ideas

If you have writing skills, one great way of meeting people in the industry is to write articles, do reviews, or interview people for local, regional, or national periodicals or newspapers. How does this work? A great deal of it depends on your situation, where you live, and what's happening in your area. If you're still in school, become involved with the school newspaper. Try to become the entertainment reporter or theater reviewer. If you live in an area where you have a lot of theatrical, musical, and other performing arts events and concerts consider calling up your local newspaper or a regional magazine and see if they might be interested in reviews of shows.

Try to develop an angle or hook for a story on an actor, playwright, composer, dancer, singer, or songwriter. For example, did the lead in a theatrical production attend your alma mater? Is the lead singer of a hot recording act the spokesperson of a national charity you're involved with on a local level? Is the producer of a play facilitating a seminar on theater arts in an area college? These are all angles or hooks you might use to entice a local or regional periodical to let you do an article.

You probably will have to give them some samples of your writing and your background sheet or resume. You might also have to write on "spec" or speculation. What this means is that when you do the story they may or may not use it. If they do, they will pay you. If not, they won't.

Your goal here (unless you want to be an entertainment journalist) is not to make money (although that is nice). Your goal is to be in situations where you have the opportunity to meet industry insiders and meeting them on a different level than if you were looking for a job.

Depending on the story you are working on you might have the opportunity to speak to a wide array of industry insiders. Press credentials can give you access to actors, producers, directors, casting directors, promoters, managers, publicists, tour managers, and a host of others you might not otherwise be able to have contact with. Use these contacts wisely.

Networking Basics

It's not always what you know but sometimes who you know. With that in mind, I'm going once again to bring up the importance of networking, especially if you're trying to succeed in any part of the performing arts industry. You can never tell who knows someone in some area of the industry so it is essential to share your career dreams and aspirations with those around you. Someone you mention them to might just say, "My uncle is a casting director," "My sister is a costume designer," or any other of a hundred different scenarios.

Think it can't happen? Think again. Need some examples? Then read on.

I was giving a speech on stress management for a convention in Las Vegas a couple of years ago. Before my presentation, I was sitting in the speaker ready room chatting with a woman who was a temp secretary for the conference management company. She asked if I could spare a few minutes after my presentation to give her a bit of advice and I agreed.

"I'm doing this part time," she said. "I just moved here a few months ago from Minnesota and don't really know too many people. It's my dream to be a working actress, but I don't know how to go about it. I acted since I was a young girl and had roles in all my school plays and then my college productions. I did some summer stock while I was still in college, but since I received my degree in theater arts, I haven't had a paying job in theater and I don't know what to do."

"Why did you move here?" I asked.

"My college roommate moved here and my aunt and uncle live here, so it seemed like a good idea at the time. I wanted to get away from the snow, and I thought there was a lot of opportunity here, but so far, nothing. What can I do?" she asked.

"Have you tried auditioning for any of the productions out here?" I asked.

"I called a couple, but they weren't looking to fill any roles at the time," she said. "I look in the paper, but I haven't seen anything."

"Do you have your head shots and your resume done?" I asked.

"Yes," she said, "I did that as soon as I got here."

"I take it your roommate knows what you want to do. Did you share your career dreams with your aunt and uncle too?" I asked.

"No, not really," she said. "I sort of mentioned it, but I didn't make a big deal out of it.

No one in my family really thinks acting is a serious career choice."

"Do your relatives work here?" I asked.

"My aunt works in marketing for one of the developers here," she said, "and my uncle works at one of the casino hotels. No one works in the entertainment part of the industry in case that's what you're asking."

"As a temp, do you ever get sent to work with any of the production shows here?" I asked.

"Not so far. My company does send out temps to a couple of the shows, but they haven't sent me."

"You need to get proactive," I said. "I want you to make up business cards and then give them out. Tell everyone what you want to do. Ask people around you if anyone has any idea. You can never tell what might happen. Don't forget to ask your aunt and uncle."

"I'll ask, but I'm sure they don't know anyone. If they did, I'm sure they would have mentioned it. I'm having dinner with them tonight. I'm going to ask," she said.

"Let me know what happens," I said.

A couple days later I received a call from the woman.

"Guess what? You were right. My aunt does know someone who is involved in the theatrical world. As a matter of fact, she knows a couple of them. One of the people moving into one of the buildings she's doing the marketing for is in the casting department for a big production which didn't open yet and another one is one of the scenic designers. I'm so excited."

"So what's the next step?" I asked.

"My aunt called the casting guy she knew and told him about me. He told her he couldn't promise anything, but he would be glad to set up an audition. She also spoke to the scenic designer. He's having an open house in two weeks and invited my aunt and uncle and *me*! He told

her a lot of the people in the Vegas entertainment industry and from Broadway would be there and told her to tell me it would be a great night to get to meet people."

A few months later I heard from her again. She had just landed a role in one of the Las Vegas production shows. She still keeps in contact with me. The last I heard she was auditioning for a new role in one of the Las Vegas–based Broadway shows.

Knowing how important networking can be to your career, let's talk about some networking basics.

The first thing you need to do is determine exactly who you know and who is part of your network. Then you need to get out and find more people to add to the list.

When working on your networking list, add the type of contact you consider each person. Primary contacts are those people who you know; your family members, teachers, friends, and neighbors. Secondary contacts are those individuals who are referred to you by others. These would include, for instance, a friend of a friend, your aunt's neighbor, your attorney's sister, and so on.

You might also want to note whether you consider each person as a close, medium, or distant relationship. Close would be family, friends, employers, and current teachers. Medium would be people you talk to and see frequently such as your dentist, attorney, or your UPS, FedEx, or mail delivery person. Distant would include people you talk to and see infrequently or those you have just met or have met just once or twice.

A sample networking worksheet appears on page 140.

It would be great to have a network full of people in the theater and the performing arts. That may not be the case—but this doesn't mean, however, that other people can't be help-

Networking Worksheet

Name	Relationship/ Position	Type of Contact (Primary or Secondary)	Closeness of Contact (Close, Medium, or Distant)
Mary Jones	Former Music Teacher	Primary	Medium
Donna Rigby	Drama Coach	Primary	Close
Jim Baker	Bank Teller	Primary	Distant
Sam	UPS Delivery Person	Primary	Medium
Matt Rodgers	Newspaper Reporter	Secondary	Distant
Laura	Sister-in-law	Primary	Close
Dr. Wells	Dentist	Primary	Medium
Bill Roberts	Attorney	Primary	Medium
Manny Binjo	Production Director	Secondary	Medium
Tim Thomas	Talent Agent	Primary	Close

ful. Your network may include a variety of people from all walks of life. These may include

◎ family members
◎ friends
◎ friends of friends
◎ coworkers and colleagues
◎ teachers or professors
◎ doctors and dentists
◎ pharmacists
◎ your mail carrier
◎ your hairstylist
◎ your personal trainer
◎ your priest, pastor, or rabbi
◎ members of your congregation
◎ UPS, FedEx, Airborne, or other delivery person
◎ your auto mechanic
◎ your attorney
◎ the server at the local diner or coffee shop
◎ bank tellers from your local bank
◎ entertainment reporter from local newspaper
◎ theater owner
◎ neighbors
◎ friends of your relatives
◎ business associates of your relatives
◎ people you work with on volunteer not-for-profit boards and civic groups

Now look at your list. Do you see how large your network really is? Virtually everyone you come in contact with during the day can become part of your network. Just keep adding people to your list.

Expanding Your Network

How can you expand your network? There are a number of ways. Networking events are an excellent way to meet people. Industry networking events are, of course, the best to attend, but don't count out nonindustry events. For example, your local chamber of commerce may have specific networking programs designed to help business people in the community meet and "network" with each other. In case you're thinking that no one in theater or the other performing arts will be there remember two things. First, as we've discussed, you don't know who people know. People you meet may know others who *are* in the industry. Second, no matter how small your area, you never really know who is involved in what. For all you know, someone in your area may be

◎ a lawyer who represents someone in theater or the other performing arts
◎ the dentist of someone in the performing arts
◎ the personal physician of someone in the performing arts
◎ the tailor or seamstress to industry executives or talent
◎ the dry cleaner for theatrical productions
◎ the caterer at arenas, theaters, or concert halls in your region

If you're under the impression that everyone who has a client, a friend, or a relative in theater or the performing arts talks about it and brags, you couldn't be more mistaken. Many people just don't think their business is someone else's. Others may not want to drop names. It might not be until someone like you says, "I wish I knew someone in the theater or the performing arts," that someone else brings their own network into the picture.

Civic and other not-for-profit groups also have a variety of events that are great for networking. Whether you go to a regular meeting or you attend a charity auction, cocktail party or large gala to benefit a not-for-profit, you will generally find business people in the community you might not know. As an added bonus, many larger not-for-profit events also have media coverage, meaning that you have the opportunity to add media people to your network.

Those who take advantage of every opportunity to meet new people will have the largest

Networking Worksheet			
Name	Relationship/ Position	Type of Contact (Primary or Secondary)	Closeness of Contact (Close, Medium, or Distant)

networks. The idea in building a network is to go *out* of your comfort zone. If you just stay with people you know and are comfortable with, you won't have the opportunity to get to know others. You want to continually meet new people; after all, you never know who knows who.

Networking Savvy

You are learning how to build your network. However, the largest network in the world will be useless unless you know how to take full advantage of it. Let's talk about how you're going to use the network you are building.

Networking is a skill. You're not born with it. You can acquire the skill to network, practice, and improve. What that means is that if you practice networking, you can get better at it, and it can pay off big in your career!

Get out. Go to new places. Meet new people. When you're in a situation where there are new people, don't be afraid to walk up to them, shake their hand, and talk to them. People can't read your mind, so it's imperative to tell them about your career goals, dreams, and aspirations.

Because of the mystique surrounding all of the performing arts, people will generally find your choice of careers interesting. If they are involved or have any contact in the industry at all, they will usually say something like: "Oh, that's neat, my best friend is a lighting designer for Broadway productions." "My cousin works at one of the major labels." "My accountant was just telling me he handles a couple of Broadway actors," or "My attorney is the lawyer for a number of the big comedians."

When you meet new people, listen to them. Focus on what they're saying. You can never tell when the next person you talk to is the one who will be able to help you open the door or vice versa.

If you're shy, even the thought of networking may be very difficult for you. However, it is essential to make yourself do it anyway. Successful networking can pay off big. It can mean the difference between getting in the industry or not, between success and failure. Isn't it worth the effort?

Just meeting people isn't enough. Whether you meet a successful casting agent, a famous director, an acclaimed producer, the director of a major orchestra, a Tony award winning actor or actress, a successful music publisher, or anyone to add to your network, the idea is to try to develop the relationship further. Just having a story to tell about who you know is not enough. Arrange a follow-up meeting, send a note or letter, or make a phone call. The more you take advantage of every opportunity, the closer you will be to getting what you want.

A good way to network is to volunteer. I've mentioned attending not-for-profit events and civic meetings to expand your network, but how about volunteering to work with a not-for-profit or civic group?

I can imagine you saying, "When? I'm so busy now, I don't have enough time to do anything."

Make the time. It will be worth it.

Why? People will see you on a different level. They won't see you as someone looking for a job or trying to succeed as a performer. Generally, people talk about their volunteer work to

---

⭐ Words from a Pro

Keep a scrapbook of articles, photos, programs, and other supporting material from volunteer events you have worked on. It will be useful when putting together your portfolio.

friends, family, business associates, and other colleagues. This means that when someone is speaking to someone else they might mention in passing that one of the people they are working with on their event or project is trying to make it as an actor or actress, trying to succeed as a singer, musician, or dancer or attempting to get into one of the other performing arts. Anyone they mention it to is a potential secondary networking contact. Those people, in turn, may mention it to someone else. Eventually, someone involved in the area of the performing arts you're zeroing in on might hear about you. Another reason is people will see that you have a good work ethic. Treat volunteer projects as you would work projects. Do what you say you are going to do and do it in a timely manner.

This also gives you the opportunity to demonstrate skills and talents people might not otherwise know you have. Can you do publicity? Can you write? How about organizing things? Do you get along well with others? What better way to illustrate your skills than utilizing them by putting together an event, publicizing it, or coordinating other volunteers. Are you trying to get exposure as an actor, actress, singer, songwriter, director, producer, etc.? What better opportunity to showcase your talents than composing a song or opening tune for a not-for-profit's big event? How about volunteering to perform at the event gratis? No, you won't get paid, but you will have great exposure and possibly get some media attention.

Tip from the Coach

A man called one day asking for advice. He had been working in the administrative end of small orchestra and was depressed becuase he couldn't seem to move into his dream career of a position in the marketing department of a major orchestra. One of the pieces of advice I offered him was to do some volunteer work.

"What do you like to do?" I asked.

"I love to cook for people," he said.

"Why don't you call a couple of not-for-profit agencies and see who is looking for someone to volunteer to cook," I suggested. A few days later he called to tell me that he would be cooking meals a few times a month for 40 people at his home and then bringing the food to a homeless shelter. He mentioned that in addition to donating his time, he would have to buy the ingredients for the meals as well. While he wasn't making much money in his job at the time, the man told me that each time he shopped, he bought ingredients that he would buy if he were cooking for his own family. He never scrimped.

The shelter director called him after three months to tell him how much the clients enjoyed the food on the nights he cooked. She invited him to a meeting for volunteers at the shelter. He went to the meeting and was introduced to other volunteers and members of the organization's board of directors. He happened to mention his dream career to one of the board members who, as it turned out, was the husband of a woman who was the orchestra director of a major orchestra. A few days later the man received a call from the man's wife. She had been at a conference and heard that one of her colleagues from another orchestra was looking for a marketing director. The man interviewed for the position and landed it. Had he not volunteered for that particular position, he might not have even heard of the job opening.

Best of all, you can use this activity in your resume. While volunteer experiences don't take the place of work experience, they certainly can fill out a resume short of it.

Don't just go to meetings. Participate fully in the organization. That way you'll not only be helping others, you will be adding to your network.

Try to keep in contact with people on your network on a regular basis. Set up a schedule of sorts to do some positive networking every day. For example, you might decide to call one person every day on your networking list. Depending on the situation you can say you were calling to touch base, say hello, keep in contact, or see how they were doing. Ask how they have been or talk about something you might have in common or that they might think is interesting. You might also decide that once a week, you will try to call someone and set up a lunch or coffee date.

Be on the lookout for stories, articles, or other tidbits of information that might be of interest to people in your network. Clip them out and send them with a short note saying you saw the story and thought they might be interested. If you hear of something they might be interested in, call them. The idea is to keep in contact with people in your network and stay visible.

Keep track of the contacts in your network. You can use the sample sheet provided, a card file using index cards or a database or contact software program on your computer. Include as

---

Tip from the Top

After you have worked on a volunteer project, ask the director or board president if he or she would mind writing you a letter of recommendation for your file.

---

much information as you have about each person. People like when you remember them and their interests. It makes you stand out.

Then use your networking contact list. For example, a few days before people's birthdays, send them a card. If you know someone collects old guitars and you see an article on old guitars, clip it out and send it. Don't be a pest, but keep in contact. People in sales have been using this technique for years. It works for them and it will help you as well.

Here's a sample Networking Contact Information Sheet. You might want to use some of the items here and then add more information as it comes up.

Making and Using Contacts in Theater and the Performing Arts

If you are interested in the talent end of the industry, make additional contacts in that area. Make contact with people who can help push your plays, compositions, and songs. Make contact with people who can cast you, book you, manage you, or just help you get your foot in the door and advance your career.

How can you catch the attention of people like this? Think creatively. Look for every opportunity. Are classes offered in playwriting? What about acting workshops? How about seminars on better ways to perform? Can you find workshops on various aspects of theater or the

---

The Inside Scoop

Volunteer to do projects that no one else wants to do and you will immediately become more visible.

Networking Contact Information Sheet

Name
_____

Business Address
_____

Business Phone
_____

Home Address
_____

Home Phone
_____

E-mail
_____

Web Address (URL)
_____

Birthday
_____

Anniversary
_____

Where and When Met
_____

Spouse or Significant Other's Name
_____

Children's Name(s)
_____

Dog Breed and Name
_____

Cat Breed and Name
_____

Hobbies
_____

Interests
_____

Things Collected
_____

Honors
_____

Awards
_____

Interesting Facts

other performing arts? Take them! Aside from learning something, you can never tell who you might meet there.

Workshops where people in the industry critique your work are especially useful. In the event that someone doesn't like your work, don't let it get to you. He or she is only one person. Use these opportunities to hone your craft and talent. Use them to meet others in the industry.

Be on the lookout for contests and competitions. They're great for exposure. If they are televised, even on a local basis, all the better. Make sure you get a tape even if you have to buy one. If the local television news covers an event and you don't tape it yourself, call them up and ask how you can get a copy. If the news happens to film you and only uses a few seconds or a minute, see if you can buy the raw tape footage that they didn't use.

Many television and cable stations are now hosting television shows showcasing talent. If you are ready, consider applying. Shows like *American Idol, Grease, You're The One That I Want*, or *Last Comic Standing* can give you major exposure and have already spawned a number of top stars. If you are talented and lucky, you could be one of them.

Depending on the area of the industry you're in, you might want to consider talent showcases.

Words from a Pro

Copyright all songs and compositions before letting anyone outside of your family listen to them. Catchy tunes often stick in people's heads. It's not uncommon for people to inadvertently think that *they* came up with a song. A copyright will protect you.

Similarly, copyright scripts you develop and write.

These opportunities help to display your talent to industry insiders. Showcases may be sponsored by a variety of industry organizations, trade associations, or other businesses. Sometimes a manager or other business associate may put together a showcase for you and invite industry professionals such as agents, promoters, producers, and record company executives.

In some cases, you may even want to showcase yourself. If you hear of a showcase for someone else and you have the opportunity to attend, go. Although it's fine to network and pick up business cards while you're there, don't overshadow the person or act being showcased. While every showcase or competition might not end up in a contract, the idea is to find opportunities to explore where you have the chance to meet industry insiders.

Finding a Mentor or Advocate

Mentors and advocates can help guide and boost your career. A mentor or advocate in the industry also often provides you with valuable contacts which, as you now know, are essential to your success. The best mentors and advocates are supportive individuals who help move your career to the next level.

Can't figure out why anyone would help you? Many people like to help others. It makes them feel good. How do you find a mentor? Look for someone who is successful and whom you respect, and ask. Sounds simple? It is simple. The difficult part is finding just the right person or persons.

While someone in theater or one of the other performing arts would be ideal, don't let that exclude those outside the industry.

Sometimes you don't even have to ask. In many cases, a person may see your potential and offer advice. They may not call it mentor-

Tip from the Coach

If someone asks you to be their mentor, or asks for your help and you can offer it, say yes. As a matter of fact, if you see someone you might be able to help, do just that. You might think that you don't even have your own career on track or you don't have time. You might be tempted to say no. Think again. You are expecting someone to help you. Do the same for someone else. There is no better feeling than helping someone else. And while you shouldn't help someone for the sole purpose of helping yourself, remember that you can often open doors for yourself, while opening them for someone else.

ing, but with any luck, that's what it turns into. Time is a valuable commodity, especially to busy people. Be gracious when someone helps you or even tries to help. Make sure you say thank you to anyone and everyone who shares his or her time, expertise, or advice. And don't forget to ask them if there is any way you can return the favor.

Internships, Apprenticeships, and More

As in many other industries, internships, apprenticeships and other programs are a wonderful method to help you get your foot solidly in the door. These programs can help you explore the career path you've chosen in more depth, learn new skills, and most importantly, make contacts you might not otherwise have had the opportunity to make.

If you are interested in a career in arts administration you should know that most orchestra, opera, and ballet companies—no matter what size—offer internship opportunities. Many theater companies have similar opportunities. As a

matter of fact, many companies involved in the performing arts industry offer internships.

How do you find them? Check out the Web sites of companies you're interested in interning. Search the Web. Talk to people. Ask industry insiders. If you are still in college, ask your advisor to help you set up an internship. If you are attending a college which has arts administration or theater arts majors, they may already have internship programs set up. Be sure to ask.

"But what if the company I want to work with doesn't offer an internship?" you ask. "What do I do then?"

Just contact the company you're interested in working with and see if you can set up an internship. Ask to speak to the director of human resources or the company director and tell them what you're interested in doing. Explain what *you* will do for them. If you're enthusiastic and persuasive, companies usually will help you arrange an internship.

Take advantage of your internship opportunity. Learn as much as you can. Even if you're not being paid, work as though you're the highest-paid employee there. Ask questions. Offer to do things you're not asked to do. Make contacts within the company in every department even if it means doing extra work. Have a great work ethic and be a positive, enthusiastic, helpful presence in the company while you're there. It can pay off big time. In many instances, companies hire interns after their internship program has concluded.

The Inside Scoop

Most of the current members of the New York City Ballet were trained at the School of American Ballet and entered through their apprentice program.

> ### ⭐ Tip from the Top
> Sometimes compensation for internships is monetary. Other times you may receive college credit. Be aware that even if internships are paid, the compensation will be nominal. The true value of internships is the contacts you can make. Take advantage of every opportunity.

> ### ⭐ The Inside Scoop
> Apprenticeships can be transitional points in your career as a performing artist, often following formal training and before becoming a professional. They can help you translate your talent from the classroom to the stage.

If your dream is a career in the talent end of the industry, try to find apprenticeships or development programs. Are you an aspiring opera singer? Then you want to become involved in a young artist development programs and apprentice singer programs. Facilitated by renowned singers, directors, and coaches, these programs will help hone your skills and propel you to the next stage in your career through training and performance opportunities.

Where do you find them? Contact the various opera companies such as the Metropolitan Opera, Santa Fe Opera, Washington National Opera, and the Seattle Opera, among others. You might also contact Opera America for more information on possible programs.

If a career in symphonies is your passion, contact midsized and major orchestras to see if they offer apprentice or training programs. Contact the American Symphony Orchestra League to learn about opportunities.

In the same vein, if you are interested in a career in ballet, look for an internship or apprentice program. Contact ballet companies or *Dance Magazine* to find opportunities. Your best bets will be well-established programs associated with professional schools.

If you are an aspiring actor, apprenticeships in theater arts can not only help you hone your skills, but can showcase your talent. Look for the best programs you can find. Talk to industry insiders. Get advice from your drama coach, acting teachers, and directors of local theater companies. Surf the net. Check out industry publications.

All programs are not alike. Some offer more opportunities. Some offer training with more established actors and directors.

Internships and apprenticeships are also useful for getting your foot in the door if you're working toward a career in any other creative aspect of theater arts including costume, lighting or scenic design, producing, directing, casting, and playwriting. Keep in mind that you usually get out of a program, what you put into it. These opportunities can help jumpstart your career. Learn as much as you can, make contacts and have fun. You're in the door and on your way to a great career!

> ### ⭐ The Inside Scoop
> The Williamstown Theatre Festival located in the Berkshires in Massachusetts has an apprentice program that is referred to by many as a "theater boot camp." In this particular program, the participants pay instead of the other way around. During the 10-week program, apprentices get involved in every aspect of theater from building sets, to passing out scripts to cleaning the stage, and more. Who would pay to do this, you ask? Reportedly mega-stars like Sigourney Weaver and Gwyneth Paltrow went through the program at the beginning of their careers.

8

THE INTERVIEW

Getting the Interview

Whether your dream is to succeed in a career in the talent or creative end of theater or in any of the other performing arts, the arts administration or business areas, or anything in between, the first step is always getting the job.

One of the keys to getting the job you want is the interview. Let's take some time to discuss how to get that all-important meeting.

The interview is your chance to shine. During an interview you can show what can't be illustrated on paper. This is the time your personality and talents can be showcased. In an industry such as the performing arts, where there are often more people who want to get in than there are jobs, obtaining an interview and excelling in the interview can help get you the job you want.

If you do it right, the interview can help make you irresistible. It is your chance to persuade the interviewer to hire you. It is your main shot at showing why you would be better than anyone else; why hiring you would benefit the company; why not hiring you would be a big mistake. So let's take some time to discuss how to get that all-important meeting.

There are many ways to land job interviews, including

◎ responding to advertisements
◎ recommendations from friends, relatives, or colleagues
◎ making cold calls
◎ writing letters
◎ working with executive search firms, recruiters, or headhunters
◎ working with employment agencies
◎ attending job and career fairs
◎ finding the jobs that have not been advertised (the hidden job market)

Responding to an advertisement is probably the most common approach people take to obtaining a job interview. Where can you look for ads for jobs in theater and the other performing arts? Depending on the exact type of job you're looking for, here are some possibilities:

◎ trade magazines (*Backstage*, *Billboard*, *Variety*, and others)
◎ association Web sites
◎ company Web sites
　▫ opera companies
　▫ symphonies
　▫ ballet companies
　▫ theaters
　▫ arts councils
　▫ casting companies

- ☐ production companies
- ☐ publicity and public relations agencies
- ☐ marketing companies
- ☐ booking agencies
- ☐ talent agencies
- ☐ literary agencies
- ◎ career-oriented Web sites
- ◎ music business-oriented Web sites
- ◎ theatrical business–oriented Web sites
- ◎ performing arts business–oriented Web sites
- ◎ newspapers

Now let's say you open up the paper or a trade magazine or even see an advertisement on the Web that looks like this:

SYMPHONY ORCHESTRA seeking the following positions: Director of Fund Raising and Development, Assistant to Music Librarian, Administrative Assistant to PR director, Box office staffer. For consideration for these positions either fax resume to (111) 222-3333, e-mail to goodorchestra@orchestra.org or mail to PO Box 1111, Some Town, NY 11111.

Once you see the ad you get excited. You have been looking for a job just like this one. You can't wait to send your resume.

Want a reality check? There may be hundreds of other people who can't wait either. But

---

The Inside Scoop

No matter where you live, you can usually view the classified ads for most of the major newspapers throughout the country online. Go to the newspaper's main Web site and look for "classifieds."

Tip from the Coach

If your career is in the talent area, the interview will most likely take the form of an audition.

---

here's the good news: With a little planning, you can increase your chances of getting an interview from the classified or display ad, and as we've just discussed, this is your key to the job.

Your resume and cover letter need to stand out. Your resume needs to generate an interview. Most importantly, on a broad sense, you want your resume to define you as the one *in* a million candidates an employer can't live without instead of one *of* the million others that are applying for a job.

It's essential that your resume and cover letter distinguish you from every other applicant going for the job. Why? Because if yours doesn't, someone else's will and he or she will be the one who gets the job.

Let's look at the journey a resume might take after you send it out in response to a classified ad. Where does it go? Who reads it? That depends. In some companies, usually smaller ones, your resume and cover letter may go to the person who will be hiring you. It may go to that person's secretary or administrative assistant. This might be the case, for example, if you're replying to an ad for a job in a small booking or talent agency or even a smaller orchestra, opera, ballet company, or theater. In some companies, usually larger ones, your resume and cover letter may go to a hiring manager or human resources director. This would probably occur if you're answering an ad for a position at a midsized to larger orchestra, opera, or ballet company, large booking and talent agencies, and major production companies.

Tip from the Top

Here is what you need to know. The requirements set forth in an advertisement are the ideal requirements that the company would like; not necessarily what they are going to end up with. While it would be great if they could find a candidate with every single requirement, it doesn't always work like that. Often a candidate has all the qualifications, yet someone who is missing one or two stands out and is the one who ultimately lands the job.

If you are replying to an advertisement placed by an employment agency, your response will generally go to the person at the employment agency responsible for that client and job.

In any of these cases, however, your resume may take other paths. Depending on the specific job and company, your response may go through executive recruiters, screening services, clerks, or even receptionists. Whoever the original screener of resumes turns out to be, he or she will have the initial job of reviewing the information to make sure that it fits the profile of what is needed. But—that doesn't mean that if you don't have the exact requirements you should not reply to a job.

The trick is to tailor your resume as much as possible to the specific job and write a great cover letter. For example, let's say the job requirements for a position at a theatrical production company in the publicity department look something like this:

Creative, enthusiastic individual to publicize new touring theatrical production show. Must have strong organization skills and excellent verbal and writing skills. Ability to work without direct supervision.

Minimum requirements include bachelor's degree and six years experience in entertainment publicity and nationwide entertainment media contacts.

Now let's say that while you are creative and enthusiastic and have excellent verbal and writing skills, you don't have six years experience working in entertainment publicity. Instead, you have three years of experience handling corporate publicity and public relations. You have national media contacts, but they're in the business industry. Should you not apply for the job? If you want it, go for it.

Here is what you need to know. When you are developing your resume and cover letter in response to an ad, remember that skills are transferable. Skills for specific areas might need to be fine-tuned, but sales skills are sales skills, writing skills are writing skills, and publicity and public relations skills are publicity and public relations skills. Stress what you have done successfully, not what you haven't done. Use your cover letter to help showcase these accomplishments.

Whoever your resume and cover letter go to, you want to increase your chances of it being looked at and passed on to the pile of resumes from people who will ultimately end up getting called for an interview. Whoever the screener of the resumes is, he or she will probably pass over anything that doesn't look neat and well thought out or any applications with obvious errors.

What can you do? First, go over your resume. Make sure it is perfect. Make sure it is neat. Make sure it is tailored to the job you are going after. If you are going to mail it, make sure it's printed on high-quality paper.

Human resources departments dealing with entertainment-oriented companies often receive hundreds of responses to ads. While most people use white paper, consider using off-white or

Tip from the Coach

If mailing your resume and cover sheet, use an envelope large enough to fit the paper, so you don't have to fold it. That way it comes in flat and looks neat when it arrives. If faxing any documents, remember to use the "fine" option on your fax machine. While this may take a bit longer to send, the recipients will get a better copy.

even a different color such as light blue or light mauve. You want your resume to look sophisticated and classy, but still stand out in a professional way. While the color of the paper will not change the content of your resume, it will at least help your resume get noticed in the first place.

If the advertisement directs you in a specific method of responding to the ad, use that method. For example, if the ad instructs applicants to fax their resumes, fax it. If it says e-mail your resume, use e-mail and pay attention to whether the ad specifies sending the file as an attachment or in the body of your e-mail. The company may have a procedure for screening job applicants.

When is the best time to send your response to an ad in order to have the best chance at getting an interview? If you send your resume right away, it might arrive with a pile of hundreds of others. Yet if you wait too long, the company might have already found a candidate and stopped seriously looking at new resumes.

Many people procrastinate, so if you can send in your response immediately, such as the day the ad is published or the very next morning, it will probably be one of the first ones in. At that time the screener will be reading through just a few responses. If yours stands out, it stands a good chance of being put into the "initial interview pile."

If you can't respond immediately, wait two or three days so your resume doesn't arrive with the big pile of responses. Your goal is to increase your chances of your resume not being passed over.

If you are trying to land an interview through a recommendation from friends or colleagues, cold calls, letters, executive search firms, recruiters, headhunters, employment agencies, people you met at job fairs, through other networking events, or any aspect of the hidden job market, the timing of sending a resume is essential. In these cases you want the people receiving your information to remember that someone said it was coming, so send it as soon as possible. This is not the time to procrastinate. If you do, you might lose the opportunity to set up the interview.

Persistence is the word to remember when trying to get an interview. If you are responding to an advertisement and you don't hear back within a week or two, call to see what is happening. If after you call the first time, you don't hear back for another week or so (unless you've been given a specific time frame), call back again. Don't be obnoxious, but call.

If you're shy, you're going to have to get over it. Write a script ahead of time to help you. Don't read directly from the script, but practice so it becomes second nature. For example: "Hello, this is John Cromwell. I replied to an advertisement you placed in the paper for the director of development position at your ballet. I was wondering who I could speak with to find out about the status of the position."

When you get to the correct person, you might have to reiterate your purpose in calling. Then you might ask, "Do you know when interviewing is starting? Will all applicants be notified one way or the other? Is it possible to tell me whether I'm on the list to be contacted?" Don't be afraid to try to get as much information as possible, once again making sure you are being pleasant.

Remember that becoming friendly with the secretary or receptionist is a good thing. These people are on the inside and can provide you with a wealth of information.

Be aware that there is a way that you can get your resume looked at, obtain an interview, and beat the competition out of the dream job you want in the performing arts. Remember that we discussed the hidden job market? We know that some jobs are not advertised. Following this theory, all you have to do is contact the company and land the job you want *before* it is advertised.

"How?" you ask.

Take a chance. Make a call or write a letter and ask. You might even stop in and talk to the human resources department or one of the department heads. There is nothing that says you have to wait to see an ad in the paper. Call up and ask to speak to the human resources department or hiring manager. Write a script ahead of time so you know exactly what you want to say. Ask for the hiring manager or human resources department. Ask about job openings. Make sure you have an idea of what you want to do and convey it to the person you are talking to.

If you are told there are no openings or that the company doesn't speak to people unsolicited, be persistent. Ask if you can forward a resume to keep on file. In many cases, they will

agree, just to get you off the phone. Ask for the name of the person to direct your resume, then ask for the address and fax number. Thank the person you spoke to and make sure you get his or her name.

Here's a neat trick. Fax your resume. Send it with a cover letter that states that a hard copy will be coming via mail. Why fax it? Did you know that when you fax documents to a company they generally are delivered directly to the desk of the person you are sending them to? They don't go through the mailroom where they might be dumped in a general inbox. They don't sit around for a day. They are generally delivered immediately.

Now that your resume is in the hands of the powers that be, it's your job to call up, make sure they received it, and try to set up an interview. The individual's secretary might try to put you off. Don't be deterred. Thank the individual and say you understand his or her position. Say you're going to call in a week or so after the boss has had a chance to review your material. Send your information out in hard copy immediately. Wait a week or so and call back. Remember that persistence pays off.

Sometimes you might reach someone who tells you that "if they weren't so busy, they'd be glad to meet with you." They might tell you when their workload lightens or a project is done, they will schedule an interview. You could say thank you and let it go. Or you could tell them, that you understand that they're busy. All you are asking for is 10 minutes and not a minute longer. You'll even bring a stopwatch and coffee if they want. Guarantee them that 10 minutes after you get in the door, you will stand up to leave.

If you're convincing, you might land an interview. If you do, remember to bring that stopwatch.

★ Tip from the Coach

Don't be in such a rush to get your resume out that you make errors or don't produce a neat and tailored resume.

⭐ ## Tip from the Coach

When I was first trying to get into the music business, I met a young man who was a comedian. He wasn't a very good comedian, but he said he was a comedian and did have a good number of jobs performing, so I guess he was a comedian. During this time, I was trying to land interviews with everyone I could so I could get my own dream job in the music industry.

I made contact with a booking agent with whom I had developed a business relationship. Every week I'd call, and every week he would tell me to call him back. It wasn't going anywhere, but at least *someone* was taking my calls. This went on for about three or four months.

One day when I called, the owner got on the phone and said, "Do you know Joe Black? [Not his real name.] He said he has worked up in your area."

"Yes, he works as a comedian," I told him.

"What do you know about him?" he asked.

"Well, he's not a great comedian, but he seems to keep getting jobs. He's booking himself," I replied.

"That's interesting," he said. "He has called me over 25 times looking for a job as an agent. What do you think?"

I was wondering why he was asking my opinion, because I had yet to get into his office myself. "If he can book himself, he can probably do a great job for your agency," I said. "You have great clients. I bet he would do a good job."

"Thanks," he said, "I might just do that."

"What about me?" I asked.

"I still can't think of where you might fit in," he said. "Why don't you give me a call in a couple of weeks."

I waited a couple of weeks, called back and asked to speak to the owner.

"Hello," he said. "Guess who's standing next to me?"

He had hired Joe Black the comedian to work as an agent in his office.

"He had no experience, outside of booking himself, " the agent said. "But I figured if he was as persistent making calls for our clients as he was trying to get a job, he'd work out for us. Why don't you come in and talk when you have a chance. I don't have anything, but maybe I can give you some ideas."

I immediately said that I had been planning a trip to the booking agent's city the next week. We set up an appointment.

Did the agent ever have a job for me? No, but while in his office, he introduced me to some of the clients he was booking, who introduced me to some other people who later turned out to be clients of mine when I opened up a public relations business. Whether you want a job in any part of the performing arts—or any industry at all for that matter—the moral of the story is the same. Networking and persistence always pay off.

Introduce yourself, put the stopwatch down on the desk in front of you and present your skills. You must practice this before you get there. Give the highlights of your resume and how hiring you would benefit the company. When your 10 minutes are up, thank the person you are meeting with for their time, give them your resume, any supporting materials you have brought with you and your business card. Then leave. If you are asked to stay, by all means, stay and continue the meeting. One way or the other, write a note thanking them for their time.

If you have sold yourself or your idea for a position in the company, someone may just get back to you. Feel free to call in a week or two to follow up.

The Interview Process

You got the call. You landed an interview. Now what? The interview is an integral part of getting the job you want. There are a number of different types of interviews. Depending on the company and the job, you might be asked to go on one or more interviews ranging from initial or screening interviews to interviews with department heads or supervisors you will be working with.

Things to Bring

Once you get the call for an interview, what's your next step? Let's start with what you should bring to the interview.

- Copies of your resume
- Letters of reference
- References
- A portfolio of your work
- Business cards

You want to look as professional as possible, so don't throw your materials into a paper bag or a sloppy knapsack. At the very least put your information into a large envelope or folder to carry into the interview. A professional-looking briefcase or portfolio is even better.

Your Interviewing Wardrobe

You've landed an interview, but what do you wear? That depends to a great extent on the specific job for which you're interviewing. However, the rule of thumb is to dress for the job you want. With that in mind, there are a couple of things you should know. While you might see people in various areas of the performing arts wearing esoteric clothing, remember that they are not the ones going for the job. You want to dress professionally so that interviewers will see you as a professional.

First let's start with a list of what *not* to wear.

- sneakers
- flip-flops
- sandals
- microminiskirt or minidress
- very tight or very low dresses or tops
- jeans of any kind
- ripped jeans or T-shirt
- midriff top
- skintight pants or leggings
- very baggy pants
- sweatshirt
- workout clothes
- T-shirt
- heavy perfume, men's cologne, or aftershave lotion
- very heavy makeup
- flashy jewelry (this includes nose rings, lip rings, and other flamboyant piercings)

What you *should* wear:

Men
- dark suit
- dark sports jacket, button-down shirt, tie, and trousers
- clean, polished shoes

Women
- suit
- dress with jacket
- skirt with blouse and jacket
- pumps or other closed-toe shoes

Interview Environments

In most cases interviews are held in office environments. If you are asked if you want coffee, tea, soda, or any type of food, my advice is to abstain. This is not the time you want to accidentally spill coffee, inadvertently make a weird noise drinking soda, or get sugar from a donut on your fingers when you need to shake hands.

In some cases, however, you may be interviewed over a meal. Whether it is breakfast, lunch, or dinner, it is usually best to order something simple and light. This is not the time to order anything that can slurp, slide, or otherwise mess you up. Soups, messy sauces, fried chicken, ribs, or anything that you have to eat with your hands would be a bad choice. Nothing can ruin your confidence during an interview worse than a big blob of sauce accidentally dropping on your shirt—except if you cut into something and it splashes on to your interviewer's suit. Eating should be your last priority. Use this time to present your attributes, tell your story, and ask intelligent questions.

This is also not the time to order an alcoholic beverage. Even if the interviewer orders a drink, abstain. You want to be at the top of your game. If, however, the interviewer orders dessert and coffee or tea, do so as well. That way he or she isn't eating alone and you have a few more minutes to make yourself shine.

A company may invite you to participate in a meal interview for a number of reasons. They may want to see how you act in social situations, check out your table manners, see whether you drink to excess or how you make conversation. They might want to know if you will embarrass

The Inside Scoop

If you have been invited to a meal interview, generally the interviewer will pay the tab and tip. At the end of the meal, when you are leaving, thank the person who paid for the check and tell him or her how much you enjoyed the meal and the company.

them, if you can handle pressure, or how you interact with others. They might want you to get comfortable so they can see the true you. If you are prepared ahead of time, you will do fine. Just remember this isn't a social meal. You are being scrutinized. Be on your toes.

During the meal, pepper the conversation with questions about the company and the job. Don't be afraid to say you're excited about the possibility of working with them, you think you would be an asset to the company, and you hope they agree. Make eye contact with those at the table. When the interviewer stands up after the meal, the interview is generally over. Stand up, thank the interviewers for the meal, tell them you look forward to hearing from them, shake everyone's hand, and then leave.

Many companies pre-interview or do partial interviews on the phone. If the company has scheduled a phone interview ahead of time,

Words from the Wise

Never ask for a doggie bag at an interview meal. I've seen it happen and I've heard interviewers talking about it in a negative manner two weeks later.

Words from the Wise

In your effort to tell people about your accomplishments, try not to monopolize the conversation talking solely about you. Before you go to an interview, read up on the news of the day, in case someone asks your opinion about the day's happenings. You want to appear as well-rounded as possible.

make sure your "space" is prepared so you can do your best.

Here are some ideas:

◎ Have your phone in a quiet location. People yelling, a loud television, or music in the background is not helpful in this situation.

◎ Have a pad of paper and a few pens to write down the name of the people you are speaking to, notes, and to jot down questions as you think of them.

◎ Have a copy of your resume near you. Your interviewer may refer to information on your resume. If it's close you won't have to fumble for words.

◎ Prepare questions to ask in case you are asked whether you have any.

◎ Prepare answers for questions that you might be asked: "Why do you want to work for us?" "What can you bring to the company?" "What type of experience do you have?" "Why are you the best candidate?"

Timing is everything in an interview. Do not be late. If you can't get to an interview on time, chances are you won't get to a job on time. Try to time your arrival so you get there about 15 minutes before your scheduled time. When you arrive, tell the receptionist your name and with whom you have an appointment. When you are

directed to go into the interview, walk in, smile sincerely, and shake hands with the interviewer or interviewers and sit down. Look around the office. Does the interviewer have a photo of children on the desk? Is there any personalization in the office? Does it look like the interviewer is into golf, or fishing, or some other hobby? Do you have something in common? You might say something like:

◎ "What beautiful children."
◎ "Is golf one of your passions too?"
◎ "Do you go deep sea fishing?"
◎ "Those are amazing orchids. How long have you had them?"
◎ "What an incredible antique desk. Do you collect antique furniture?"

Try to make the interviewer comfortable with you before the questions start.

Interview Questions

What might you be asked? The performing arts industry is like every other industry. You will probably be asked a slew of general questions and then depending on the job, some questions specific to your skills and talent.

◎ Why should we hire you?
  ⊡ This is a common question. Think about the answers ahead of time. Practice saying them out loud so you feel comfortable. For example, "I believe I would be an asset to the company. I have the qualifications. I'm a team player, and this is the type of career I really want to pursue. I'm a hard worker, a quick study, and I'll help you achieve your goals."

    You can then go on to explain one or two specific reasons. For example, "In my current position, I developed a publicity plan which has generated 10 front-page articles as well as a number of feature stories for our theater, just this year alone. I would love the opportunity and challenge to work with a larger, more prestigious theater like yours, to do an even bigger, more exciting campaign."

◎ What makes you more qualified than other candidates?
  ▫ Another common question. How about saying something like, "I believe my experience first working as an intern and then in a paid summer position while in college gave me a fuller understanding of the inner workings of a ballet company in both the talent and business area. As an intern, I rotated through almost every department and then over last summer I worked in the special events office. I brought my portfolio so you can actually see some of the projects I worked on. You indicated today one of the challenges of your ballet company was funding. Last year I volunteered with our local community theater and wrote a number of large grants that we won. I also assisted in a big special event which raised over $35,000."

◎ Where do you see yourself in five years?
  ▫ Do not say, "Sitting in your chair." People in every business are paranoid that someone is going to take their job, so don't even joke about it. Instead, think about the question ahead of time. It's meant to find out what your aspirations are and if you

have direction.

One answer might be, "I hope to be a successful member of this company. I grew up attending performances at this theater, and as a child, always looked at everyone who worked here and envied them. I would love to think that I can have a long career here."

◎ What are your strengths?
  ▫ Be confident but not cocky when answering this one. Toot your horn, but don't be boastful. Practice ahead of time reciting what your greatest strengths, talents, and skills are. "I'm passionate about what I do. I love working at something I'm passionate about. That's one of the main reasons I applied for this position. I also have great organizational skills, I'm a people person, and I'm a really good communicator. I pride myself on being able to solve problems quickly, efficiently, and successfully."

◎ Where are your weaknesses?
  ▫ We all have weaknesses. This is not the time to share them. Be creative. "My greatest weakness is also one of my strengths. I'm a workaholic. I don't like leaving a project undone. I have a hard time understanding how someone cannot do a great job when they love what they do."

◎ Why did you leave your last job?
  ▫ Be careful answering this one. If you were fired, simply say you were let go. Don't go into the politics. Don't say anything bad about your former job, company, or boss. If you were laid off, simply say you were laid off, or, if it's

true, that you were one of the newer employees and unfortunately, that's how the layoff process worked. You might add that you were very sorry to leave because you really enjoyed working there, but on the positive side, you now are free to apply for this position. If you quit, simply say the job was not challenging and you wanted to work in a position where you could create a career.

Never lie. The world of the performing arts is small. You can never tell when your former boss knows the person interviewing you. In the same vein, never say anything bad about anyone or any other company. The boss you had yesterday might end up moving over to your new company and being your new boss. It is not unheard of in the industry.

◎ Why do you want to work in the performing arts? (Depending on the specific area of the industry, the question might be: "Why do you want to work in theater?" "Why do you want to work in an orchestra?" or "Why do you want to work in a ballet company?"

◎ Do you like theater (or music, dance, or whatever area of the performing arts in which you are seeking a job)?
   ▫ The answer here should be, "Yes, I love theater (or music, dance, etc.)." You might add something like, "My parents instilled a love of theater and it has been a life-long passion. I especially love musical comedies."

◎ Who's your favorite actor?

◎ What's your all-time favorite theatrical production?
   ▫ Think about this question ahead of time and answer accordingly. Even if you love it all, come up with a specific answer. "I've always loved The Nutcracker. I've seen the majority of the new Broadway shows, but my favorite has got to be The Lion King. I love the scenery and the music."

◎ Do you have a favorite piece of music?

◎ What's your favorite ballet?

◎ What's your favorite genre of music?

◎ Are you a team player?
   ▫ Companies want you to be a team player, so the answer is, "Yes, it's one of my strengths."

◎ Do you need supervision?
   ▫ You want to appear as confident and capable as possible. Depending on the specific job and responsibilities, you might say, "I work well with limited supervision." Or "No, once I know my responsibilities, I have always been able to fulfill them."

◎ Are you free to travel?
   ▫ You might be required to travel for some jobs. A publicist for a touring theatrical production or a traveling orchestra or ballet may need to go on the road. A marketing executive might need to travel to various locations. Scenic designers and lighting designers who are working with touring productions may need to travel as well. Be honest here. If the job you are applying for requires travel and that is a problem, now is the time to straighten it out. If you're

not sure what type of travel the position entails, ask. You might ask how often travel will be required and if it is scheduled ahead of time.

◎ Do you get along well with others?
  ▫ The answer they are looking for is yes. Do not provide any stories about times when you didn't.

◎ Every now and then, you get a weird question or one that you just don't expect. If you could be a car, what type of car would you be and why? If you were an animal, what animal would you be? If you could have dinner with anyone alive or dead, who would it be? These questions generally are just meant to throw you off balance and see how you react.
  ▫ Stay calm and focused. Be creative but try not to come up with any answer that is too weird.
  ▫ An interviewer might ask what was the last book you read, what newspapers you read, what television shows are your favorites, or if you read the trades.
  ▫ Be honest, but try not to say things like, "I don't have time to read" or "I don't like reading." You want to appear well-rounded.

◎ What type of salary are you looking for?
  ▫ This is going to be discussed in detail below, but what you should know now is that this is an important matter. You don't want to get locked into a number before you know exactly what you will be responsible for. You might say something to the effect of, "I'm looking for a fair salary for the job. I really would like to know more about

the responsibilities before I come up with a range. What is the range, by the way?" You might turn the tables and say something like, "I was interested in knowing what the salary range was for this position." This poses the question back to the interviewer.

What You Might Want to Ask

Just because you're the one being interviewed doesn't mean you shouldn't ask questions. You want to appear confident. You want to portray yourself as someone who can fit in with others comfortably. You want to ask great questions. Depending on the specific job, here are some ideas.

◎ Was the last person who held this job promoted, or did he or she leave the company?

◎ Does the company promote from within as a rule or look outside?

◎ Is there a lot of longevity of employees here?

◎ How will I be evaluated? Are there periodic reviews?

◎ How do your measure success on the job? By that I mean, how can I do a great job for you?

◎ What are the options for advancement in this position?

★ Tip from the Top

If you have an extreme emergency and absolutely must be late for an interview, call and try to reschedule your appointment. Do not see if you can get there late and come up with an excuse when you get there.

- To whom will I report? What will my general responsibilities be?
- Feel free to ask any questions you want answered. Don't, however, ask questions like: "How many famous people will I meet?" "Do I get to go to the performances for free?" "Do I get free tickets to concerts?" "Can my family and friends get free tickets to the theater?"
- It's normal to be nervous during an interview. Relax as much as you can. If you go in prepared and answer the questions you're asked, you should do fine.

Salary and Compensation

As much as you want a job in the performing arts, you're not going to work for free. Compensation may be discussed generally at the interview or may be discussed in full. A lot has to do with the specific job. One way or another, salary will generally come up sometime during your interview. Unless your interviewer brings up salary at the beginning of an interview, you should not. If you feel an interview is close to ending and another interview has not been scheduled, feel free to bring it up when asked if you have any questions.

A simple question such as "What is the salary range for the job?" will usually start the ball rolling. Depending on the specific job, your in-

---

Tip from the Top

Try not to discuss salary at the beginning of the interview. Instead, wait until you hear all the particulars about the job and you have given them a chance to see how great you are.

---

terviewer may tell you exactly what the salary and benefits are or may just give you a range. In many cases, salary and compensation packages are only ironed out after the actual job offer is made.

Let's say you are offered a job and a compensation package. What do you do if you're not happy with the salary? What about the benefits? Can you negotiate? You certainly can try. Sometimes you can negotiate better terms for salary, better benefits, or both. A lot of it depends on how much they want you, how much of an asset you will be, and what they can afford.

When negotiating, speak in a calm, well-modulated voice. Do not make threats. State your case and see if you can meet in the middle. If you can't negotiate a higher salary, perhaps you can negotiate extra vacation days. Depending on the company and specific job, compensation may include salary, vacation days, sick days, health insurance, stock options, pension plans, or a variety of other things. When negotiating, look at the whole package.

Over the years I have seen many people who are so desperate to get the job of their dreams in the performing arts that when offered the job they will take it for almost anything. Often when asked about salary, they come up with salary requirements far below what the company would have offered. In your quest to get a job in the performing arts, don't undersell yourself.

The Inside Scoop

Accepting a job offer below your perceived salary "comfort level" often results in you resenting your company and coworkers and, even worse, whittles away at your self worth.

Things to Remember

To give yourself every advantage in acing the interview, there are a few things you should know. First of all, practice ahead of time. Ask friends or family members for their help in setting up practice interviews. You want to get comfortable answering questions without sounding as though you're reading from a script.

Here are some other things to remember to help you land an offer.

◎ If you don't have confidence in yourself, neither will anyone else. No matter how nervous you are, project a confident and positive attitude.

◎ The one who looks and sounds most qualified has the best chance of getting the job. Don't answer questions in monosyllables. Explain your answers using relevant experience. If you're asked if you have good organizational skills, for example, you might say something like, "Yes, I have great organizational skills. When I was an intern at the Grand Theater, I developed a system for organizing the names and information of people who had purchased single tickets over the last few years, all our season ticket holders, and individuals who had come to any of our special events. We then used the names and addresses to send out monthly newsletters that not only promoted our shows and special events, but had information for people who wanted to make donations. I have a letter in my portfolio from my supervisor indicating the increase in donations from doing that." Use your experiences in both your work and personal life to reinforce your skills, talents, and abilities when answering questions.

◎ Try to develop a rapport with your interviewer. If your interviewer "likes" you, he or she will often overlook less than perfect skills because you "seem" like a better candidate.

◎ Smile and make sure that you have good posture. It makes you look more successful.

◎ Be attentive. Listen to what the interviewer is saying. If he or she asks a question that you don't understand, politely ask for an explanation.

◎ Turn off your cell phone and beeper before you go into the interview.

◎ When you see the interview coming to a close, ask when a decision will be made and if you will be contacted either way.

◎ When the interview comes to a close, stand up, thank the interviewer, and then leave.

Here are some things you should not do:

◎ Don't smoke before you go into your interview.

◎ Don't chew gum during your interview.

◎ Don't be late.

◎ Don't talk negatively about past bosses, jobs, or companies.

◎ Don't use words like *ain't*, *heh*, *uh-huh*, *dunno*, and the like. It doesn't sound professional and suggests that you have poor communication skills.

◎ Don't interrupt the interviewer.

◎ While you certainly can ask questions, don't try to dominate the conversation to try to "look smart."

◎ Don't drop names. People in entertainment and the performing arts industry frown on this.

◎ Don't swear, curse, or use off-color language.

Thank-You Notes

It's always a good idea to send a note thanking the person who interviewed you for his or her time. Think a thank-you note is useless? Think again. Take a look at some of the things a thank-you note can do for you:

◎ show that you are courteous and have good manners

◎ show that you are professional

◎ give you one more shot at reminding the interviewer who you are

◎ show that you are truly interested in the job

◎ illustrate that you have good written communication skills

◎ give you a chance to briefly discuss something that you thought was important yet forgot to bring up during the interview

◎ help you stand out from other job applicants who didn't send a thank-you note

Try to send thank-you notes within 24 hours of your interview. You can handwrite or type them. While it's acceptable to e-mail or fax them, I suggest mailing.

What should the letter say? It can simply say thank you, or it can be longer. For example:

Dear Mr. Cooper:

Thanks for taking the time to interview me yesterday for the assistant marketing director position for the Emerald Touring Theater Company. As I indicated during our meeting, I am sure the experience I gained handling the marketing for CBC Bank will transfer over well, especially because I did the marketing for six theatrical events the bank cosponsored last year.

I feel that I would be a good match for the job and an asset for the Emerald Touring Theater Company. I look forward to hearing from you and hope that I am able to help with the push to make your touring company number one in the country!

Thanks once again.

Sincerely yours,
Christa Graver

Waiting for an Answer

You've gone through the interview. You've done everything you can do. Now what? Unfortunately, now you have to wait for an answer. Are you the chosen candidate? Hopefully, you are.

If you haven't heard back in a week or so (unless you were given a specific date when an applicant would be chosen), call and ask the status of the job. If you are told that they haven't made a decision, ask when a good time to call back would be.

If you are told that a decision has been made and it's not you, say thank you, tell them you appreciate the consideration and request that your resume be kept on file for the future. You might just get a call before you know it. If the company is large, you might ask if other positions are available and how you should go about applying if you are interested.

If your phone rings and you got the job, congratulations! Welcome to your great job in the performing arts. Once you get a call telling you that you are the candidate they want, depending on the situation, they will either make an offer on the phone or you will go back to the company to discuss your compensation package. If an offer is made on the phone, you have every right to ask if you can think about it and get back to them in 24 hours. If you are satisfied with the offer as it is, you can accept it.

Depending on the job, you may be required to sign an employment contract. Read the agreement thoroughly and make sure that you are comfortable signing it. If there is anything you don't understand, ask. Don't just sign without reading. You want to know what you are agreeing to.

Interviewing is a skill. The more you do it, the more comfortable you'll be going through the process. The more prepared you are ahead of time, the better you'll usually do. Good luck!

9

THE THEATRICAL AUDITION

The Audition Process

If you're pursuing a career in the business or administrative segment of theater or any of the other performing arts, you generally begin the process by going through an interview. In these cases, the interview is your chance to shine. If, on the other hand, you're pursuing a career in the talent area of the industry, even if you also have interviews, you will more than likely need to go through the auditioning process as well.

Auditions can either be an exciting, positive part of your life in the performing arts or a major stumbling block, depending on how you deal with them. While a lot of it has to do with your attitude, preparation can help tremendously. One thing is for sure: In order to succeed in the talent area of the performing arts, it's essential that you give yourself every opportunity to get an edge over others auditioning for the same role.

The audition is your one shot at showing the director and casting director why *you* would be better than anyone else to play the role that is being cast; why having you in the cast will benefit the production; and why *not* casting you would be a big mistake.

Auditions, like interviews, can help make you irresistible. Performing well at an audition can help persuade the casting director that you are the actor who will be the best at playing the character he or she is casting. So let's take some time to discuss some of the elements of the audition process.

First of all, you're going to need to prepare a monologue. A good monologue can mean the difference between an agent saying, "Thanks for coming in" when you leave and a callback. The idea is to wow the casting people with your monologue. With that in mind, it's essential to choose your monologue carefully.

What exactly is a monologue? In the broadest sense, for the purpose of auditions, a monologue is a scene or a part of a script in which an actor will speak without interruption. It is a speech that will hopefully showcase the actor providing insight into the particular character he or she is portraying. In essence, your monologue is like a short scene in a one-person show, and you are the star.

Why do you need a monologue? The main reason is because it helps the casting director evaluate your acting talents and abilities.

There are various types of monologues, ranging from parts of plays to parts in movies and everything in between. Some are contemporary while others are classical. Some may

Tip from the Top

If you are going to be auditioning for a part in a theatrical production, try to find a monologue from a play. Unless specifically requested, don't use a monologue from a play for which you are auditioning. If you do and the casting director doesn't have your vision of how the character is played, you might have lost the role before you get started.

be dramatic while others are humorous. When choosing your monologue, make sure it is geared toward the type of character for the role you are trying to land.

Most actors and actresses find it a good idea to have a couple of different monologues ready depending on the talents they are trying to showcase. As a matter of fact, in some situations, a casting director may expressly ask you to perform two totally different types of monologues so he or she can see how you perform in a variety of situations.

You might, for example, prepare one monologue for showcasing your comedic talents and another for showcasing roles that are dramatic.

How do you find that perfect monologue? Where can you look? There are books of monologues available at the library and in bookstores. You might also want to talk to your drama coach. If you already have a manager, he or she might give you some tips as well.

Once you choose your monologue, make sure you are comfortable with it. If you aren't, you will look and sound uncomfortable when you need to present it and it will not serve you well.

Memorize your monologues. Practice until they are perfect and then rehearse them some more. You might first practice in front of a mir-

ror. As you feel more comfortable, try them out on your family and friends, your drama coach, manager, and anyone else you can find.

Break down your monologue. What does the character in the monologue want? What does the character get? What is he or she like? The more you can feel the character, the better you can portray him or her.

When you are doing your monologue, visualize the person to whom you would be speaking. Try to picture the reactions he or she would have.

Get feedback and constructive criticism when you can and keep on working on your monologues. As you do, you will be honing your craft and giving yourself an edge over others.

How do you perform your monologue when you're at an audition? Try to keep movement to a minimum. Don't use props unless they are essential to the role.

When you are called to do your monologue, introduce yourself and the monologue you are going to do. For example: "Hello, I'm Anthony King. I'll be doing a scene from [the name of the play] by [playwright] and be playing the part of [the character]." Speak slowly and clearly. Give them a chance to write down information or ask you any questions they may have.

The Inside Scoop

When trying to memorize your monologue, it often helps to record it on a cassette, CD, or DVD so you can play it back until you remember it. After you have memorized your monologue, try to find a friend to videotape your performance. Watch it and critique it yourself. While this is difficult for many people to do, it can immensely help you improve your performance.

When you're ready, take a breath and go into character. Don't look directly at the casting director, directors, or any one of other auditors for that matter. Instead, try to look past them to an imaginary audience.

Remember to project your voice. You want to be heard, but don't screech. You may or may not be given a microphone or cordless mike. Adjust your voice accordingly.

Make sure your monologue fits into the permitted time limit. While this varies, it generally is between one and four minutes. Don't go over your time. If someone says "that's enough," or "thank you," stop speaking immediately. Don't say something like, "Can't I just finish?" or "I'm almost done."

Don't assume that just because the casting people are talking, it's bad news. It may not be. They may be discussing how well you would fit into the role.

If you forget a line or mix up a word, just keep going. Never apologize for what you feel is a bad audition. Never say anything negative about your audition or acting or be self-deprecating in any manner. Never ask, "Can I do it again?" or "How was I?"

When you're on stage, try to illustrate that you have a charismatic, magnetic stage presence. Most people can remember a monologue. Reciting it back without any enthusiasm or passion will *not* get you the role. What makes a good actor is the ability to bring a character to life—the ability to show passion and emotion. The personality you project when delivering your monologue can make all the difference in your audition.

Show that you're professional. When you're done, smile and thank the casting panel for their time. Don't move out of your space so quickly that if the casting director or any of the other auditors want to ask you questions or want you to perform something else, you're already out of the room. They may want you to perform your monologue in a different manner, do a reading, stick around for a bit, or may thank you for coming and tell you that you can leave. Keep alert so you know what to do.

Sometimes you won't need your monologue at all. Instead, you may be asked to read a scene from the play for which you are auditioning.

Broadway, Off Broadway, Off-Off Broadway, dinner theater, regional, repertory, and children's theater are all classified as "straight," "legitimate," or "legit" theater. When you are doing an audition for one of these types of productions, in many cases you may be able to get a copy of the script or at least the sides. (*Sides* are pages or scenes from the script which will be used in auditions.) This will give you the opportunity to prepare for the exact part for which you are auditioning. If you have an agent, he or she should generally be able to get you a copy of the script or the sides if they are available. If you don't have an agent, you might want to call the casting assistant to see if they're accessible.

Given the option of a prepared reading (one where you get the script ahead of time and can prepare) or a cold reading where your first look at the script is when you walk into the audition, your best bet will usually be the prepared reading.

Tip from the Coach

Get to auditions early. That way you'll have time to relax and compose yourself before your big moment.

If you get a copy of the entire script ahead of time, take some time to read it. Knowing the story and seeing the characters will help you prepare for the role for which you are auditioning. If all you get are the sides, read it over a few times and prepare. Don't just give it a once over and think you will do fine. Remember that a good audition can get you the role. Don't skimp on the preparation.

How do you deal with a cold reading? When you go into the audition and are given the script, don't waste time. Use every minute you have to read over the script or sides while you are sitting there. Mentally prepare the way you will deliver your lines. You might also excuse yourself for a few minutes, go into the rest room or hallway and read your lines out loud.

In many cases when you are doing a reading of the script for an audition you will be reading with someone else. This might be anyone else from another actor to the stage manager.

Try not to get too stressed when doing your reading. Directors and casting people know it is difficult. Many have auditioned for parts themselves over the years. No matter what anyone tells you, the directors and casting people are not your enemy. In reality, these people want you to succeed so they can choose a great cast for the production.

If you are doing a cold reading, no one expects you to memorize your lines. On the other hand, you don't want to keep your head down to the script while you are reading. Try to look down, grasp the line and then look at the other person you are doing the reading with so it looks like you are in an engaging conversation.

Musical Theater

If you are auditioning for a musical, you are also going to have to prepare a couple of songs

as well. When choosing your songs, pick those that showcase what you can do, not what you can't. It seems like simple advice, but I've been to auditions where people struggled with songs because they thought they would be better off with a more complicated tune that they just couldn't pull off, instead of an easier song that they could do perfectly.

What kind of songs should you choose for a professional theatrical audition? A good choice is to prepare one ballad and one up-tempo tune. If you are auditioning for a theatrical production, show tunes are a good choice. Just as you shouldn't use a monologue from the play you're auditioning for, it's not usually a good idea to sing a song from the show for which you're auditioning. The only exceptions would be if you are specifically asked to prepare one of the songs from the show.

It also isn't a good idea to choose a very popular show tune. Why? Because the casting director, musical director, and everyone else has probably heard the tune a thousand times...sometimes by the star who originally made it popular. In those cases, you're competing against the way it was done originally.

"But what if I put a different spin on it?" you ask. "What if I do a different arrangement? I know I sound better. They will be blown away with my performance. Can't I do it then?"

You can, but it is still a risk. It's risky having someone compare you to the original singer. And if you change the arrangement, they might not like your arrangement. You're not trying to be an arranger at this point. You're auditioning for a role. Focus in on what you are going after.

Ideally, you want to find songs that will showcase your talents while building a connection with the show or the role. Your audition songs should suit your voice and have some sort of extended notes that can highlight your vocal ability.

If you look at the cast breakdowns in audition notices, you can often get some ideas on choosing the best songs. The casting notice may, for example, describe the character as a young, slim, thirty-something, dark-haired female soprano or a tall, muscular male who can sing in the belt style.

Build up a repertoire of various songs in an array of styles. That way, you will always be ready. If you have a vocal coach, he or she can help you do this.

Bring sheet music in the correct key to the audition for the accompanist. Make sure it is clean and clearly marked. While you are going to prepare full songs for your auditions, you often don't get to sing your entire song.

If you don't get to finish your song, you generally end up singing about 16 bars. Clearly mark the 16 bars you will be singing for the piano player, so he or she knows where to start.

Remember to be nice to the accompanist. Don't say things like, "No, don't play it like that," "You're going too fast," or "Can you speed up the tempo?"

When you give your music to the piano player, you might say something like, "I'll be doing this in the key of C with an upbeat tempo. Thanks." Be professional. Remember, your audition starts when you walk in the door. Every thing you do and say might be scrutinized.

If, when you start your audition, the accompanist starts in the wrong key or too slow or fast a tempo, just keep going with the way you have rehearsed your song. Most accompanists are professionals and will follow your lead.

While most of the time there is an accompanist available when you audition for musical theater, there may be some situations where this

> ### ⭐ Tip from the Top
> Before you audition for a musical, you will generally need to know the cast breakdowns, so you know if you will qualify for the role. Cast breakdowns might include, for example, the musical range for the specific character.

is not the case. What do you do then? Bring a cassette or CD with your music.

When you finish your song, the casting people may just say thank you, may ask you to do another song, or might even ask you to do some scales just to hear your range. If you're lucky, they might even ask you to return for a callback.

Dance Auditions

If you are auditioning as a dancer for a production, you generally will be brought in to audition with a group of other dancers. A choreographer or choreographer's assistant will then perform a combination of moves or steps and the dancers will be instructed to repeat them in groups.

The choreographer will then pull out the dancers he or she likes, putting them into other groups and dismissing the others. Eventually, there will be just a small group of dancers left. Depending on the situation, you may be told on the spot that you have the job or may be asked to return for a callback.

One of the keys to success in these auditions is being able to learn the routines quickly and accurately. If you have been taking dance classes along the way, you probably won't have a problem.

The ability to show energetic enthusiasm helps set you apart. When you go for an audition as a dancer, be ready to dance. No matter how long the audition is, don't groan and complain that you are tired.

Unless instructed otherwise, dress in dance wear or rehearsal attire. Wear clothing that allows you to move easily. Generally, it is a bad idea to wear bulky clothing or sweats.

Women might choose to wear leotards, tights, footless tights, jazz pants, dance sweaters, or dance skirts. Men might wear tights, jazz pants, shorts, and neat T-shirts. Depending on the audition, dancers might need character shoes, jazz shoes, or ballet slippers. If you're not sure, ask ahead of time or bring along extra shoes in a tote bag.

Your Audition Wardrobe

Now that we've discussed what dancers should wear to their auditions, let's talk a bit about the audition wardrobe of actors.

First impressions are always important in every situation, and going to auditions is no exception. Choosing your audition wardrobe is an integral part of your audition preparation. What should you wear? The most important advice I have here is that you should wear something that is comfortable and makes you feel confident. It should be neat, clean, pressed, and flattering to your figure. You want your clothing to be loose enough so you can move, yet form-fitting enough so the casting panel can see your body type.

If you have an agent, check with him or her before the audition to see if there are any special attire requirements. You can also check to see if there are any requirements in the casting notice.

Prepare a few outfits that you will always have ready for auditions. Make sure everything is clean, pressed, and ready to go at a moment's

notice. Don't just include the major components of what you plan to wear. Include underwear, socks, panty hose, scarves, ties, shoes, and other accessories you choose. Having everything ready ahead of time means you don't have to stress out about what to wear when you have an audition. Instead you'll be able to spend your time preparing for the audition.

So what should you wear? Everyone has a different opinion. Try to put together specific outfits that are appropriate for various situations. You might include a business look, a casual look, and a sporty look, for example.

Women might want to wear either a dress or a blouse and skirt or pants and maybe a jacket or blazer. If you want to appear more casual, you can take off the jacket. Don't wear flashy jewelry, which will distract from your performance.

For men, a pair of pants and a shirt or turtleneck will work. Depending on the audition you might want to wear a sports jacket and tie. If you want to look more casual, you can take off the tie or jacket when you get to the audition.

Keep notes on what you wear to auditions. When you get a callback, you know what you wore to the original audition. Why is that important? When you go back, you want to look as much like you did at the original audition as possible. Yes, that means wearing the same thing.

There are always people at our seminars who question this. There is always someone

---

⭐ **Words from the Wise**

Unless you are instructed to do otherwise, don't dress in costume when going to an audition.

Voice of Experience

Have you ever gone to a party and dressed in casual attire and when you walked in the door everyone else was in dressy clothes? On occasion, that kind of situation happens when going to an audition. You dress in something you feel is appropriate and when you get there, you find you look totally out of place. What can you do? Be prepared. Bring a change of clothing with you just in case.

Oliver Thomas: Early 30s, dark hair and eyes; slim build, nerdy looking; accountant, LEAD. **Ms. Joan Brown:** Late 20s, early 30s, slender, attractive, blond; secretary. LEAD. **Mr. Evans:** late 50s, graying hair, tall, husky build, obnoxious boss with a comedic edge, supporting role. **Mrs. Thomas:** Late 50s, Oliver's pushy, overbearing mother, graying hair, well dressed; supporting role. Males and Females: 18+ to play various office workers.

Keep in mind that roles have different requirements. Some roles may require the ability to sing, dance, or both. As we've discussed throughout the book, the more versatile you are, the better your chances of success.

Every role is not a lead. There are supporting roles, and chorus members. No matter what role you get, remember that you are an integral part of the show.

who says, "But if I wear the same thing, they will think it's all I own. It's embarrassing."

Trust me, the audition panel is not thinking about your clothing. But they might have seen hundreds of actors and actresses. What they might remember is that you were the actor with the black pants and blue scarf.

When you return for a callback, you want them to remember you the way you looked when you were there the first time. So, if you wear a pair of black pants, white shirt, and blue scarf to the first audition, make sure you wear black pants, a white shirt, and blue scarf to your callback.

Character Breakdowns

How do you know what types of roles are being cast? How do you know what the requirements are? If you have an agent, he or she may get breakdowns from directors and casting people on shows they are casting. If you don't have any agent, you're going to have to look at the character breakdowns in the casting notices yourself.

Character breakdowns are synopses of characters in the script. What does that mean? In essence, character breakdowns are thumbnail descriptions of the cast of characters. For example:

Audition Locations

Where are auditions held? Depending on the specific audition they may be held at theaters, producers offices, or rehearsal studios. If you read about a casting call and it is in a location which you are unfamiliar with or you are not sure whether it on the level, check it out ahead of time. In your zeal to find auditions or land a role do *not* take chances. Make sure productions, producers and casting people are legitimate before putting yourself in an unsafe situation. Be wary if a producer or casting director you have never heard of, tells you the audition is in his or her apartment.

The Casting Panel

By now you might be wondering who will be at your audition. Who will be in charge of your fate? That depends to a great extent on the specific situation.

Some of the people who might be there include the director, director's assistant, casting director, casting assistants, producers, playwright, actors , and stage manager.

Be pleasant to everyone you meet at auditions, even your competition. Remember that your audition starts the minute you walk in the door. Having an attitude toward anyone at all can affect your chances of getting a role. People want to know that you will be pleasant to work around. A bad attitude in theater is no more accepted than a bad attitude in any other industry.

While you want to appear confident, you don't want to appear cocky. Trying to make yourself feel better by making someone else feel worse is not a good idea. Resist the temptation to do things like walking out of an audition and saying to a fellow actor who is going for the same role, "I was awesome. The director loved me. The casting director loved me. I already was asked to a callback."

Things To Bring to an Audition

What should you bring to your audition? Here's a list of some things you shouldn't be without:

◎ **Your head shots and resume.** Bring a few copies. You can never tell when you need an extra one.
◎ **A change of clothing.** In case you are wearing the totally wrong thing.
◎ **Extra pantyhose.** For women wearing a dress or skirt; in case you get a run in your stockings.
◎ **A brush or comb and/or makeup for touch-ups.** You want to look your best.
◎ **Water.** You can never tell how long you will be at an audition.

◎ **Pens.** In case you need to fill in applications.
◎ **Your appointment book.** That way when you are asked if you can come to a callback you can check to make sure you don't have a conflict. You can also write down the information immediately so there are no mix-ups about when you are supposed to be back.

More Audition Advice

In any situation, there are always things you can do which help give you the edge over others. Most of the time, they don't take too much extra effort, but they can make a difference. As auditioning is competitive in itself, you want to do everything possible to put yourself in the best possible situation.

Let's look at some things that can help you succeed at your audition.

◎ Be on time.
◎ Don't miss your appointment.
◎ Don't leave before your audition. This sounds simple, but there are people who don't wait around to be called. They sign in, it takes longer than they thought, and they leave. One thing I can pretty much guarantee you is that unless you are very well known and have a reputation which precedes you (and a number of Tonys), you won't get the role unless you audition.
◎ When you go into the audition location, smile. Make sure you look like you want to be there.
◎ Be pleasant to everyone. Aside from it being good manners, you can never tell who someone you meet might be.
◎ Be prepared. This will give you extra confidence.
◎ Be confident.

◎ Follow directions. If the production assistant asks you to fill in something, fill it in legibly and fully. They might need this information to contact you. If the director asks you to do a scene from a different perspective, do the scene from the perspective he or she requested.

◎ Be positive and have a positive attitude. People are drawn to positive people. Given the choice between a actor with a positive attitude and an actor who walks around with an attitude that the world is going to end, the director will generally choose the one with the positive attitude.

◎ Don't name-drop. It is frowned upon in the industry.

◎ Don't smoke before you go into your audition or at any time during your audition. This means that you should not go out while you are waiting and have a cigarette.

◎ Don't chew gum at any point during the audition process. This means don't even enter the building chewing gum.

◎ As nervous as you might be, don't go to an audition under the influence of alcohol or drugs. That means don't even have one drink before you audition.

◎ Don't talk negatively about anyone…in the industry or out.

◎ Don't say, "uh-huh" or "don't know" or other similar things. It doesn't sound professional or suggests that you have poor communication skills.

◎ Don't audition for a role that you *know* really isn't for you. If you are auditioning for a musical and you know you will have to sing and you are tone deaf, this is not the role for you. If the character breakdown is for a slender woman in her

20s and you are a shapely woman in your 40s, it probably isn't the role for you.

◎ Turn off your cell phone. Nothing is more distracting than your phone ringing during your audition. Nothing is ruder than having it ring during someone else's.

◎ Don't wear heavy perfume to an audition. Some people are either sensitive to odors or allergic to perfume. If it makes them sick, they will remember you as the one who gave them the migraine and you will not get the role.

◎ Don't forget your head shots and resume. It looks unprofessional.

◎ Don't lie about experience on your resume or when they are asking you questions. It is too easy to check out.

◎ After an audition, don't ask when they will make their decision.

◎ After an audition, don't ask when they will do callbacks.

◎ After your audition, don't try to pressure the casting director into telling you whether you got the role because you have to make a decision on another role. It will backfire on you.

◎ Try to relax. You will have a better audition.

How to Find Auditions

Now that you're prepared, let's take some time to discuss how to get auditions. Where do you hear about casting calls?

If you are represented by a talent agent, hopefully he or she will actively seek out auditions for you. He or she may receive notices or calls from casting directors, directors, and producers regarding their casting needs and then send you out on auditions for which you are qualified.

Keep in mind that even if you do have an agent, you should take a proactive role in your career. Remember that your agent has more than one client. Don't just hope he or she will call you. Initiate the calls. Ask about roles. Ask about productions you have heard will be casting.

The trades often list casting notices and auditions for roles as well. Some, such as *Backstage,* also have online versions, meaning that you can see the notices on a very timely basis. While you can read basic information and some news for free, you can also purchase a subscription, which gives you access to the entire site. If you are serious about your acting career, this is a good investment that I highly recommend.

You might also check out local newspapers and entertainment-oriented periodicals. Many either list or advertise auditions or discuss upcoming productions in the area. You might contact theaters directly to ask where they advertise openings for their productions.

The Internet is another good source of information. Check out theatrical and performing arts sites and search out articles about new productions that are being cast. Appendix II at the back of this book lists a number of Web sites to get you started.

If you make it a habit to consistently read the trades and visit Web sites that discuss the theater industry, you will also have a better chance of hearing about productions that are being cast. You can do some investigative work on your own or give the information to your agent.

There are also breakdown services, which for a fee provide detailed casting information about productions that are being cast. In many cases, however, these services are only available to legitimate talent representatives.

What if you don't have an agent? How do you let casting directors know you exist? The fastest way to make sure casting directors know about you is by simply sending them a cover letter along with your head shot and resume. Make sure your contact information is printed on all material you send out.

Will they look at it? The job of the casting director is to find the perfect cast for a production. If your head shot catches his or her eye and your resume shows you have what's needed, you'll get a call.

As you look through casting notices, be aware that certain roles require that you be a member of Actors Equity, a union. If you are a member of the union, you can find out about theater auditions at the local union office.

Networking also is helpful in finding out about auditions. Talk to fellow actors, drama coaches, vocal coaches, and people in your acting classes. They may know of roles that are being cast for which you may be perfect.

What about open casting calls? Open casting calls are casting calls where anyone who fits the requirements of the production can show up regardless of whether or not they have representation. The problem with these is hundreds of people can show up. If you are just starting your career and don't have representation, an open casting call may help you get your foot in the door. At the very least, it will give you some experience with the casting process.

Whether you go on an open casting call or your agent sends you to a casting call for an audition, here are some basic tips to help you succeed:

◎ Bring at least two copies of your head shot and resume.
◎ Be professional.
◎ Try to illustrate that you are flexible.

◎ Try to illustrate that you are a team player. The casting director's job is to bring together a team of actors who all work well together.

◎ Don't act like a prima donna.

◎ Be prepared for readings.

◎ If the casting director asks you to do something, listen and try to accommodate him or her. Show that you can follow direction.

◎ Don't cop an attitude at the casting call.

◎ Don't be annoying.

◎ Make a good first impression.

◎ Be confident, not cocky.

After an audition, if you do not get a call back or you do and you don't land the role, remember this: It is only one audition. It is only one role. While at the time, you may feel that your career is over, it is not.

Don't beat yourself up because you drop a line, forget a word, get confused, or don't perform as well as you wish you had. We are all our own worst critic. There will be other auditions and other roles. If you are persistent, you will eventually make it.

If you don't get the callback, look at the audition as a learning experience. Next time, you will feel more confident, more relaxed. The next audition you have may get you the role of your dreams.

Tip from the Top

If you have an extreme emergency and absolutely must be late to an audition, either call ahead yourself or have your agent call to see if you can reschedule. Do not see if you can get there late and come up with an excuse when you get there.

The Audition Process in a Nutshell

We've discussed a lot about auditions here, but let's discuss it a little more so you're more comfortable when you go on one. Here's a rundown of how it might go.

You are going to arrive early for your appointment with your 8-by-10 head shots and resume in hand. When you get to the audition, there usually will be a sign-in sheet. Information you're asked to provide on this sheet will vary depending on the type of audition. Casting calls for union actors, for example, may ask for different information than casting calls for nonunion actors.

If you will be performing your monologue, you will take a seat and wait to be called. If you are doing a cold reading, you will be given the sides or script and hopefully given a few minutes to read it over and prepare. Instead of chatting with other actors waiting for their auditions, you will be mentally preparing yourself and going over your audition material.

When you are called to do your monologue or reading, go up on stage or to the audition space and introduce yourself and your audition piece. One of the auditors (the people who will be auditioning you) might ask you some questions. Answer them honestly in a clear voice. Try not to chitchat too much because you're nervous. When the questions are done and you're ready, take a breath and start your monologue or reading.

The director may stop you and ask you to perform one of your other monologues or may ask you to read the script with a different interpretation. Listen to what he or she is asking you for and follow directions. The director and casting crew are trying to evaluate your work and see if you would be perfect for the role.

When you're done, you will thank them, smile, and get ready to leave. They may ask you some additional questions and may or may not tell you about callbacks. They may just thank you for coming and you will leave.

Leave your audition with a strong, confident and professional finish. You won't ask when you will hear something. Much as you want to know, you will not ask if you got the part.

You are going to have to play the waiting game. There are a few things that can happen. You (or your agent) may then either get a callback, get the role, or not get the role.

When you've done the best you can, just let it go. Not getting a role doesn't mean that you are a bad actor. It doesn't mean you aren't talented. All it means is that you were not right for *that particular role*. Don't beat yourself up. Don't go into a depression. Don't give up your dream.

Another role is right around the corner just waiting for you to audition for it. Have faith in yourself and your talent and you will get where you want to in your career.

10

Marketing Yourself for Success

What Marketing Can Do for You

What do hot trends, hit theatrical productions, blockbuster movies, top television shows, hot CDs, mega-superstars, and even hot new toys have in common? They all utilize marketing in some manner.

Do you want to know the inside information on becoming successful and getting what you want no matter what part of the industry in which you're interested? It's simple; all you have to do is market yourself.

Many people think that marketing techniques are reserved for businesses or products. Here's something to think about. From the moment you begin your career until you ultimately retire, you are a product. It doesn't matter what direction your career is going or what area you pursue.

Thousands of people want to be actors, dancers, musicians, singers, songwriters, playwrights, costume designers, set designers, comedians, composers, or directors. Some make it, and some don't. Is it all talent? A lot of it has to do with talent, but that is not everything. Thousands of talented individuals haven't made it, so what is the key to success? In addition to talent, luck, and being in the right place at the right time, another factor that seems to set one person apart from another is the way they are marketed or market themselves.

Whether you are seeking a career on the business or administrative end of the industry or in the talent or creative area, marketing can help you become one of the hottest commodities around.

"Can't my talent and creativity just get me the job? Why do I have to market myself?" you ask.

Here's the answer in a nutshell. If you aren't marketing yourself, the next person who *is* marketing himself will have an advantage over you. One of the keys to success is taking advantage of every opportunity. Marketing yourself is an opportunity you just can't afford to miss.

What is marketing? On the most basic level, marketing is finding markets and avenues to sell products or services. In this case, you are the product. The buyers are employers if you are looking for a traditional job, or fans, managers, talent and booking agents, casting directors, producers, and so on if you are a performing artist.

To be successful, you not only want to be the product; you want to be the brand. Look at Nabisco, Kellogg's, McDonalds, and Disney. Look at Donald Trump, a master marketer who

177

believes so strongly in this concept that he successfully branded himself. He continues to illustrate to people how he can fill *their needs*. Then he finds new needs he can fill. If you're savvy, you can do the same.

If you know or can determine what you can do for an employer or what can help them, you can market yourself to illustrate how you can fill those needs. If you can sell and market yourself effectively, you can succeed in your career; you can push yourself to the next level and you can get what you want.

Is there a secret to this? No, there really isn't a secret, but it does take some work. In the end, however, the payoff will be worth it.

Do you want to be the one who gets the job? Marketing can help. Want to make yourself visible so potential employers will see you as desirable? Marketing can help. Do you want to set yourself apart from other job candidates? Guess what? Marketing can help. It can also distinguish you from other employees. If you have marketed yourself effectively, when promotions, raises, or in-house openings are on the horizon, your name will come up. Marketing can give you credibility and open the door to new opportunities.

If you're pursuing a career on the talent or creative end of the industry, marketing is just as important if not more. Do you want to stand out from every other actor, singer, musician, songwriter, composer, comedian, playwright, costume designer, set designer, director or producer? You know what you have to do. Market yourself!

Do you want to become more visible? Get the attention of the media? Do you want to get the attention of talent and booking agents, casting directors, managers, labels, promoters, and other important people? Do you want to open up the door to new opportunities? Do you want to become a star? Market yourself!

"Okay," you're saying. "I get it. I need to market myself. But how?"

That's what we're going to talk about now. To begin with, understand that in order to market yourself or your act effectively, you are going to have to do what every good marketer does. You're going to have to develop your product, perform market research, and assess the product and the marketplace.

Is there any difference between marketing yourself for a career in the business or administrative areas of the performing arts or as a performing artist? Of course there are going to be some differences, but in general, you're going to use a lot of the same techniques. Read the following section and see which techniques and ideas will work best for you. As long as you are marketing yourself in a positive manner, you are on the right track. Now let's get busy.

The Five Ps of Marketing and How They Relate to Your Career

There are five Ps to marketing, whether you're marketing your career, a hot new restaurant, a new product, your acting, dancing, music, composing, scriptwriting or anything else. They are *product*, *price*, *positioning*, *promotion*, and *packaging*. Let's look at how these Ps relate to your career.

◎ *Product*: In this case, as I just mentioned, the product is *you*. "Me," you say. "How am I a product?" You are a package complete with your physical self, skills, ideas, and talents. If you're on the talent end of the industry, your product might also include your acting, your songs, your dances, and other parts of your creativity and talent.

◎ *Price*: Price is the compensation you receive for your work. As you are aware, there can be a huge range of possible earnings for any one job. On the talent end of the industry, there can be an even greater range. While one actor might be paid $250 for his or her role in a theatrical production, another may command thousands. One singer might be paid $100 to perform for an evening and another may receive thousands. One of your goals in marketing yourself is to sell your talents, skills, and anything else you have to offer for the best possible compensation.

◎ *Positioning*: What positioning means in this context is developing and creating innovative methods to fill the needs of one or more employers, agents, casting directors, producers, directors, record companies, fans, or other potential clients. It also means differentiating yourself and/or your talent from other competitors. Depending on your career area this might mean differentiating yourself from other employees, actors, singers, songwriters, dancers, musicians, composers, playwrights, costume designers, scenic designers, and so on.

◎ *Promotion*: Promotion is the promotion and implementation of methods that make you or your act visible in a positive manner.

◎ *Packaging*: Packaging is the way you present yourself.

Putting Together Your Package

Now that we know how the five Ps of marketing are related to your career, let's discuss a little more about putting together your package.

The more you know about your product (you), the easier it is to market and sell it. It's also essential to know as much as possible about the markets to which you are trying to sell. What

do you have to offer that a potential buyer (employer) needs? If you can illustrate to a market (employer) that you are the package that can fill their needs, you stand a good chance to turn the market into a buyer.

Assess what you have to offer as well as what you think an employer needs. We've already discussed self-assessment in Chapter 4. Now review your skills and your talents to help you determine how they can be used to fill the needs of your target markets.

While all the Ps of marketing are important, packaging is one of the easiest to change. It's something you have control over.

How important is packaging? Very! Good packaging can make a product more appealing and more enticing and make you want it. Not convinced? Think about the last time you went to the store. Did you reach for the name brand products more often than the bargain brand? Not convinced? How many times have you been in a bakery or at a party and chosen the beautifully decorated desserts over the simple un-iced cake? Packaging can make a difference—a big difference—in your career. If you package yourself, your talent, or your act effectively, people will want it.

Want to know a secret? Many job candidates in every industry are passed over before they get very far in the process because they simply don't understand how to package themselves.

Tip from the Coach

While you can't tell a book by its cover, it's human nature to at least look at the book with an interesting cover first. You might put it back after looking at it, but you at least gave it a first shot. That is why it is so important to package yourself as well as you possibly can.

What does this mean to you? It means that if you get the concept, you're ahead of the game. In the competitive world of theater and the performing arts, this one thing can give you the edge. Knowing that a marketing campaign utilizes packaging to help sell products means that you want to package yourself as well as you can. You want potential employers, casting directors, managers, record labels, managers, agents, producers, directors, and others to see you in the most positive manner possible. You want to illustrate that you have what it takes to fill their needs.

So what does your personal package include?

People base their first impression of you largely on your appearance. Whether you are going for an interview for a hot job or currently working and trying to move up the ladder of success, appearance is always important.

It might seem elementary, but let's go over the elements of your appearance. Personal grooming is essential. What does that mean?

◎ Your hair should be clean and neatly styled.
◎ You should be showered with no body odor.
◎ Your nails should be clean. If you polish them, make sure that your polish isn't chipped.
◎ If you are a man, you should be freshly shaved and mustaches and beards should be neatly styled.
◎ If you are a woman, your makeup should look natural and not overdone.
◎ Your breath should be clean and fresh.

Good grooming is important whether you're on the talent end of the industry or the business end. Of course, there might be situations in the talent or performance areas of the business where you are building a specific type of image and some of these points don't apply.

Tip from the Top
Make sure you have mints or breath strips with you when you go on auditions or to interviews. You don't want bad breath when speaking with an agent, casting director, or interviewer.

Now let's discuss your attire. Whether you're going on interviews, in a networking situation, or already on the job, it's important to dress appropriately. What's appropriate?

That depends to a great extent on what area of the industry you're involved and your specific job. If you're working in the business end of the industry, you want to look professional, but like other creative fields, certain segments of the performing arts may be more accepting of fashion trends than other industries. This means you might have more leeway in the dress code at a job at a talent or booking agency, public relations firm, or record label than, for example, a job at a bank, insurance company, or even a symphony, ballet, or opera company. Miniskirts might not be appropriate for working in a corporate attorney's office, but they might be acceptable at a talent agency. Similarly, jeans might not be appropriate for working at a symphony, but might be very appropriate working at a recording studio or for a set designer.

Always dress to impress. Employers want to see that you will not only fit in, but that you will not embarrass them when representing the company. What should you wear?

If you are going on an interview, dress professionally. If you're a man, you can never go wrong in a suit and tie or a pair of dress slacks with a jacket, dress shirt, and tie. Women might wear a suit, a professional-looking dress, a skirt and jacket, or a skirt and blouse. Once you're

Words from a Pro

Even if you are interviewing for an entry-level job, dress professionally. You want your interviewer to see that you are looking for a career, not just a job.

hired, learn the company dress policy. It's okay to ask. No matter what the policy is, observe what everyone else is wearing. If the policy is casual and everyone is still dressed in business attire, dress in business attire.

"But I'm going for a job in the creative end of the industry," you say. "Why would I get dressed up?"

The answer is simple: You want to make a good impression. You want to look like you care and you want to look like you're serious about your career. You want to look professional.

A common question people always ask at our seminars is, "How should I dress if I'm on the talent end of the performing arts What's the best way to dress then?"

If you're performing on stage in a play, dancing in production, singing in an opera, or playing in an orchestra, your clothing or costumes will most likely be chosen for you. If you are a performing artist in other genres of the industry, you'll have to put some time and thought into what you want your stage persona to be and then dress accordingly. There are, for example, comedians who come out on stage in suits, while others' stage attire is jeans and T-shirts. Whatever you decide to wear, it's important to remember that you should choose your stage attire to reflect the image you want to project.

If you're a performer, you might also want to think about your image when you're *not* on stage. Why is this important? While the world of the performing arts can be very large at times,

it can also be very small. If you project an unprofessional image offstage, it can possibly affect your career in a negative manner.

Communication Skills

Your communication skills, both verbal and written, are yet another part of your package. What you say and how you say it can mean the difference between success and failure in getting a job or succeeding at one you already have. You want to sound articulate, polished, strong, and confident.

Do you ever wonder how others hear you? Consider using a tape recorder, recording yourself speaking, and then playing it back.

Is this scary? It can be if you've never heard yourself. Remember that no matter what you think you sound like, it probably isn't that bad.

When you play back your voice, listen to your speech pattern. You might, for example, find that you are constantly saying "uh" or "uh-huh." You might find that your voice sounds nasal or high pitched or that you talk to quickly. If you're not happy with the way you sound, there are exercises you can do to practice changing your pitch, modulation, and speech pattern.

There are even exercises to change your accent, if you have one. Accents generally are acquired by being around others who speak in a certain way. Can a casting director tell you're from New York City, Boston, Alabama, South Carolina, or England just by talking to you?

The Inside Scoop

It's always easier to make yourself look more casual than it is to make yourself appear dressed more professionally. If you're in doubt about what to where, err on the side of professional.

If you're an actor or actress, you need to be aware of the type of accent you have. In some cases accents can be helpful. In other, they can be a hindrance. It all depends what the casting director wants.

If you feel you need to change your accent, look for a speech therapist or speech or vocal coach. These individuals can also be helpful in helping you to pick up dialect you might need for roles. For example, a breakdown of a character may illustrate that a casting director is looking for an actress who has a Scottish inflection. A good vocal coach can help you pick up the accent.

Because you can't take words back into your mouth after you say them, here are some *don'ts* to follow when speaking.

◎ Don't use off-color language.
◎ Don't swear or curse.
◎ Don't tell jokes or stories that have either sexual or racial undertones or innuendoes.
◎ Don't interrupt others when they are speaking.
◎ Don't use poor grammar or slang.

We've discussed your verbal communication skills; now let's discuss the importance of your written communication skills. Whatever your career choice, you need at least basic written communication skills. You need to be able to compose simple letters, memos, and reports. If you are uncomfortable with your writing skills, either pick up a book to help improve them or consider taking a basic writing class at a local school or college.

Your body language can also tell people a lot about you. The way you carry yourself can show others how you feel about yourself. We've all seen people in passing who are hunched over or look uninterested or just look like they don't care. Would you want one of them working for you? Neither do most employers.

What does your body language illustrate? Does it show that you are confident? That you are happy to be where you are? Do you make eye contact when you're speaking to someone? Are you smiling? What about your demeanor? Common courtesy is mandatory in your life and your career. Polite expressions such as "please," "thank you," "excuse me," and "pardon me" will not go unnoticed.

Your personality traits are another part of your package. No one wants to be around a whiner, a sad sack, or people who complain constantly. You want to illustrate that you are calm, happy, well-balanced, and have a positive attitude. You want to show that you can deal effectively with others, are a team player, and can deal with problems and stress effectively.

You might be surprised to know that in many cases employers will lean toward hiring someone with a bubbly, positive, and energetic personality over one with better skills who seems negative and less well balanced. And that's not only on the business end of the industry, it's on the talent end as well.

Last but not least in your package are your skills and talents. These are the things that make you special. What's the difference between skills and talents?

Skills can be learned or acquired. Talents are things that you are born with and can be embellished. Your personal package includes both.

What you must do is package the product so the buyer wants it. In this case, the product is you and the buyer is a potential employer, casting director, manager, agent, fans, and so on.

Now you know what goes into your package, and you're going to work on putting together your best possible package. What's next?

Marketing Yourself like a Pro and Making Yourself Visible

How can you market yourself? If you're like many people, you might be embarrassed to promote yourself, embarrassed to talk about your accomplishments, and embarrassed to bring them to the attention of others. This feeling probably comes from childhood when you were taught it wasn't nice to brag.

It's time to change your thinking. It's time to toot your own horn! If you do this correctly, you won't be bragging; you will simply be taking a step to make yourself visible. Want to know the payoff? You can move your career in a positive direction quicker. Career success can be yours, but you need to work at it.

Visibility is important in every aspect of business, and the performing arts are no exception. Whether you want to make it on the talent end of the industry or the business side, visibility can help you attain your goals. What can visibility do for you?

To start with, it can help set you apart from others who might have similar skills and talents.

Tip from the Coach

Be positive about yourself and don't be self-deprecating, even in a joking manner. Many people start doing this because they want the person with whom they are speaking to say, "No you're not." The truth is, when you're self-deprecating you will start believing it and so will the people with whom you are speaking.

How can you make yourself visible?

◎ Tell people what you are doing.
◎ Tell people what you are *trying* to do.
◎ Share your dreams.
◎ Send out press releases.
◎ Send out postcards or flyers to industry insiders and the media to tell them what you're doing.
◎ Toot your own horn.
◎ Make it happen.

When you make yourself visible, you will gain visibility in the workplace, the community, the media, and more. This is essential to getting what you want and what you deserve in your career, whether it's the brand-new job you want in the music business, a promotion pushing you up the career ladder, or your shot at success as a performer.

We'll discuss how you can tell people what you're doing without bragging later, but first, let's discuss when it's appropriate to toot your own horn. Here are some situations:

◎ When you land a new role
◎ When you get a new job
◎ When you get a promotion
◎ When you get a good review
◎ When you sign a record deal
◎ When you sign a contract with a performing arts company
◎ When you are honored
◎ When you go on tour
◎ When you sign an agreement with a booking or management agency
◎ When you have a special appearance scheduled
◎ When you're doing a showcase
◎ When you are going to be (or have already appeared) on television or radio
◎ When you sign a publishing agreement
◎ When someone produces your play

- ◎ When someone records your song
- ◎ When you have a major accomplishment
- ◎ When you receive an honor or an award
- ◎ When you chair an event
- ◎ When you graduate from school, college, or a training program
- ◎ When you obtain professional certification
- ◎ When you work with a not-for-profit organization on a project

And the list goes on. The idea isn't only to make people aware of your accomplishments, but to make yourself visible in a positive manner. These are the reasons you would toot your own horn, but how do you do it? Well, you could shout your news from a rooftop or walk around with a sign, but that probably wouldn't be very effective.

One of the best ways to get the most bang for your buck is by utilizing the media.

"I don't have money for an ad," you say.

Well, here's the good news. You don't have to take out an ad. You can use publicity. Newspapers, magazines, and periodicals need stories to fill their pages. Similarly, television and radio need to fill airspace as well. If you do it right, your story can be among the ones filling that space and it will cost you next to nothing.

How do you get your news to the media? The easiest way is by sending out press or news releases.

Tip from the Top

A press release is not an ad. Ads cost money. There is no charge to send press releases to the media. Press releases are used by the media to develop stories or can be edited slightly or published as is.

Words from a Pro

Many of the stories you read in newspapers and magazines or hear on the radio or television are the direct result of press releases. Don't make the mistake of not sending out press releases because you think the media won't be interested.

There are also many books, classes, seminars, and workshops which can help you learn how to write press or news releases effectively.

To get you started, you should know that news releases are composed of answering the five Ws:

- ◎ Who
  - ▫ Who are you writing about?
- ◎ What
  - ▫ What is happening or has happened?
- ◎ When
  - ▫ When did it happen or is it happening?
- ◎ Where
  - ▫ Where is it happening or has it happened?
- ◎ Why
  - ▫ Why is it happening or why is it noteworthy or relevant?

While it would be nice for everyone to have their own personal press agent or publicist, this is not generally the case. Until you have one, you are going to have to be your own publicist. To market yourself, you'll have to find opportunities to issue press releases, develop them, and send them out. You want your name to be visible in a positive manner as often as possible.

Let's look at an example of how visibility might help your career. A woman who first came to a seminar and then became a client shared her story with me. I've changed the names because of confidentiality issues.

Debra was an actress who had just graduated with a bachelor's degree in theater arts. While in school, she had starred in a number of college productions as well as in stock productions during the summers. She also had landed a couple of national television commercials.

Debra had been reading the trades, networking, and landing small parts on her own, but she wanted more. She wanted to elevate her career as an actress. Her short-term goal was finding an agent to represent her, yet she was finding it difficult to get anyone to return her calls.

Debra was reading the newspaper one day when she saw an article about some teens who were discussing their dreams. She noticed that a number of the young people were interested in ultimately working in the entertainment industry and performing arts. Some wanted to work in the music industry while others wanted to be actors or actresses.

Debra had an idea. While she was waiting for her own dreams to come true, why not see if she could put together a program to help others realize their dreams? She called the local community center and set up a meeting. She explained that she would like to give a workshop to the youngsters to help them prepare for the career of their dreams.

During the workshop, Debra saw how excited the teens were. They were hungry to perform, yet other than a once a year school play or talent show there were no opportunities. Debra had another idea. She talked to the community center director to see if she could produce a musical production where the kids would all have a chance to perform.

Debra began sending out press releases on a variety of subjects ranging from inviting teens to become involved in the project to looking for other adults to help put the production together to garnering community support. Throughout the project she continued sending out press releases on a regular basis. In each press release Debra always had stock paragraphs that mentioned her career and her involvement in the project. For example:

> The Acting Teens project was initiated by Debra James. James recently graduated from State College with a major in theater arts. While waiting for her own big break, James saw a need in the community and stepped up to the plate. "I remembered how much I wanted to perform when I was younger," said James "and there were limited opportunities. The Acting Teens project offers young people the chance to not only perform but to see if the performing arts is the direction they want their career to take."
>
> James has appeared in numerous stock productions including *Dial M For Murder, West Side Story, Seven Brides For Seven Brothers,* and *South Pacific,* and she held the lead role in *Grease.* She has also been in a number of national commercials.

I can almost hear you asking, "How can doing any of this help her career as an actress, let alone mine?" Here's the answer. When you become visible, other people who might be helpful in your career sometimes surface. In this case, the program Debra started snowballed. The media picked up on it and did a number of feature stores. Coincidentally, a talent agent had a vacation home in the area and saw one of the stories. She contacted Debra and asked if she could come to a rehearsal during the week, give the young people a pep talk and tell them a little about the business end of the industry.

Of course Debra agreed. The teens were thrilled. After rehearsal, Debra asked the talent agent if she wanted to join her for coffee. The two spoke and James explained that she had started this volunteer project while looking for an agent as well as telling her a little about her acting career. She was hoping that the agent would say, "Well I would be glad to sign you," but she didn't. Instead the agent said she enjoyed the opportunity to help and she hoped the show went well. She told Debra she would love to come to the production, but she planned to be on the West Coast during that time.

Debra was disappointed but, caught up in the production, she didn't dwell on what had or hadn't happened.

A few weeks later, the musical production opened and received rave reviews for the three-day weekend run. On Monday morning Debra received a phone call. It was from the director of a performing arts organization who saw the show, heard the story, and wanted to talk to Debra about a possible paying job doing what she had just done on a volunteer basis. She was tempted because she needed the money, yet taking the job in Debra's mind meant giving up her dream of being an actress. On the other hand, she really had fun with the project. She set up an appointment with the organization executive director for later that week to discuss it.

Wednesday evening the phone rang again. This time it was the talent agent. She told Debra she had been at the performance on opening night and then had to catch a plane to the West Coast. She congratulated Debra and told her how much she enjoyed the show.

During the conversation she told Debra how impressed she was with her not only with the production, but as an actress. Evidently, the agent had checked out some of the reviews from Debra's prior performances and spoken to a few of the directors and was interested in signing her.

"Well, that's a nice story," I can hear you saying. "But in the real world does that kind of thing happen?"

You might not hear about it all the time, but those situations do happen. The key here is that in order for them to unfold, you have to be visible.

Make sure your press releases look professional by printing them on press or news release stationery. This can easily be created on your computer. Include the words "News" or "News From" or something to that effect someplace on the release so the media is aware it is a press release. Also make sure to include your contact information. This is essential in case the media wants to call to ask questions about your release. In many instances, the media just uses the press release as a beginning for an article. Once you pique their interest, they use the press release as background and write their own story.

★ Voice of Experience

It's difficult to proofread your own press releases to catch errors. Always have someone else read them not only for errors but to make sure they make sense.

You've developed a press release. Now what? Whether it's about getting a promotion, being named employee of the month, signing a contract, or anything else, developing a great press release is just the first step. Once that's done, you have to get the releases to the media.

How do you do this? You're going to have to send, fax, or e-mail them to the media. First you need to put together a list so you can reach the correct people. Look around your area. Get the names of your local media. Then find regional media. If your stories warrant it, national or trade media should also be included. Don't forget any Web or online publications.

Call up each and ask to whom press releases should be directed. Sometimes it will be a specific person. Sometimes it may just be "News Editor" or "Entertainment Editor." Then get their contact information. Put together a database consisting of the name of the publication or station, contact name or names, address, phone, and fax numbers, e-mail, and any other pertinent information. Try to find out the publication's deadline. The deadline is the day you need to get the information to the publication so that your news can be considered for the next issue.

Becoming an Expert

Want another idea to make yourself visible? Become an expert. You probably already are an expert in one or more areas either in or out of the performing arts. Now it's time for you to exploit it.

Many people are used to the things they know well. They don't give enough credence to being great at them. It's time to forget that type of thinking!

Everyone knows how to do something better than others. One of the wonderful things about being an expert in any given area is that people will seek you out.

"Okay," you say. "Let's say I'm a gourmet chef. But what does that have to do with the performing arts?"

It might have nothing to do with the performing arts on the surface. However, if it can help you gain some positive attention and visibility, it will give you another avenue to get your story out. This will help you achieve the career success you desire. So with that in mind, it has everything to do with it.

Let's begin by determining where your expertise is. Sit down with a piece of paper and spend some time thinking about what you can do better than anyone else in or out of the music business. What subject or area do you know more about than most?

Need some help? Can't think of what your expertise is? Here are some ideas to get you started:

◎ Are you a gourmet cook?
◎ Do you bake the best brownies?
◎ Are you a trivia expert?

⭐ Words from the Wise

Just because you send a press release doesn't mean it will get into the publication. Small local publications are likely to eventually use your press releases. Larger publications are more discriminatory. Do not call up media and insist that they use your release. This will make you look like an amateur and they will probably ignore your releases from that day forward. While you don't want to write a press release about nothing, anytime you have anything noteworthy to send out a press release about, you should.

◎ Are you a master gardener?

◎ Do you design jewelry?

◎ Can you speak more than one language fluently?

◎ Do you love to shop?

◎ Do you know how to coordinate just the right outfit?

◎ Do you know how to write great songs?

◎ Can you write a play?

◎ Do you know how to write great press releases?

◎ Do you know how to pack a suitcase better than most people?

◎ Are you an expert organizer?

◎ Do you know how to arrange flowers?

◎ Are you a great fund-raiser?

◎ Have you set a world record doing something?

◎ Do you volunteer teaching people to read?

◎ Do you have special skills or talents that others don't?

Are you getting the idea? You can be an expert in almost any area. The way in which you exploit it can make a difference in your career.

You want to get your name out there. You want to draw positive attention to yourself. You want others to know what you can do. That way, you can market yourself in the areas in which you are interested.

Find ways to get your name and your story out there. How? Developing and sending out press releases is one way, but what else can you do?

You can become known for your expertise by talking about it. Most areas have civic or other not-for-profit groups that hold meetings. These groups often look for people to speak at their meetings. Contact the president of the board or the executive director to find out who schedules the meeting speakers. In some areas, the chamber of commerce also puts together speaker lists.

You might be asking yourself, "Unless I'm a rocket scientist, why would any group want to hear me speak about anything? What would anyone want to know about me knowing how to pack a suitcase?" or "Why would anyone be interested in my organizing ability?"

Here's the answer: They might not, *unless* you tailor your presentations to their needs. If you create a presentation from which others can learn something useful or interesting, they usually will. For example, if you're speaking to a group of businesspeople, you might do a presentation about "The Stress-Free Bag: Packing Easily For Business Trips," "Organize Your Career, Organize Your Life," "Helping Children in Need," or "Using Acting Techniques to Help You Succeed in Business." Depending on your audience, you might do presentations on "Making Money In Music," "Beginning Your Acting Career," "Getting Into the Performing Arts," or "Understanding Opera." Whatever your subject matter is when you speak in front of a group, whether it be 20 or 2,000 people, you will gain visibility. When you are introduced, the host of the event will often mention information about your background to the audience. Make sure you always bring a couple of paragraphs with you to make it easy for the emcee to present the information you want to convey.

For example, the emcee might introduce you like this: "Good afternoon, folks. Our luncheon speaker today is John Robertson. John is a professional actor and has appeared in numerous theatrical productions on and off Broadway. Some of you might recognize John from his appearances in the Fuller Garden Products commercials. Others of you might have been lucky enough to see him perform in *Grease, The Odd Couple,* or in the role of Scrooge last winter in a *Christmas Carol* or in his current role as Josh in the musical *Sorry* at the Solutions Theater. Today he will be sharing some tips for using acting techniques to improve your sales presentations. Let's have a warm welcome for John Robertson."

As you can see, John is getting exposure, which is not only an asset to his career, but may help ticket sales as well.

On a local level, you will do most of these types of presentations for no fee. The benefit of increased visibility, however, will be well worth it. When you are scheduled to do a presentation, make sure you send out press releases announcing your speech. If it was a noteworthy event, you might also send out a release after the event as well. Many organizations will also call the media to promote the occasion. Sometimes the media will call you for an interview before the event. Take advantage of every opportunity.

It's exciting once you start getting publicity. Keep clippings of all the stories from the print media. Make copies. If you have appeared or have been interviewed on television or radio, get clips. Keep these for your portfolio. Every amount of positive exposure will help set you apart from others and help you market yourself to career success.

★ Words from a Pro

The media works on very tight deadlines. If they call you, get back to them immediately or you might lose out.

More Strategies to Market and Promote Yourself

If you aren't comfortable speaking in public, how about writing an article on your area of expertise instead? You might also consider writing articles or columns for newspapers or magazines on any subject. The idea once again is to keep your name in the public's eye in a positive manner.

How do you get your articles in print? Call the editor of the publication you are interested in writing for and ask! Tell them what you want to do and offer to send your background sheet, resume, or bio and a sample. Small or local publications might not pay very much. Don't get hung up on money. You are not doing this for cash. You are doing it to get your name and your story before the public.

If you are a good writer, enjoy writing, and are already working in a performing arts company and want to move up the career ladder, think about offering to put together a periodical column for your company's newsletter. They don't have one? Offer to put one together. Why? It will bring you visibility. You will have opportunities to meet and converse with higher-ups who you might not otherwise have met.

Don't forget to tell media editors about your expertise. Call or send them a short note asking that they put you on a list of experts for your specific area of expertise. When they're working on a story that relates to your subject, they may call upon you as a resource.

What can your expertise do for you? It will get your name out there. It will give you credibility and it will give you visibility. When you're at meetings or speaking to the media, be sure to network. Tell people what you do. Tell people what you want to do. Give out cards. This technique works effectively whether you're trying to succeed in the business or talent segment of the industry.

Join professional associations and volunteer to be on committees or to chair events that they sponsor. Similarly, join civic groups and not-for-profit organizations volunteering to work on their projects.

"I don't have time," you say.

Make time. Volunteering, especially when you chair a committee or work on a project, is one of the best ways to get your name out there, obtain visibility, and network.

The radio and television talk show circuit is yet another means to generate important visibility. Offer to be a guest on radio, cable and television station news, variety, and information shows.

"Who would want me?" you ask.

You can never tell. If you don't ask, no one will even know you exist in many instances. Check out the programming to see where you might fit. Then send your bio with a letter to the producer indicating that you're available to speak in a specific subject area. Pitch an idea. A producer just might take you up on it.

Here's a sample pitch letter to get you started:

David Thomas, Producer
WGEE Radio
Talk Today Show
PO Box 2222
Anytown, NY 33333

Dear Mr. Thomas:

It has been said that most people dread speaking in public more than dying. As a professional comedian, I understand that thought. Yet, I have been working onstage making people laugh for over five years now. While it's my job to make people laugh, as I travel throughout the country, I have found that people do the same for me. People are funny.

I will be in Anytown on October 20 through October 30 performing at the Great Anytown Hotel and Casino. I would love to share some of my road stories with your audience and am sure your listeners would enjoy the show.

I have heard your program on prior visits to the area and believe the subject matter fits in with your show's format.

I have included a press kit and my background sheet for your review. Please let me know if you require additional information.

I look forward to hearing from you.

Sincerely,
Gina Hastings

Wait a week after sending the letter. If you don't hear back, call the producer. If there is no interest, say thank you, and request that your background sheet be kept on file.

Remember that people talk to each other, so that every person you speak in front of, who reads an article about you, who hears you on radio, or sees you on television has the potential of speaking to other people who might then speak to others.

As we've discussed, networking is one of the best ways to get a job, get a promotion, and advance your career. If you're on the talent end of the industry, the same concept applies. Even if your expertise is something totally not involved in the performing arts, you can use your expertise to boost your career.

If your expertise happens to be something related to theater or the performing arts, that's even better. What might that be? You might be an expert in getting publicity. You might have expertise in successfully going through the audition process. You might be an expert in various dialects. Whatever your expertise, exploit it and it wiil help your career move forward.

More Marketing Techniques to Get You Noticed

Many charities and not-for-profit groups sponsor charity auctions. If you're a performer and looking for a way to get noticed, here's an idea: Donate your services.

"What's in it for me?" you ask.

Aside from doing some good for a worthwhile organization, you probably can get a ton of exposure. There are a couple ways to do it. You can offer to perform gratis at the event or you can donate your services for the auction.

Depending on what your talent is, you could, for example, donate a one- or two-hour concert to the winning bidder. If you're a comedian, you might donate a forty-five minute or hour set or might offer to emcee the event. Most people bidding at these types of auctions are connected to the community and its businesses in some manner. You will be building goodwill. You will be opening up new markets for your act and have opportunities to network.

Here's another idea that can get you noticed: A feature story in a newspaper or magazine. How do you get one of these? You have to develop an angle to catch the attention of the media and contact a few editors to see if you can get one of them to bite. Before you call anyone, however, think out your strategy. What is your angle? Why are you the person someone should talk to or do a story on? Why would the story be interesting or unique or entertaining to the reader?

How do you develop an angle? Come up with something unique that you do or are plan-

ning to do. What is the unique part of your package? Were you the runner-up in a talent competition? Everyone wants to talk to the winner. How about giving the story from the one who didn't win?

Send a letter with your idea, a background sheet or bio, and press kit if you have one. Wait a week and then call the editor you sent your information to. Ask if he or she received your information. (There is always a chance it is lost, if only on the reporter's desk.) If the answer is no, offer to send it again. Sometimes you get lucky. Your angle might be just what an editor was looking for or what they might need to fill in a space with an interesting story.

Opening the Door to New Opportunities

If you keep on doing the same old thing, things might change on their own, but they probably won't. It's important when trying to create a more successful career to find ways to open up the door to new opportunities.

Start to look at events that occur as new opportunities to make other things happen. If you train yourself to think of how you can use opportunities to help you instead of hinder you, things often start looking up.

Do you want to be around negative people who think nothing is going right or people who think they are losers? Probably not. Well neither does anyone else. Market yourself as a winner, even if you are still a winner in training. The old adage "misery loves company" is true. One problem people often have in their career and life is that they hang around other people who are depressed or think that they're not doing well. Remember that negative energy attracts negative results, so here's your choice: You can either stay with the negative energy, help change the

---

⭐ **Tip from the Top**

Many people lose out because they just don't follow up. They either feel like a nuisance or feel that they are being a pain. No matter how awkward and uncomfortable you feel, follow up on things you are working on. Be polite, but call to see what's happening.

negative energy, or move yourself near positive energy. Which choice do you want to make?

Work on developing new relationships with positive people. Cultivate new business relationships. When doing that, don't forget cultivating a business relationship with the media. How? Go to events where the media is present. Go to chamber of commerce meetings, not-for-profit organization events, charity functions, entertainment events, meetings, union events, and other occasions.

Walk up, extend your hand, and introduce yourself. Give out your business cards. Engage in conversation. If a reporter writes an interesting story, drop him or her a note saying you enjoyed it. If a newscaster does something special, drop a note telling him or her. The media is just like the rest of us. They appreciate validation.

Don't just be a user. One of the best ways to develop a relationship with the media or anybody else is to be a resource. Help them when you can.

Want to close the door to opportunity? Whine, complain, and be a generally negative person who no one wants to be near. Want the doors to opportunity to fly open? Whatever level you are at, more doors will open if you're pleasant, enthusiastic, and professional.

Dreams can come true. They can either happen to you or happen to someone else. If you want it bad enough and market yourself effectively, you will be the winner.

It's essential in marketing yourself and your career to move away from your comfort zone even if it's just a little way. Find new places to go, new people to meet, and new things to do. You are the number-one factor in creating your success. Don't let yourself down!

11

SUCCEEDING IN THE WORKPLACE

Learning As You Go

No matter how it looks, there are very few overnight successes. Appearances can be very deceiving. While it may seem that actors, singers, or other performing artists suddenly just appear on the scene and within a short time are stars, it generally doesn't happen like that.

While there are exceptions, more than likely, the performing artists you *think* are overnight successes have been working at it and preparing for their dream career. Many of them were probably in the same position you are now.

What looks like an overnight success generally was a well thought-out plan, a lot of work, some talent, a bit of luck, and of course being in the right place at the right time. And if you think that it's only in the talent area, you're wrong. Achieving success in the business, administration, and creative areas of the performing arts requires similar plans.

Unfortunately, just getting your foot in the door is not enough. Whatever area of the performing arts in which you are seeking a career, once you get in, it's essential to take positive actions to climb the ladder to success. Theater and all the performing arts as other entertainment based industries, have keen competition in both

the talent and business areas. If you don't take those actions, someone else will.

So let's begin by discussing some of those positive actions you might take in the business and performance ends of the industry. Now that you've got the job, what can you do to increase your chances of success and turn your job into the career of your dreams? Lots of people have jobs, but you don't just want a job. You want a great career! In order to move up the career ladder, you have to do more than is expected of you and put some extra effort into getting what you want.

Once you get your foot in the door, do what you can to get to the top. You want to create your perfect career. Getting a job is a job in itself. However, just because you've been hired, doesn't mean your work is done. It's essential once you get in to learn as you go. If you look at some of the most successful people, in all aspects of life and business, you'll see that they

Tip from the Coach

While success does sometimes just fly in the window, it always helps to at least open the window.

continue the learning process throughout their life. If you want to succeed you'll do the same.

Learning is a necessary skill for personal and career growth and advancement. Many people feel that your ability to learn is linked to your success in life. This doesn't necessarily mean going back to school or taking traditional classes, although sometimes that's a good idea. In many cases, it means life learning.

What's life learning? Basically, it's learning that occurs through life experiences. It's learning that occurs when you talk to people, watch others do things, work, experience things, go places, watch television, listen to the radio, hear others talking, or almost anything else. Every experience you have is a potential learning experience. And almost everyone you talk to can be a teacher. If you're open to it, you can usually learn something from almost everyone you come in contact with.

Look for opportunities. Be interested. Everything you learn might not be fascinating, but it might be helpful; maybe not today or tomorrow, but in the future. Sometimes you might learn something work related, sometimes not. It doesn't matter. Use what you can. File the rest away until needed.

Challenge yourself to learn something new every day. Not only will it help improve your total package, but it will make you feel better about yourself. Whether it's a new word, new skill, new way to do something, or even a new way to deal better with people, continue to learn as you go.

How else can you continue to learn? Take advantage of internships, formal and informal education, company training programs, and volunteer opportunities. Many companies in and out of the performing arts have formal volunteer programs. If yours does, take advantage of it. If yours doesn't, you might want to get your company involved in one.

The payoff for volunteering can be priceless for many reasons, one of which is knowledge.

What can you learn volunteering? The possibilities are endless. You might learn a new skill or a better way to get along with others. You might learn how to coordinate events, run organizations, or publicize programs. You might learn new acting techniques, new dance routines, or how to direct a production. You might learn almost anything…if you're out there. And as a bonus, if you volunteer effectively, you might obtain some important visibility.

Don't discount books as a learning tool. There are tons of books on various aspects of theater and the performing arts. The more you read, the more you'll know. Books often hold the answers to many of your questions. They give you the opportunity to explore opportunities.

Trade journals offer numerous possibilities as well. They'll keep you up to date on industry trends and let you know about industry problems and solutions. What else can you find in the trades? Advertisements for job openings, casting calls, notices for trade events, and current news. There are a number of trade publications geared toward the theater industry. *Backstage*, for example contains the latest casting news. *Playbill*

⭐ Tip from the Coach

Don't assume that because someone is under you on the career ladder they know less than you or you are above them. Career progression in the performing arts does not always follow traditional paths. The receptionist at your talent agency today may be a talent agent next month or even the newest Broadway star. You just never know.

Tip from the Top

Check out your company's policy on private e-mail. Be aware that in many situations, you may not be allowed to send private e-mail.

On-Line often lists job openings. *Billboard,* the best-known trade in the music industry, often is full of ads for jobs on both the business and talent ends of the industry. *Dance Magazine* offers opportunities in dance.

If you're not prepared to buy a subscription yet, you can often locate the trade in which you're interested in your local library, the newsstand, or bookstores. If you are already working in the industry, these trades may also be available in your workplace. Be sure to check out the online versions of trade publications. While many require subscriptions to access some areas, they still often carry the latest news and job openings in the free section.

How about workshops, seminars, and other courses? In addition to learning new skills in or out of the performing arts industry, there are a number of added benefits including expanding your network. Classes, seminars, and workshops also help stimulate your creativity.

"But," you say, "I'm already working as a costume designer [or a playwright, or any other creative job]. I'm busy enough without doing extra work. Is this really necessary? Do I have to take classes?"

No one is going to make you do anything, but you should be aware that they can help take your career to a new level. Even successful playwrights, composers, songwriters, scenic designers, costume designers, and others in the creative end of the industry often take classes, workshops, and seminars to help give them new ideas or look at things from a different perspective.

Many successful actors, musicians, and singers continue taking classes, workshops, and seminars and so should you. Whether you're taking a workshop in acting, a class in dialects, private vocal training, a seminar in dance techniques, or go to a drama coach, you will be learning new techniques and honing your craft. The results can only help you in the quest to be the best at what you do.

If you continue to navigate your way through formal and informal learning experiences throughout your life and career, you will be rewarded with success and satisfaction.

Workplace Politics

To succeed in your career in the performing arts, it's essential to learn how to deal effectively with some of the challenging situations you'll encounter. Workplace politics are a part of life. And in the performing arts, the "workplace" can be almost anyplace.

The real trick to dealing with workplace politics is trying to stay out of them. No matter which side you take in an office dispute, you're going to be wrong. You can never tell who the winner or loser will be, so try to stay neutral and just worry about doing your job. Is this easy? No. But for your own sake, you have to try.

Will keeping out of it work all the time? Probably not, and therein lies the problem. There's an old adage that says the workplace is a jungle. Unfortunately that's sometimes true.

If you think you're going to encounter politics only in the office, think again. As we just mentioned, in the performing arts, the workplace can be almost anyplace. What that means is that if you're working in the talent and creative end of the industry, you often may have additional challenges. In many cases, workplace politics will now be expanded to every area of your life from your personal relationships to your family to work. With this in mind, let's learn more about them.

Why are there politics in the workplace? Much of it comes from jealousy. Someone might think you have a better chance at a promotion or are better at your job than they are at theirs. Someone might think you slighted them. Believe it or not, someone just might not like you. In any business setting there are people who vie for more recognition, feel the need to prove themselves right all the time, or just want to get ahead. There really is nothing you can do about workplace politics except stay out of them to the best of your ability.

On the talent end of the industry, these feelings sometimes escalate. There are many reasons for this. Someone may feel they are more talented than you. They may not understand why *you* got the role and they didn't. They may not understand why you have a top-10 record and they can't get on the charts. They may not understand why you are a featured dancer and they are still in the chorus line. Sometimes people may want to protect themselves from feeling like a failure or may just be frustrated with their career (or lack of one).

In these situations, many lash out and talk about others. These words can hurt. Worse than

that, on the talent end of the industry, your words can come back to haunt you.

Office Gossip

Gossip is a common form of office politics. Anyone who has held a job has probably seen it and perhaps even participated in it in some form. Have you? Forget the moral or ethical issues. Gossip can hurt your career.

Here's a good rule of thumb. Never, ever say anything about anyone that you wouldn't mind them hearing and knowing it came from you. If you think you can believe someone who says, "Oh, you can tell me; it's confidential," you're wrong.

"But she's my best friend," you say. "I trust her with my life."

It doesn't matter. Your friend might be perfectly trustworthy, but trust is not always the problem. Sometimes people slip and repeat things during a conversation. Other times a person might tell someone else whom they trust what you said and ask him or her to keep it confidential, but then that person tells another person and so it goes down the line. Eventually, the person telling the story doesn't even know it's supposed to be confidential and might even mention it to a good friend or colleague of the person everyone has been gossiping about. In the entertainment industry, it might even get into the press.

The reason people gossip is because it makes them feel like part of a group. It can make you feel like you're smarter or know something other people don't. Most of the time, however, you don't even know if what you're gossiping about is true, yet once a gossip session gets started, it's difficult to stop.

How do you rise above this? Keep your distance. People generally respect that you don't

---

⭐ ## Words from the Wise

Do not get into a personal relationship with a boss, supervisor, director, producer, or agent thinking that it will improve your career. In many cases it does just the opposite.

want to be involved. Don't start any gossip, and if someone starts gossiping around you, just don't get involved.

On the business end of the performing arts, office gossip may lead to bigger problems. Depending on your work environment, you might be privy to private stories about actors, singers, musicians, dancers, directors, producers, or other prominent people. You might, for example, hear that an actor got drunk and missed a show even though he said he had the flu. You might hear about some personal problems an actress in the hottest play on Broadway has or you might be privy to contract negotiations.

Office gossip is bad enough, but gossip regarding those in the performing arts or any other part of the entertainment industry often gets to the media and can get totally blown out of proportion. Gossiping about what happens in the office, what you hear, or what you know (even if it is true) can ruin your career, especially if it leads to embarrassment for powerful people.

It's essential to your success in the industry not to spread rumors, either in the office or out. Don't talk about the inside information you have, whether it's good or bad. Don't be surprised if friends and family pump you for information on performers or businesspeople with whom they know you work. Learn to simply say, "Sorry, that's confidential."

Money, Money, Money

How distressed would you be if you knew another actor you thought you were as talented as was making more money than you? How unhappy would you be if you found out a dancer or singer with similar talent was being compensated better than you were? How upset would you be if you found out that a coworker who had a job similar to yours was making more money than you? Probably pretty upset.

Whether it's what you're making, your coworker is making, or someone else is making, money is often a problem in the workplace. Why? Because everyone wants to earn more. No matter how much money people are paid, they don't think they're getting enough. If they hear someone is getting paid better than them, it understandably upsets them.

Here's the deal. If you know you're making more than someone else, keep it to yourself. If you're making less than someone else, keep it to yourself. No matter what your earnings are, keep it to yourself. Don't discuss your earnings with coworkers, other actors, actresses, the media, or anyone else. The only people in the workplace you should discuss your earnings with are the

> ### ⭐ Tip from the Coach
>
> There is a tremendous amount of money to be made in the various aspects of the performing arts. Top directors, playwrights, composers, actors, singers, dancers, and musicians make the big bucks. It's very easy to start comparing your earnings with those of others and start feeling sorry for yourself. Try not to compare yourself, your job, or your earnings to anyone else. Instead of concentrating on what they're making, try to concentrate on how you can get there.

human resources department, your supervisors, your agent, and/or your manager

Why would one person be earning more than another in a similar position? There might be a number of reasons. Compensation for many positions is negotiated, and the person might be a better negotiator. He or she might have more experience, more education, seniority, or different skills.

In the talent area, some people may be bigger draws. They may have proven they can attract large audiences and fill seats. They may have better agents. They may have recently won awards or generated more publicity making them more attractive.

"But it's frustrating," you say.

Worry about your own job. Don't waste time comparing yourself to your coworkers, colleagues, or others in position you consider similar. Definitely don't whine about it in your workplace. It will get on people's nerves.

What can you do? Make sure you are visible in a positive way. Make sure you're doing a great job. If you're already doing a great job, try to do a better job. Keep notes on projects you've successfully completed, ideas you've suggested

which are being used and things you are doing to make the company better. Then, when it's time for a job review, you'll have the ammunition to not only ask for but get the compensation you deserve.

If you're working in the talent or creative area of the industry, keep tear sheets and clips of publicity you've garnered, awards you've received, and quotes from industry insiders. Then, when all your ducks are in a row, strike while the iron is hot.

Dealing with Colleagues

Whatever area of theater or the performing arts you choose to work in, you're going to be dealing with others. Whether they are superiors, subordinates, or colleagues, the way you deal with people you work with will affect your opportunities, your chances of success, and your future.

Many people treat colleagues and superiors well, yet treat subordinates with less respect. One of the interesting things about the performing arts and all other segments of the entertainment industry is that career progression doesn't always follow a normal pattern. That means that with the right set of circumstances someone might jump a number of rungs up the career ladder quicker than expected. The result could be someone who is a subordinate might become either a colleague or even a superior. It's essential to treat everyone with whom you come into contact with dignity and respect. Aside from being common courtesy, you can never tell when the person making you coffee today will be at a desk making a decision about your future.

Want to know a secret about dealing effectively with people? If you can sincerely make every person you come in contact with feel special, you will have it made. How do you do this? There are a number of ways.

When someone does or says something intelligent or comes up with a good idea you might tell him or her. For example, "That was a great idea you had at the meeting, Katrina. You always come up with interesting ways to solve problems."

Sometimes you might want to send a short note instead. For example:

Mark,

While I'm sure you're ecstatic that the press conference is over, I hope you know how impressed everyone was with the event. You handled the coordination like a seasoned pro. No one would ever have guessed that this was the first one you ever put together.

Everything was perfect. But the real coup was getting the story on every major television station. You did a great job. I'm glad we're on the same team.

Evan

If another actor gives an exceptional performance, write a note. It doesn't make you any less talented, and your words can not only make someone else's day, but help you build a good relationship with a colleague.

Everyone likes a cheerleader. At home, you have family. In your personal life, you have friends. If you can be a cheerleader to others in the workplace it often helps to excel yourself.

Never be phony and always be sincere. Look for little things that people do or say as well. "That's a great tie, John." "Nice suit, Amy. You always look so put together." "Great show, John. The audience loved you in the last scene."

Notice that while you're complimenting others, you're not supposed to be self-deprecating. You don't want to make yourself look bad, you want others to look good. So, for example, you wouldn't say, "Nice suit Amy. You always look so put together. I couldn't coordinate a suit and blouse if I tried." or "Great job on the press conference. I never could have coordinated an event like that."

The idea is to build people up so they feel good about themselves. When you can do that, people like to be around you, they gain self-confidence, and they pass it on to others. One of them might be you. Best of all, you will start to look like a leader—a very important image when you're attempting to move up the career ladder.

Dealing with Superiors

While you are ultimately in charge of your career, superiors are the people who can help either move it along or hold it back. Depending on what area of the performing arts you are involved in, your superior might be a boss, a director, a producer, or a section leader. Try to develop a good working relationship with your superiors whoever they are in your career. A good boss can help you succeed in your present job as well as in your future career.

One of the mistakes many people make in the workplace is looking at their bosses as the enemy. They get a mind-set of us against them. Worse than that, they sit around and boss-bash with other colleagues.

Want to better your chances of success at your job? Make your boss look good. How do you do that?

◎ Don't boss-bash.
◎ Speak positively about your boss to others.
◎ Do your work.
◎ Cooperate in the workplace.
◎ If you see something that needs to be done, offer to do it.
◎ Volunteer to help with incomplete projects.
◎ Ask if he or she needs help.

"But what if my boss is a jerk?" you ask. It's still in your best interest to make him or her look good. Believe it or not, it will make you look good.

While we're on the subject, let's discuss bad bosses. With any luck, your boss will be a great person who loves his or her job. But every now and then you just might run into a bad boss.

He or she might be a jerk, a fool, an idiot.

"I could do a better job than him or her," you say. Well, you might be able to, but not if you can't learn to deal so you still have a job. In many cases, your boss has already proven him or herself to the company and is therefore more

of a commodity than you are at this point. So just how do you deal with a bad boss and come out on top?

Let's first go over a list of *don'ts*:

◎ Don't be confrontational. This will usually only infuriate your boss.
◎ Don't shout or curse. Even if you're right, you will look wrong.
◎ Don't talk about your boss to coworkers. You can never tell who is whose best friend or who is telling your boss exactly what you're saying.
◎ Don't send e-mails to people from your office about things your boss does or says.
◎ Don't talk about your boss to clients.
◎ Don't cry in your workplace. No matter how mad your boss makes you, no matter how bad you flubbed your lines on stage, no matter what nasty or obnoxious thing someone says about your talent, keep your composure until you're alone. If you have to bite your lip, pinch yourself, or do whatever you have to do, keep the tears under control.

Now let's go over a list of *dos* that might help.

◎ Do a good job. It's hard to argue with someone who has done what they are supposed to do.
◎ If you are in the talent end of the industry, attend every scheduled rehearsal and always be on time for every performance.
◎ Keep a paper trail. Keep notes when your boss asks you to do things and when you've done them. Keep notes regarding calls that have been made, dates, times, and so on. Keep a running list of projects

you've completed successfully. Do this as a matter of course. Keep it to yourself. If and when you need something to jog your memory, you can refer to it.

◎ Wait until no one is under a time constraint to finish something and ask your boss if you can speak to him or her. Then say you'd like to clear the air. Ask what suggestions he or she can give you to do a better job. You might for example say, "Mr. Johnson, I just wanted to clear the air. We're on the same team and if there is something I can be doing to do a better job, just let me know. I'll be glad to try to implement it." Or, you might say something like, "Joan, you weren't happy with my performance during rehearsal. Can you give me suggestions how to make my character come to life?"

◎ Think long and hard before you decide to leave. If your boss is as much of a jerk as you think, perhaps he or she will find a new job or be promoted.

No matter what type of boss you have, learning to communicate with him or her is essential. Everyone has a different communicating style and it's up to you to determine what his or hers is and make it work for you.

Words from the Wise

Do not put anything in an e-mail that you wouldn't mind someone else reading. No matter what anyone tells you, e-mail is not confidential. Furthermore, be aware that in many situations your e-mails, private or business, may be classified as company property. What this means is management may have the right to access your e-mail.

Tip from the Top

If you carry a personal cell phone, set it to the vibrate mode while in the office. Getting constant calls from friends in the office even on your cell phone is inappropriate. This applies to performing artists as well. While we're on the subject, if you're an actor, singer, dancer, musician, or any other performing artist, do not break up rehearsals—or even worse, performances—to take a call, no matter whom it's from.

A great deal of business is also done by phone. Good phone etiquette is essential. Whether you're on a business phone in the office, your cell phone on the road, or your home phone speaking to your agent or manager or a reporter doing an interview, the phone is a major communications tool. Learn how to use it effectively.

It's important to realize that you have a choice in your career. You can sit there and hope things happen or you can make them happen. You can either be passive or pro-active. In order to succeed in your career, proactive is usually a better choice.

You can go to work and let your boss tell you what to do or you can do that little bit extra, share your dreams and aspirations, and work toward your goals. On the business or administrative end of the industry, your boss and supervisors can help you make it happen.

In the talent and creative segments of the performing arts, it's up to you to be proactive. Don't leave your career solely in the hands of your agent and manager. Be proactive and work with them to help you achieve the success you want and deserve.

Dealing with Fans

If you're on the talent end of the industry, treating people respectfully is critical. What is essential to remember is that whether you're an actor in a summer stock production or a Broadway show, if people don't come to see your performances, you're out of business. Fans are what make you and break you whether you're an aspiring performing artist or a top star.

No matter what area of the performing arts you're in or what level your career is at, when you are a performing artist you will have fans. Building a fan base is essential to success in your career as a performing artist. Keeping your fan base once you have it is crucial. In order to do this, it is vital that you treat your fans, both current and potential, with respect and dignity.

The first few times someone asks for your autograph, you probably will be flattered. You'll stop, smile, say a few nice words to the person asking and excitedly sign your name. As you become more popular and giving autographs becomes more commonplace, don't get caught up thinking you are too busy, too famous, or too *anything* to treat your fans well.

"I can't wait for someone to ask me for my autograph," you say. "I'll never be like that."

I've heard that same thing from a lot of performing artists. Most embrace their fans. Unfortunately, there are a few who down the line, after experiencing a bit of fame, forget that fans helped them get where they are. What this often results in is either being nasty to fans or ignoring them totally.

Be aware that acting in this manner has the potential of slowly but surely destroying your career. If you absolutely cannot stop to sign autographs, or talk to a fan, try to at least briefly give an explanation.

"I am so flattered," you might say. "but I can't stop right now. I have to catch a plane. I'm sorry."

★ The Inside Scoop

A friend of mine who worked on Broadway once spent a couple of hours after a Saturday matinee performance signing autographs outside the backstage door in the rain. By the time he finished, it was almost time to get ready for the Saturday evening show.

I asked him why he stood outside so long and he replied, "Those are my fans. They were standing out in the rain waiting for me. I couldn't disappoint them. Every one of them will go home and tell at least one other person about the show and about me. Every one of them will probably tell someone else. Before you know it, I have a whole new set of fans. They might come see me here or they might see me in another show down the line, but the one thing I'm sure of is they will remember me."

As a performer, it is normal for others to want to talk to you, tell you how much they enjoyed your performance, take a picture, or just shake your hand. Acting appropriately is part of your job. When dealing with fans be pleasant, genuine, and try to make *them* feel important.

Ethics, Morals, and More

We all have our own set of ethics and morals. They help guide us on what we think is right and wrong. In your career you may be faced with situations where a person or group of people want you to do something you know or feel is wrong. In return for doing it, you may be promised financial gain or career advancement.

Would you do it? "Well," you might say. "That depends on what I'd have to do and what I'd get." Here's the deal. No matter what anyone wants you to do, if you know it's wrong—even if you only think it *might* be wrong—it probably is a bad idea.

"But they told me no one would know," you say. Hmm…most people are not that good at keeping secrets and if they get caught, you're going down too. If you're just getting started in your career, you might be looking at ending it for a few dollars. If you're already into your career, are you really prepared to lose everything you worked that hard to get?

"But they told me if I did this or did that, they'd remember me when promotions came up," you say. But how do you know someone isn't testing you to see what your morals are? And exactly what are you planning on doing after you do whatever the person asked you to do and he or she doesn't give you the promotion? Report them? Probably not.

Throughout the book, we've discussed that while the theater and the performing arts industry is large, the performing arts world is small. This means that everyone important knows everyone else who is important. With this in mind, do you really want to take a chance doing something stupid? Probably not.

And forget getting caught. Do you want to build a great career that you can be proud of on unethical activities? Once again, the answer is probably not.

How do you get out of doing something you don't want to do? You might simply say something like "My dream was to work in this industry. I am not about to mess it up for something like this." Or "I've worked so hard to get where I am now, I really don't want to lose what I have." How about, "No can do. Sorry," or "Sorry, I'm not comfortable with that."

But what do you do if a supervisor wants you to do something unethical? How do you handle that? You can try any of the lines above, but if your job is on the line you have a bigger problem to deal with. In cases like this, docu-ment as much as you can. Then, if you have no other choice, go to human resources, a higher supervisor, or someone you think can help.

Accountability

No one is perfect. We all make mistakes. No matter how careful anyone is, things happen. Accept the fact that sometime in your career you are going to make one too. In many cases it's not the mistake itself that causes the problem, but the way we deal with it.

The best way to deal with it is to take responsibility, apologize, try to fix it, and go on. Be sincere. Simply say something like, "I'm sorry, I made a mistake. I'm going to try to fix it and will make sure it doesn't happen again." With that said, it's very difficult for anyone to argue with you.

If, on the other hand, you start explaining mitigating circumstances, blame your coworkers, your secretary, your boss, the director, another actor, or make excuses, others get on the defensive. Similarly, when you're wrong, just admit it and go on. People will respect you, you'll look more professional, and you'll have a lot less turmoil in your life. For example, "I was wrong about the marketing campaign. You were right. Good thing we're a team." Or, "I am so sorry I missed my cue. I'll make sure it doesn't happen again. I don't think the audience noticed because you reacted so quickly. Thanks for covering for me."

What happens if someone else makes a mistake and you're blamed or you're the one who looks like you're unprepared? Let's say, for example, you are working in the fund-raising office of a ballet company and find that the name of a major benefactor has inadvertently been spelled wrong on an engraved plaque that is supposed to be presented at a luncheon in 45 minutes.

What do you do? Blame the engraver? Blame your assistant? Blame your secretary?

The benefactor probably doesn't care or want to know if you have an incompetent staff. It's not their problem. The best thing to do in these type of situations is to acknowledge the problem, apologize, and see what you can do to fix it. "I'm sorry. I should have triple-checked the spelling on your plaque before I brought it to the luncheon. I've already called the engraver to rectify the situation and asked him to make a new plaque. I personally will get you the new plaque with the correct spelling tomorrow. I hope you can forgive me." The result? What could have been a major faux pas is now just a minor inconvenience that no one will probably even remember a few weeks down the line.

Time, Time Management, and Organization

Here's a question for you. What is one thing that every person on the planet has the same amount of? Do you know what it is? Here's a hint. I have the same amount you have. Bill Gates has the same amount I have. Oprah Winfrey has the same amount Bill Gates has. William Shakespeare had the same amount as Oprah Winfrey does. Do you know what it is yet?

Every person in this world, no matter who they are or what they do has the same 24 hours a day. You can't get less and you can't get more, no matter what you do. It doesn't matter who you are or what your job is. You don't get more time during the day if you're young, old, or in between. You don't get more time if you're a millionaire or you're making minimum wage. You don't even get more time if you are starring in a school play or the hottest show on Broadway.

With all this in mind, it's important to manage your time wisely. That way you can fit more of what you need to fit into your day and get the most important things accomplished.

To start with, let's deal with your workday. Try to get to work a little earlier than you're expected. It's easier to get the day started when you're not rushing. On occasion, you might also want to stay late. Why? Because when superiors see you bolting at five o'clock (or whenever your day ends), it looks as though you're not really interested in your job.

If you're working on the business end of the industry, you should also keep in mind that certain parts of the industry may be bicoastal. This means that if you're working in New York you may still need to deal with people on the West Coast and visa versa. Generally that means that there is a three-hour time difference.

If you're on the talent end of the industry, you want to get to work a little earlier than expected as well. You want to be relaxed before you go onstage, not stressed because you got stuck in a traffic jam and started worrying that you were going to be late getting to the theater. You also can never tell if there's someone important who wants to meet you before the show, an opportunity to talk to someone in the media, or some other fantastic big break just waiting for you. If you're not there, you might miss it.

⭐ The Inside Scoop

The time period before everyone else gets in or after everyone has left the office is usually less formal and less stressed. If you make it a habit to come in when the big brass comes in and leave when they leave, you will become visible to higher-ups. You will also often have the opportunity to ask a question, make a comment, or offer a suggestion.

No matter what your career choice in theater and the other performing arts, in order to be successful, you will need to learn to prioritize your tasks. How do you know what's important?

If your boss needs it now, it's important. If you need to rehearse for an opening, it's important. If your play is opening tomorrow, it's important. If you promised to do something for someone, it's important. If things absolutely *need* to get done now, they're important.

Generally what you need to do is determine what is most important and do it first. Then go over your list of things that need to get done and see what take precedence next.

The more organized you are, the easier it will be for you to manage your time. Make lists of things you need to do. You might want to keep a master list and then a daily list of things you need to do. You might also want a third list of deadlines that need to be met.

It's important to remember that just making lists won't do it. Checking them on a consistent basis to make sure the things that you needed to do actually got done is the key.

Writing things down is essential to being organized. Don't depend on your memory or anyone else's. Whatever your job in the industry, it will be filled with lots of details, things that need to get done, and just plain stuff in general. The more successful you get, the busier you will be and the more things you'll have to remember. Don't depend on others reminding you. Depend on yourself.

You might want to keep a notebook to jot things down as they occur. Date each page so you have a reference point for later. Then make notes. Like what?

◎ The dates people called and the subject of the conversation.
◎ The dates you call people and the reason you called.
◎ Notes on meetings you attend. Then, when someone says something like, "Gee, I don't remember whether we said May 9 or May 10," you have it.
◎ Names of people you meet.
◎ Things that happened during the day.

After you get used to keeping the notebook it will become a valuable resource. You might, for example, remember someone calling you six months ago. "What was his name?" you ask yourself. "I wish I knew his name." Voila! Just look in your notebook.

"It seems like a lot of trouble," I hear you saying.

Well, it is a little extra effort, but I can almost guarantee you that once you keep a notebook like this for a while, you won't be able to live without it. You won't be looking for little sheets of paper on which you have jotted down important numbers and then misplaced. You won't have to remember people's names, phone numbers, or what they said. You won't have to remember if you were supposed to call at 3:00 or 4:30. You'll have everything at your fingertips.

A Few Other Things

It's important to realize that while of course you want to succeed in your career, everything

---

⭐ **Words from the Wise**

In prioritizing, don't forget that you must fit in the things you promised others you would do. Don't get so caught up in wanting to be liked or wanting to agree or even wanting to be great at your job that you promise to do something you really don't have time to get done. Doing so will just put you under pressure.

you do may not be successful. Every idea you have may not work. Every project you do may not turn out perfectly. Every audition might not turn into the role you hoped for. Every role may not work out.

Things take time. Careers take time—especially in the performing arts. None of these situations mean that you are a failure. What they mean simply is that you need to work on them a little bit more.

Be aware that success is often built on the back of little failures. Take a look, for example, at some of the top actors, composers, producers, directors, dancers, singers, musicians, and comedians. Most had a string of rejections and failures before they got where they were going. Eventually after plugging away, they landed better roles or jobs, signed contracts, received great reviews or starred in hit shows.

If you're working on the business end of the industry you may have similar situations. You might not get the promotion you wanted right away. You might not get the job of your dreams . . . yet. That does not mean it won't happen. Keep working at it and success will come your way.

Most successful people have a number of key traits in common. They have a willingness to take risks, a determination that cannot be undone, and usually an amazing amount of confidence in themselves and their ideas.

Can they fail? Sure. But they might also succeed, and they usually do. What does this have to do with you? If you learn from the success of others, you can be successful too. If you emulate successful people, you too can be on the road to success.

Don't be so afraid of getting things right that you don't take a chance at doing it a better way, a different way, or a way that might work better. Don't get so comfortable that you're afraid to take on a new role, move to a new position, take a promotion, or accept a new job or new responsibilities. Be determined that you know what you want and how to get it . . . and you will.

Take advantage of opportunities that present themselves, but don't stop there. Create opportunities for yourself to help launch your career to a new level by using creativity and innovative ideas.

If you want to succeed in your career and your life, I urge you to be confident and be willing to take a risk. Success can surprise you at any time.

12

SUCCEEDING ON THE TALENT END OF THE INDUSTRY

How many times have you sat in a theater looking up at the stage wishing you were the one acting in the show? How many times have you watched a play unfold wishing you were the director of the production? How many times have you seen scenery during a show wishing you were the one who had designed the set?

How many times have you gone to a concert and wished you were the one on stage—that you were the singer, the musician, or the conductor?

How many times have you turned on the radio and wished it was your CD everyone was listening to and requesting? How many times have you heard a song and wished it was you who wrote it?

How many times have you watched a dancer and wished you were the one pirouetting across the stage, tapping to the beat, or performing the modern dance yourself? How many times have you sat in the audience and laughed at a comedian and wished you were the one telling the jokes?

How many times have you been in an audience when the curtain came down and heard the thundering applause and the cheering and joined as everyone stood up in unison giving the performers onstage a standing ovation? How many times during situations like these did you wish it was you standing on that stage and imagine yourself receiving the accolades?

I'm betting if you are reading this section of the book, there's a good chance you see yourself in one of these scenarios.

There is certainly nothing wrong with wishing. It definitely can't hurt, and in fact it sometimes helps you focus more clearly on what you want. But wishing alone can't make something happen. To succeed on the talent end of the performing arts, it's essential to take some positive actions.

It's no secret that the industry is competitive, but someone has to be on top. Why shouldn't it be you? While of course talent is important in the performing arts, it is only one factor in success. No matter how talented you are, you need to be aware that talent alone doesn't guarantee success in this industry. Fully understanding the business end is just as important.

This section will discuss things that might help you if you want to move ahead on the talent end of the industry.

Breaking Into the Performing Arts

It's important to remember that the theater and the performing arts industries are a business, and no matter what type of career you're pursuing, it's crucial to your success that you understand this fact and treat it as such.

Yes, it can be fun; it can be exciting; it can be glamorous; and it can be something you love to do, but in the end, the performing arts is part of show business and show business is just that; it is a business. In order to succeed you need to act in a professional manner in every situation. How can you be professional? Present yourself professionally. If you say you're going to be someplace, be there. If you say you're going to call somebody, call them. If someone calls you and leaves a message, call them back on a timely basis. If you say you're going to do something, do it.

Be prepared. If you are auditioning for a role, have your monologue perfected. If you're given sides, have them rehearsed. If you're going onstage, know your lines. If you're auditioning for a musical, know your song. If you're auditioning for an orchestra, know your piece. If you are auditioning for a dance company, have your audition piece down perfectly.

⭐ Tip from the Top

In a theatrical situation, your lateness can impact an entire production and potentially even your career. Always leave enough time to get where you are going. Be prepared for unforeseen circumstances. No one in the audience is going to care if you were in a traffic jam, you couldn't get a cab, or you ran out of gas on the way to the theater.

Be on time for everything. There is nothing worse for your career than being known as the performer who is always late—or who even has been late once!

It is totally unprofessional to drink or use drugs before you go onstage. It is not fair to your audience. You might *think* that you are doing a better job, but no matter what you have heard, you will not do a better job if you are under the influence.

Professionalism doesn't only mean the way you act. It also encompasses how you present yourself. Are you ready to step onstage? Are you ready to make it? Be honest with yourself. If you're not ready, take the steps you need to prepare.

A lot of preparation has to do with the area of the performing arts you're pursuing. Do you have a monologue polished so you can audition at a moment's notice and execute it perfectly? Do you have songs ready for an audition? Can you play an audition piece perfectly? Is your stage show together? What about your material? Have you worked out all of the kinks? Are your jokes timely?

Do you have professional head shots? What about your resume, your bio, and/or your press kit? If you want industry professionals to take you seriously, make sure everything you do is professional.

"I'm talented," you say. "Isn't that all anyone is really interested in anyway?"

Talent is what industry professionals are looking for, but it's not that simple. There are a lot of talented actors, singers, dancers, musicians, and comedians. You want to give yourself the best shot possible at success. You don't want someone to say, "She's a good actress, but she can't remember her lines," or "What a great voice, but I hear he doesn't show up for every show." Or even, "What a great talent, but I hear she fights constantly with everyone."

> ### ⭐ Tip from the Top
>
> The more you know about the industry, the less of a chance that someone will try to take advantage of you. Make it part of your routine to find out at least one new thing about the industry every day. Learn something new every opportunity you get.

You want everything about you to stand out from others in a positive manner. Even if you're not a professional yet, you want it to appear that you are. A professional in the performing arts stands out from the crowd. He or she performs at the highest level and comes through in a pinch. You've no doubt heard the old adage, "the show must go on." A true professional makes sure that happens…no matter what.

To give yourself the best chances at success in the performing arts, learn as much as possible about the business. The more you know, the more you can help yourself in your quest for success.

It is imperative to learn everything you can about the industry. You've already started by reading this book. Don't stop here. Read everything you can about every aspect of theater and the performing arts.

Take classes, workshops, and seminars, both in your talent and craft and in the business of the industry. Why? You will gain valuable information, learn new skills, hone your craft, and have the opportunity to network and make important contacts. And that is what can help you on the talent end of the industry.

Moving Up and Taking the Next Step

There is a big difference between being an amateur performing artist and working as a professional in the field. As a professional, you will continually work toward building success in your given field and building a career. You need a strategy and a plan.

Have you decided that you're ready to commit to a career as a professional in the performing arts field? Are you ready to put in the hard work and perseverance that's necessary? Do you have the passion? Are you ready to pursue your dream? If your answer is a definitive yes, let's take some time to discuss some additional actions that can help you get where you want to go.

What's your next move if you're an aspiring actor and ready to take the next step? What's your next move if you have honed your skills and you're a dancer or singer or musician? What do you do if you have a group together and you're ready to take the next step? What's your next move if you're a singer or a musician? What do you do if you're a prolific songwriter or composer with a box full of lyrics and music you've written, or a talented writer with plays you've completed? How do you move from amateur to pro?

Whatever the case, no matter what area of the performing arts in which you aspire to success, you need to take stock of where you are in your career and get ready for the journey to success.

Get as much experience as you can. Work in amateur productions, summer stock, and dinner theater productions. Don't overlook community theater, orchestras, operas, and choruses. Perform every chance you can and actively seek out opportunities.

One of the most exciting things about deciding to become a performing artist is that you can do it at any age and any stage of your life. Many decide early that they want be performing artists. There are thousands who start their career in the performing arts as children. Some retire after a few years. Others keep going. Look at veteran star Mickey Rooney, whose career has spanned over 50 years and included vaudeville, films, and theater.

There are also some people who decide to take their avocation to a new level and craft a career in the performing arts later in life. While I've discussed it before, I want to reiterate that whatever your age, it is never too late to pursue your dream.

It also bears repeating that no matter what you *think* you want to do and how far you have gone in your career, you are allowed to change your mind. You may, for example, work toward becoming a successful theatrical actress and decide along the way that you really would rather be directing or perhaps you might want to work in the business end of the industry.

One of the other great things about the performing arts is that you can work in various genres of the industry. There is nothing that says you have to work in the theater genre exclusively. Flexibility is the key to a career to succeeding in the performing arts. On the journey to your destination as a theatrical actor you may perform in various other mediums.

Do you want to be the next great Broadway star? Picking up a script, trying to create a character, and practicing your role is not enough. Make sure you are constantly honing your craft. Take classes. Find a drama coach. Learn new dialects. Learn how to perfect your movements on stage in relation to movements if you are acting for film. Take voice lessons. Take singing lessons. Take dance lessons. Learn to do comedy. Make sure your package is diverse. That way you'll be ready for a variety of roles and have a better chance at landing them. Before you say, "But I don't want to be a dancer, I just want to act on Broadway," or "I don't want to sing," remember this: You may not want every role, but you at least want the opportunity to

The Inside Scoop

There are a number of different types of talent agents. Legitimate agents, which are also referred to as "legit agents," represent actors for projects in theater, television, and film. Commercial agents represent actors for projects in the areas of on-air commercials, promos, voice-overs, and industrials.

turn it down. Every legitimate role you take at this point will help build your resume and help you get your talent out in the public. One of the best ways to learn acting is to act. In order to do that, you need roles.

How do you find these coveted roles? There are a number of ways. You might go to casting calls you hear about or read about in the trades, you might have an agent searching out roles for you, or if you're very lucky you might even have people seeking you out!

Remember that acting is a business. You are the product. Whether you are preparing for an audition, looking for an agent, trying to land a role, or acting in your dream role, it is still a business. Why do I keep stressing this? Because I believe that if you keep that fact in mind, you will have a better chance at success. When you start looking at yourself as the product, you will start looking for ways to exploit and market your talent.

While you are working toward your big break in theater, you will want to find other ways to earn money. Of course you can get a day job. But you might also want to look into some other options that involve your talent.

What can you do? What about contacting advertising agencies? They often need professional actors for voice-over work, commercials, print ads, and more. What about contacting video producers and production companies? They often need professional actors and actresses for similar work. Some may do music videos. Others may do training films. Some may produce commercials. What about contacting large corporations? They too may need talent for training films or to represent the company at trade shows. What about contacting local television or radio stations? They might need talent for commercials or voice-overs. Get creative.

What do you say to these people when you call? Introduce yourself. Ask to speak to an account representative. Tell them a little about yourself. Ask if you can send your head shots and resume.

While you might want to work in legitimate theater, while you're working toward that goal, you want to make sure you have enough money to live and support yourself. While there is certainly nothing wrong with a day job, wouldn't you rather your day job be related in some manner to your acting career?

In acting, as in other segments of the performing arts, you are going to have to have a thick skin. No matter how much you want a role, not getting it does not necessarily mean you are a bad actor. What it means is that the casting director saw something that they liked in someone else better. While it is very easy to start feeling like it's you or feeling rejection or feeling any other number of emotions, try to stop yourself. Train yourself not to take it personally.

You not only have to have a thick skin when you don't get roles, you have to have a thick skin once you get them too. At some time in the career of every actor, he or she gets a bad review. If you get a bad review from a critic, let it be that—one person's opinion, one person's perception. If you can learn anything from it, do so. If not, let it go.

The Inside Scoop

Sides are a few pages or a scene from a script that is used in auditions. Generally, you receive the sides prior to auditioning so you can prepare.

While Broadway may be your ultimate goal, it's important to realize that if your passion is acting and your dream career is working onstage in front of a live audience, there are a variety of options for you to explore.

I consistently get calls over the years from people who want to work in theater yet don't live in New York City. I also get calls from people who work in New York City but haven't yet broken into Broadway. If either of these scenarios are yours, read on.

Even though New York City is the theatrical capital of the world and a role on the Great White Way might be the ultimate job, there is a wide array of other options to keep you going until you get to that point.

As a matter of fact, most large culturally active cities host theatrical opportunities. New York City, Chicago, Los Angeles, Boston, Atlanta, and Philadelphia are just some of the cities where hundreds of shows are produced every year.

Many actors and actresses also find work in regional, dinner, stock, or repertory theaters located throughout the country. Depending on the specific theater, these venues may be not-for-profit or for-profit, large or small, more prestigious or less well known.

If you have the ability to travel and enjoy living out of a suitcase, you might want to consider auditioning for a role with a national touring company. What about working on a cruise ship? Many now host theatrical shows, cabaret reviews, and more.

With theatrical productions becoming more popular as entertainment, theme parks are another option for actors and actresses. Casinos and other resorts around the country are yet another possibility. Las Vegas has always hosted production shows. Now they are also bringing in Broadway productions.

Continually scout out other opportunities, remembering to think outside of the box.

Unified Auditions

The United Professional Theatre Auditions holds combined auditions annually for actors who are available to work full time. Professional theater companies attend this event to see actors audition in a central location. Producers go to the UPTA for the sole purpose of locating talent for their productions.

UPTA also holds interviews at this event for production personnel and producers. While there are a number of qualifications necessary to participate in this program, if you can take part in it, you will have an opportunity to audition for those who can put you on stage in paying roles. To check out more about this program, visit http://www.upta.org.

Another similar unified audition program is conducted by the Southeastern Theatre Conference. The SETC, billed as the country's regional theater association, connects individuals in theater through a variety of opportunities such as conventions, auditions, networking opportunities, and job opportunities. The SETC conducts auditions for professional, Equity, and screened pre-professional actors for summer and year-round employment. They audition in front of professionals from regional, dinner, stock, musical, summer, and repertory theaters as well as individuals from theme parks, cruise lines, and more. Check out more about the SETC at their Web site at http://www.setc.org.

The New England Theater Conference is a not-for-profit group that offers a myriad of services for its members. The NETC holds annual unified auditions for performers as well as producers, directors, musical directors, and technical people. Theater professionals from both Equity and non-equity theaters, summer and year-round theaters, dinner theaters, professional theater training programs, theme parks, touring companies, and casting agencies attend. Check out more about NETC and its programs at their Web site, http://www.netconline.org.

Strawhat Auditions is another similar group whose main activity is conducting unified auditions annually in New York City for actors for non-equity summer stock and regional theaters. They additionally have a Web site where technical people can post their resumes for these theaters. Casting directors, producers, directors, and other theater and entertainment professionals attend the auditions. Check out more about StrawHat Auditions at their Web site at http://strawhat-auditions.com.

Succeeding in the Music Industry

Let's say your dream is to work as a performing artist in the music business instead. Is your music great? Do you have great songs? What about your stage show? Is it polished and professional? Can you perform a set without wondering what song is next? Does your show flow smoothly? Do you have stage presence? Do you exude charisma?

"Stage show? Stage presence? Charisma? Huh? What do mean?" you ask.

Let's discuss this aspect of your career for a bit. Think about some of the successful acts you love watching in concert. What's their stage show like? Do the singers just stand there? Does the band just play their instruments looking bored? Probably not. What do you look like on stage? Do you want to know?

Here's an idea. Next time you do a show, have a friend videotape your performance. If you don't have a show scheduled, videotape your rehearsal. Then watch the video. It's often difficult to see yourself without being overly critical. Don't be hard on yourself. That's not the point. What you want to do is watch to see how you look to others when you're on stage.

Are you just standing in front of a microphone singing your songs? Are you making eye contact with the audience? Are you gazing up while playing the drums or looking down at the floor while playing the guitar? Are you smiling and having fun or does it look like being on stage is a chore?

Once you see what you look like to your audience, decide what you want to change. What should you try? Every performer is different. What works for one, might not work for another. You have to be comfortable. Try interacting with the audience. Banter a bit. Have fun. Don't just stand there. Move around and be active. Develop unique segments of your show that you become known for; fans will hear about these signature segments and wait for them when they see you perform. Experiment with different things to see what works. If something does work, great. If not, come up with other ideas.

What you want to do is make sure your audience is entertained. You want them to have fun and you want them to look forward to the opportunity to see you again. Take some time to develop your stage show. Whatever you choose, it doesn't necessarily have to *look* like it's staged, but you want your show to look polished. Every appearance is important because every appearance is an opportunity.

Classical Music

Is classical music your passion? Is it your dream to play an instrument in a major symphony? Conduct? Be a musical director? You're going to have to pay your dues, take classes, and perfect your skill. If this is your dream, make sure that you check out the American Symphony Orchestra League Web site (http://www.orchestra. org). You'll find a plethora of useful information ranging from seminars to apprenticeships to the name, address, and phone numbers of member orchestras and more.

If you are still in school, look for young musician programs. These will be helpful in putting you in a musical environment around highly trained professionals who can help guide your career. Many of these programs are held in conjunction with major orchestras throughout the country.

Search for apprenticeships. Find a mentor. Learn new techniques and practice, practice, practice. Attending a conservatory will often open up doors which might not otherwise open and give you opportunities and contacts you might not otherwise have. You also are going to want to contact orchestras to learn about opportunities, training programs, and openings.

Actively seek out competitions. These can help give you the edge over others and bring your talent to the forefront.

Let's take some time to discuss some of the possible methods used for professional orchestral auditions. In some instances, there will be open auditions where anyone who wants to audition for the committee is invited to do so. In other cases, when there is an opening, a number of qualified people are invited to audition. Qualifications might be based on their professional reputation, experience, or resume. In some situations, the committee will both invite a group of qualified people to audition and encourage others to send audition tapes. Sometimes the committee may require audition tapes of all applicants.

As a rule, there will be one or more audition committees in charge of filling the openings. The goal of these committees is to find the best musician for the orchestra. The committee may be judging applicants against each other or against an ideal in their mind. The only thing you can do is your best.

How do you find orchestral openings? Check out orchestra Web sites, read the newspaper, look in the classifieds, talk to people at arts councils, and network, network, network. Don't forget to go through the *International Musician*, the monthly newspaper put out by the American Federation of Musicians, for orchestral vacancy notices.

Once you hear about an audition, you need to know the requirements. Write a short cover letter to the orchestra's personnel manager or director and send it with a copy of your resume. In the letter, simply state your interest and ask for information regarding the date, time, and location of the audition as well as the repertoire.

You will be giving yourself an edge by doing this even if you know the requirements. You are introducing yourself in a professional manner and sending your resume. If a tape is required, the personnel manager will also send you detailed instructions on how your tape should be made, what it should include, and, in many cases, the music you should play on the tape.

Orchestral auditions are like other auditions. You need to prepare, you need to relax, and you need to do your best. In the end, there can only be one person chosen for each opening. If you are chosen, congratulations. If you're not, it doesn't mean that you aren't a talented musician. It simply means that the audition committee felt someone else would fit into the orchestra better this time.

Don't beat yourself up. Don't go into a depression. Don't think you aren't good enough. Don't give up your dream. Just keep moving forward until you reach your goal.

If your goal is to become an operatic singer, conservatory and/or operatic singing programs are essential. Young singer programs are also extremely helpful, not only in helping you to break into the field, but training your voice in the proper manner.

While many professionals stress that the world of operatic singing is not for everyone, it may still be your dream and goal. If it is, I urge you not to let others dissuade you from pursuing your dream. Be aware, however, that as in other classical genres of the performing arts, a career in opera requires a tremendous amount of discipline—in voice, movement, acting, and more. Don't let that stop you. Instead let it inspire you because dreams stoked by talent and hard work do come true.

Opera America is the organization for those interested in a career in opera. Check out their

The Inside Scoop

If you are a member of the American Federation of Musicians, you automatically get the *International Musician* as part of your union membership. If you're not a member, check out your local library to see if they have a copy. You can also purchase a subscription directly from the AFM. Be sure to go through the newspaper when it comes in instead of waiting. You don't want to find out about an orchestral opening three days after the audition process.

Web site at http://www.operaamerica.org to get information on careers, auditions, training, resources and more. Their conferences offer a wide array of networking possibilities and will give you the opportunity to make contacts within the industry.

Dancing

Is dancing your passion? There are many options for you. Is it your dream to be a prima ballerina? A dancer in a Broadway musical? A modern or contemporary dancer? Whatever your choice, you will need training.

You're going to want to study dance at a college, university, or conservatory. Many ballet companies also provide training. People often ask why they should bother going to college if they want to be dancers. There are a number of reasons.

A degree in dance will be immensely helpful in preparing you for your career as a per-

former. Additionally, college often opens doors and gives you opportunities which you might not have otherwise had. A degree will also offer you various options for careers in the future. This is an important consideration because depending on the area of dance you choose, careers can be short.

As in other areas of the performing arts, you're going to want to look for apprenticeships, internships, training programs, and competitions. You want as much experience performing on stage as possible. This will not only give you experience, but help build your resume.

Most dancers continue their training throughout their career. Learning new techniques and honing your talent will help you succeed in this field.

I pretty much can guarantee that when you share your dream of a career in dance, no matter what the genre, there will be those who tell you how difficult it will be and the almost certain impossibility of success. I can also promise you that if this is *your* dream, you probably won't listen. If you have the passion, talent, determination, and drive, with a little bit of luck, you can make it—if you don't give up.

Comedy

Is comedy your passion? Has it been your dream to be a stand-up comedian? If so, the best advice I can give you is try it. As a former stand-up, I can tell you that if you don't at least give it a shot, you will probably never get it out of your system.

How do you get started? Start training yourself to *think* funny. Begin to look for the humor in every situation. Being a stand-up comedian is more than telling jokes. You need to learn timing. You need to come up with routines—more than one. Being a comedian is not like being a singer or a musician. After hearing your show for the first time, people may laugh at it a second time, they might even laugh at it a third time, but you're going to have to change your show and come up with some new stories and new routines.

Where do you get material for your routines? While there are some comedians who hire writers, most develop their own material. How do you do it? Observe things that are going on around you. Write about things you know. Many seasoned comedians suggest that you carry around a notebook and write down things that you find humorous. Keep a file of jokes, situations, and moments that you can pull together to create a routine. If you can find any classes, seminars, or workshops that are geared for writing comedy, take them. They will be extremely useful.

Getting on stage to do stand-up comedy the first time can be frightening, to say the least. Classes in public speaking or improvisational acting will help. Some comics tell a series of jokes, while others tell stories. When putting together your show, try to decide where your talent lies.

Once you have your material written, work on remembering it. Rehearse in front of the mir-

> ### Words from the Wise
> Whatever you do, don't steal another comic's material.

ror. Get your timing down. Then try your material out on friends or family. Once you think you're ready, look for a comedy club to try out your material in public. You probably will need between five and ten minutes. If you go on and you're great, they may offer you a good time slot for next time. In most of these situations, however, be aware that you won't be getting paid.

How do you get the paying jobs? After you've worked out all of the kinks in your material, your timing is great, and you're confident that you can handle an audience, you're on your way. You're going to need between 20 and 45 minutes of material for each show. You can then either contact clubs yourself or work with an agent to get you jobs.

Where else can you work? Many comedians work at conventions, on cruise ships, at casinos, and at nightclubs. As you become more successful, you might also perform in concert at large arenas, get roles in television shows and movies, and star in television specials or even your own series.

George Carlin, Chris Rock, Jerry Seinfeld, Ray Romano, Steve Martin, Kevin James, Rosanne Barr, Whoopi Goldberg, Robin Williams, Bill Cosby, Jay Leno, and David Letterman are all prime examples of what you can do if you're talented, funny, persistent, and have a bit of luck. You can join the list if you follow your dream.

I've mentioned throughout this book that I believe you should always live your dreams; that you should never look back and say, "I wish I

> ### Tip from the Top
> In order to improve your skills as a comedian, learn from the best. Study successful comedians. How do they present themselves? What do they do that makes them funny? Is it only their words or is it also the way they stand, their facial movements, or the persona they have created? How do they do their timing? Go to live shows, watch comedians on television, and rent videos.

had done this or that." I also mentioned earlier that I would tell you a little about my career in stand-up. So here's my story.

In school I was known as the class clown. In reality, as early as first grade (maybe earlier) I was getting ready to go on stage. Quite simply, I felt it was my job to make other people laugh.

My teachers really said, "Ms. Field, if it's so funny, perhaps you'd like to come up to the front of the room and share it with the rest of us." I remember as early as first grade being put in the corner for trying to make the rest of the class laugh and not being able to stop laughing myself. I remember teachers sending notes home that said, "Shelly laughs too much in class and makes the rest of the class laugh, please stop her." I even remember my mom writing notes back that said, "I will not stop my daughter from laughing. If you can't control the class perhaps you shouldn't be teaching." (As I've mentioned before, I always had a supportive family.)

By the time I got to sixth grade, I remember rolling up toilet paper (clean, but it was toilet paper just the same) and putting it in my mouth and pulling it out piece by piece while my classmates were giving their weekly book reports. (I had seen a magician do something like that and at that age, I didn't know they had special paper.) The problem was, I would start hysterically laughing myself to the point of tears.

I didn't like school (as a matter of fact, I hated it), but making people laugh almost made it tolerable. With all this being said, it was not surprising that at some point in my life I was going to want to at least try stand-up comedy. While it was always a dream, it for the most part stayed in the back of my mind. Yet, every time I saw one of my clients in the music industry go on stage or even saw another comedian performing, I always had that gnawing feeling that

I wanted to be on stage. Over the years, people kept telling me how funny I was, and in many cases even suggesting that I go on stage.

Did I ever get there? Definitely. I was working in the music industry at that point, doing publicity for recording groups, and decided that it was time. To be perfectly honest, I was not prepared. I went to a couple of clubs that held open mike nights, but every time I had the opportunity to get on stage (in front of the 10 other people in the room) I chickened out. The only way to live my dream, I believed, was to get on a real stage in a big club, not a comedy club or a club with an open mike night—a real club where people paid to come in and be entertained.

I called a couple clubs and told them I wanted to try stand-up, but no one was interested. So I got creative.

Because I was working in the music industry at the time, I had the lists of all the clubs in the country at my fingertips complete with the names of the club owners and agents. I called up clubs, using a pseudonym, and told the agents or club owners I was booking me—Shelly. I also told them I was great. (I hadn't been on stage yet, so I at least thought I would be great.) Some people have stage names; I had a stage booking agent—me.

Coincidentally, this method worked. (Yes, you need a lot of nerve to do something like this, but calling up and saying I wanted to do stand-up comedy and had no experience wasn't really getting me any takers.) I got my first booking. I was going to do a set at a club in Philadelphia.

I wrote my set and tried to memorize it. I at least remembered the first two lines every time I rehearsed. I came up with what I thought was a genius idea. I would write my routine on bandaids and stick them all over my hand. (It might have been a good idea, but it never worked because I forgot that it is dark in clubs and the spotlight blinds you.) At any rate, I picked out an outfit and was off to Philadelphia.

I remember the night like it was yesterday. I went alone because I didn't want anyone to see me if I was bad. I made sure everyone I knew in the entire Philadelphia area was out of town—way out of town.

I went on stage that night and tasted what I had dreamed of. I forgot the majority of my act, but I ad-libbed with the audience, something I was much better at than remembering an act. People laughed. People applauded. And it was over. I wasn't great, but no one booed me. Afterward, a few people in the audience even told me I was funny.

I still wanted to remain anonymous. My thought was, who would ever remember seeing me? It was a good thought until the next morning when I went to a shopping center in Philadelphia, and a security officer standing near the escalator said, "Didn't I see you on stage last night?"

"Yes," I said.

"I thought so," he replied. "You weren't that funny. You need to work on it." Well, there you have it. I had rejection from a mall security officer. It could have stopped me, but surprisingly I still wanted to do it again.

Over the next few months, I found new opportunities. I started getting comfortable on stage. I got better. Sometimes I was okay. Other times, I wondered why I was struggling.

At one point, I worked in a club where they actually had my name on the marquee. The advertisement in the paper said I was opening for some rock-and-roll group. I was pretty excited. The night of the show, I got to the club. What I remember about that night is the stage was very big and very high.

I was introduced, I started my show, and the audience started actually yelling, "Sex, drugs, and rock and roll," over and over and louder and louder. Evidently, they wanted music; they did not want to hear a comedienne.

Unless you have ever been in a situation like that, I don't think you can imagine how mortifying it could be. Remember I said the stage was real big and real high? I remember that because if it wasn't I might have jumped right off the stage and run out of there. With that not being an option, I finished my set. It was 20 minutes of torture.

Amazingly enough, the club owner came over when I was done and said, "Good set. Let's talk about when you can come back." Trust me—the set was not good and there was no way I would ever go back.

I went back on the road doing publicity for recording acts. Unfortunately, I still wanted to be on stage. Once again, I found clubs to work in. I actually started getting good. But it was always a struggle.

What I found was that in many situations, as a stand-up comic you were actually challenging the audience to laugh. They came to laugh, they paid to laugh, and by golly, they wanted you to work for it. The whole situation got very stressful.

Flash forward. In between all this I was still doing publicity as well as giving seminars on various subjects. I realized that while I was leading seminars and giving speeches I was making people laugh. I also realized that as much as I wanted to be on stage making people laugh, I wanted to find a better way. I used my experience as a stand-up comedian as a stepping-stone. Now instead of working in a club, I make people laugh when facilitating seminars or working as a motivational speaker. Do I feel like I failed? Absolutely not. I look back and say to myself, I'm glad I tried comedy. If I hadn't, I probably would never have found my new passion was making people laugh telling true-life stories while giving motivational presentations.

Why did I share my story? For a number of reasons, but most of all to help you realize that it's okay to have a dream—work toward it, and then change your dream.

Could I have eventually succeeded as a stand-up? There's not a question in my mind that if I hadn't given up and still had the passion, I could have. But, as I've told you throughout this book, the person who doesn't succeed at something just gave up one day too soon.

Other Performing Artists

The performing arts, is not just acting, singing, dancing, playing music, or doing comedy. For performing artists, there are a wide array of opportunities limited only to your imagination and talent. It's really up to you. Talented, creative people can turn almost anything into a performing art.

There are puppeteers, mimes, circus performers, street performers, hypnotists, magicians, and more. If any of these are your choice,

---

⭐ The Inside Scoop

A brilliant performing artist, Fan Yang, does an amazing stage show blowing soap bubbles, and he is not alone. There are a number of artists who crisscross the country and go around the world with their entertaining bubble shows, illustrating that if you can find a way to entertain and wow an audience, you can even turn a child's plaything into a performing extravaganza.

---

and we haven't discussed it specifically, try to take the suggestions from some of the other career options and apply them.

Getting the Gigs

No matter which area of the performing arts you are interested in pursuing, in order to earn a living, you're going to have to find a way to get the gigs, land the roles, and get hired.

Let's spend some time discussing this aspect of the business. We've already discussed how to find work as an actor or actress. Let's discuss getting gigs if you're in the music industry, comedy, or other part of the performing arts.

One of the ways musical talent, comedians, and other performing artists generate income is by performing live. Competition can be fierce. Whether you are just starting out or you're already successful, you're competing for the public's entertainment dollars.

There are basically two main ways to get gigs. You can go out looking for them or you can wait until they come to you. Whether you're booking the gigs yourself or booking them through an agent, if you want your calendar to be full, as in every other part of the entertainment industry, you're going to have to be proactive.

If you're just starting out, you probably are going to be booking your own gigs. Are you ready to be your own booking agent? It means you have to find ways to get engagements, negotiate fees, and deal with contracts. As your career moves ahead, you may begin dealing with agents. Either way the goal is to get more engagements, better engagements, and higher fees. You want to move out of your local market and find ways to reach more lucrative major markets.

How do you do that? It's going to depend to a great extent on where you are in your career, but generally marketing and promotion have a lot to do with it. Let's briefly review the relationship between marketing and booking engagements. Marketing can open doors for you. Why? Because all successful companies use marketing to sell products, and you need to look at yourself or your act as a product. Done correctly, marketing can tell your story, differentiate you from other acts, and convince potential talent buyers why they should hire you instead of another act. The result of good marketing in this case will be the booking or the *selling* of your live performances.

A major component of marketing is promotion. While it is useful at any level of your career, if you're just starting out or you don't have anyone else working on the task, self-promotion can help dramatically. How do you do this? There are many options. Whatever you choose, you want to create as much buzz about yourself (or your act) as possible. You want your name to be as prominent as possible before the public. That way, when people have entertainment needs, they might think of you.

Unless you are signed to an agent on an exclusive basis and have someone working on this for you, create a list of potential talent buyers to target. The people included on this list will depend on where you are in your career.

Let's look at a few possibilities to get you started.

◎ Booking agents
◎ Bar owners
◎ Comedy clubs
◎ Casino entertainment buyers
◎ Chambers of Commerce
◎ Civic groups
◎ Club owners and entertainment bookers
◎ Coffee houses
◎ College/university directors of activities
◎ College and university student unions
◎ Convention center directors
◎ Convention planners
◎ Corporate party planners
◎ Corporations and other business human resource directors
◎ Cruise ship line entertainment directors
◎ Destination management companies
◎ Dinner club entertainment directors or owners
◎ Exposition managers
◎ Fair and festival entertainment directors or talent bookers
◎ Governmental agencies
◎ High school and junior high school administrative offices
◎ Hotels and motels owners and entertainment bookers
◎ Not-for-profit organizations
◎ Radio station general managers, music directors, promotion directors
◎ Television station program directors, producers, guest coordinators
◎ Record labels
◎ Resort entertainment directors, entertainment bookers, or marketing directors
◎ Television station general managers, human resource directors, marketing directors
◎ Trade association executive directors
◎ Trade show directors
◎ Wedding planners

What do you send your potential talent buyers? You're going to start by sending that press kit/promo package that we talked about earlier. If you have a preview video and/or a CD, send that as well. You also want to send a list of your upcoming engagements. That way, people can check you out. Word of mouth and personal recommendations are the best advertising you can get.

> ### ⭐ Tip from the Top
>
> Keep a card file noting the date you called potential talent buyers, what their response was, and any other information you might pick up during the conversation. For example, the first time you call, the potential buyer may say in passing, "I'm swamped here; we're in the middle of remodeling the club." The next time you call, you might ask, "Last time I spoke to you, the club was being remodeled. How did it go?" Then go on to your sales pitch.

Don't just stop at one mailing. Send mailings to potential buyers on a regular basis so your act's name is constantly in front of them. Send out an updated engagement list every month with a flyer or even a one-page newsletter showcasing you or your act.

Don't always send the same exact mailing. Try to be creative while maintaining some consistency. One act I know always sends a list of interesting facts along with their information. Another sends monthly engagements on a calendar that also contains better-known as well as obscure special days of that month. (For example, National Ice Cream Day, National Eat a Bagel Day, National Smile Day, and so on.) It's neat to look at, so most people always open it. As a matter of fact, people start to look forward to getting it.

Keep sending your information and your updates. The more people see your name, the better the possibility they will remember you when they need talent. Having your act's name out there will give you an advantage over other acts who don't actively promote themselves.

Now that you've introduced your act to potential talent buyers with your information do

you just sit back and wait for them to call you? Well, you can, but it's not a very effective approach. What do you do? Booking engagements is selling your product, so get on the phone and call your potential buyers. Creating a personal contact with potential buyers often makes the difference between them booking your act or not. Why? Because you're putting a voice to your material. When you get on the phone you can *sell* yourself better than just some print information. It might take a few calls, but that's okay. Persistence often pays off.

What are some other ways to get gigs? Many acts advertise their services. Where should you advertise? That depends to a great extent on where you are in your career and where you're trying to go. Many newer or local acts advertise in the local newspaper or the local entertainment media. Established acts as well as lesser-known acts often place ads in entertainment directories.

If you live in an area where there are a number of entertainment venues consider renting a billboard. I've seen a number of up-and-coming acts use billboards to successfully fill up their calendar.

"Aren't billboards expensive?" you ask.

They can be depending on the location and the billboard company's rates, but they can also be worth the investment.

Does booking yourself seem like a lot of work? Well, it is. At the beginning of your career, there might not be anything you can do about it. Your goal, however, should be to have agents book you. You're still going to have to promote yourself, but you can cut out a lot of the work.

Booking agents match acts with the venues or promoters who need the talent. They generally represent a number of acts. Very large agencies may represent hundreds of acts, some exclusively, some on a non-exclusive basis. It's important to understand that just because you have an agent doesn't necessarily mean you will get tons of engagements. You need to create a good working relationship with your agent. Call them weekly. Tell them what you're doing and ask how *they're* doing securing you engagements.

Always be cordial, polite, and professional to agents. Try to develop a friendly business relationship. This is important for a number of reasons. When a club calls looking for a certain type of act, the agent has a choice. He or she can probably recommend five or six acts similar to yours on the agency roster. If you've developed a good relationship with the agent and he or she knows you have a good act and that you're professional, it increases your chances of being recommended for the gig.

Who pays the agent? Generally, the artist pays. Agents receive a percentage of the fee the artist is paid for the engagement. Percentages vary, but it will generally be between 10 percent and 20 percent of the total fee.

Before we go too far, let's discuss one of the most important matters connected to performing—how you set your fees. How do you decide how much you're worth? Whether you're a singer, dancer, musician, comedian, or any other performing artist, this is a very difficult question for most people. If you're a member of a union, the union will usually set the minimum, but that's just the *minimum*. And if you're not a part of the union, you're pretty much on your own.

Do you charge what the other people are charging at your career level? Do you charge more because you feel you're worth more? Do you charge less because if you do, you might get more gigs? In many cases, especially when you're starting out, your agent or manager will help you set fees.

Here's the deal. *You* have to decide what you're worth. You have to decide what the market will bear and you have to decide what you'll accept. You also have to decide when you're willing to cut your fee. Flexibility is often the name of the game.

I know a number of former chart-topping recording artists who are still popular, yet not currently on the charts. They might have a set a fee of $25,000 per show, but they will often adjust it if they have other gigs in a given area and can schedule enough performances to make it all worthwhile. They might also lower their fee if a particular venue that they want to play does not have a budget that can handle their usual amount. While they usually get what they want or close to what they want, they are flexible.

When you are setting your fees there are a number of things you have to remember. You can always lower your fee, but once you set it, it's very difficult to raise it. If you give a club a specific fee because you want to perform there, that is the fee they will expect to pay you the next time you appear. People often undervalue their talent because they worry that if they ask for what they think they're worth, they will not get it.

While you have to be realistic, one thing is for sure. If you don't ask for the big bucks, you'll never get them. If you think you're worth more, you have to ask for more. You might be pleasantly surprised.

Would your life be easier with an agent? It might be if he or she constantly gets you good engagements. In reality, agents generally deal with a number of acts. Is it easier dealing with an agent? Sometimes. Do you need an agent? It certainly helps to have someone working for you.

Getting Exposure

To succeed in the industry, people need to know what you're doing. You need to set yourself apart. You need exposure. It's essential to your quest for success in your career. You can be the most talented actor or actress in the world, but if you can't get an acting job, no one is going to know how good you are. You can be the funniest comedian, but unless you can find places to book you and get people to your shows, you're going to be telling jokes to your mirror. You can have the greatest CD in the world, but if no one knows about it, it probably isn't going anyplace. Similarly, you can have the best stage show, but unless people know about it, it's useless.

How do you get exposure? There are a variety of ways. Advertising, publicity, promotion, and marketing help. You need to catch the eye of people in the industry, catch the eye of the media, and catch the eye of fans. Sometimes you might need a professional. Publicists, press agents, and public relations counselors are all pros in garnering publicity and media attention and finding ways to bring your act to the attention of the public. Theatrical press agents generally do the press for productions, but unless you're one of the stars, chances are you won't be the one getting the exposure.

Can you do it yourself? It depends where you are in your career, what your skills are, and how much time you have to put into it. Publicity takes time and effort, but if you know the basics, you can try. If you have already put together your press kit/promo package, you're off to a good start.

When you go to a professional publicist, press agent, or public relations counselor, you generally tell them your goal. They then will develop a plan of action. Depending on your goal, they might set up press conferences, send out a series of press releases, arrange for media interviews, send your press kits, and so on. If you're not ready to hire a professional, make a commitment to yourself to work on a plan to get exposure for your act.

How do you do it? Let's say your goal is to make people aware of your new comedy act and let them know you're a major force in the entertainment industry. Here are some things you can try.

- ◎ Develop a media list of local, regional, and national media outlets to send your press releases.
- ◎ Come up with an interesting angle or hook for a series of press releases on your act.
  - ▫ Press release on you and your comedy.
  - ▫ Press release on how you got your career started.
  - ▫ Press release announcing your engagements.
  - ▫ Press release noting attention your engagements are receiving.
  - ▫ Press release noting that a story appeared in one of the trades.
  - ▫ Press release on performing for a charity event.
- ◎ Photo of you performing at the charity event with photo caption.
- ◎ Develop some sort of interesting angle or subject or platform you can focus on to create some buzz and can garner media attention. For example:
  - ▫ Laughing and humor are stress-busters. Find something to laugh about every day. Become spokesperson for telling people to laugh everyday. Try for public service announcements.

☐ Come to see my show for your health's sake. Laugh away your troubles.

◎ Call local, regional, and even national television and radio stations to determine what news, talk, or variety shows might feature you.

◎ Send letters to television and radio show guest coordinators and producers asking about possibilities of appearances. Remember to mention your unique angle or platform to give yourself an edge.

◎ Follow up your letters with phone calls.

◎ Develop T-shirts and other promotional material and merchandise that you can give away or sell.

◎ Contact charities to offer entertainment gratis for one of their events or do a fund-raiser.

Keep doing things to create a buzz and get exposure. Get creative. The media can make or break your act. Develop a relationship with them. When someone does a story or reviews your performance, write a note and thank them. Send them a T-shirt and other merchandise with your name. If you have the opportunity to get media to attend one of your plays or shows, make sure they have passes to get in, even if you have to pay for tickets out of your own pocket. (Some media will not allow this.)

★ Tip from the Top

Try to perform at benefits or fund-raisers. They are great for exposure, great for publicity, and get your name out to people who might not know about you. This, of course, is in addition to doing something to help a group trying to raise monies. Look for charities whose cause you support and that you can align yourself with.

★ Tip from the Coach

You might be able to get another opportunity, but you can never get back the opportunity you missed.

If you're opening in a show or performing at a big club, you might even take out some ads yourself in the local media. You might even partner with a business.

If you're just starting out, your local area is really important. This is where people know you and you can develop a large fan base. As you get more successful, you're going to move into larger markets and build a larger fan base. Fans are important to every performing artist. Treat them well. Without them, it's difficult to sustain your success.

Don't forget the Internet when looking for exposure. The World Wide Web today means that even if you're just starting out you can have fans not only in your local area but on the other side of the world.

We talked about having a Web site earlier in the book. The Web is an interesting place. You can never tell who is surfing it. It might be a new fan, a potential manager, a director, a casting agent, a producer, a possible booking contact, or a media person working on a story. If you want people to know about you, you need a Web site. Make it easy for people to find you. Update your site with news about what you're doing and keep it current so that people will come back.

Your Professional Support Team

You can have a lot of talent, but without people to help get you where you need to go, it's going to be a long, difficult road. Take a minute and think about all the successful performing artists.

Whether they're actors, singers, dancers, musicians, recording artists, comedians, or any of the other possibilities in the performing arts, every one has a professional support team of some sort. Sometimes the team is smaller, sometimes it's larger, but it's a support team just the same.

What's a professional support team? In the performing arts your support team can include all the pros who help you with your career. Depending on which area of the performing arts you are in, your support team may include, among others:

◎ Attorneys to handle your legal needs and to read and negotiate contracts. If at all possible, look for an attorney who specializes in the area of the performing arts in which you are working.
◎ Personal manager to be your chief advisor, handle your career, push it in the right direction, help you make the right decisions, and be your cheerleader.
◎ Business managers/accountants to handle your financial affairs and help you make decisions on how to spend money, save money, and invest money.
◎ Talent agents to get you roles and other work.
◎ Booking agents to handle your booking needs.
◎ Publicists/press agents/public relations counselors to handle your publicity.
◎ Tour coordinator/tour manager to help coordinate and manage your affairs while on tour.
◎ Acting and drama coaches.
◎ Vocal coaches.
◎ Singing coaches.

Each person in your support team has his or her own specific job and each can help your career in some manner.

Entertainment industry attorneys know what to look for in contracts, what should be there and what shouldn't be there. They can protect you. You can have the most promising career in the world but if you're not protected, you might wind up with nothing.

Generally, personal managers use a standard management contract that includes negotiated points that have been agreed upon by both parties. Negotiating points might include the term of the contract, options, percentage paid to the manager, and areas of management. It is essential to trust your manager because in many cases the manager will want the contract to state that he or she has power of attorney for you or your act. Basically this means that manager has the power to sign contracts on behalf of your act. It also may mean that the manager can spend money on behalf of the act. A savvy attorney will list the specific areas of the artist's career where the manager has power of attorney and limit his or her authority to spend money over a certain amount without authorization. Personal managers are paid a percentage of your gross earnings, ranging from 10 percent to 20 percent.

★ Words from the Wise

Always keep track of your monies. Know what is coming in and what is going out. Even if you use a business manager, make sure you are the one who has control over your monies. Some entertainers over the years have gone from being very wealthy to having nothing. In most of these cases they indicated that one of the main problems was they didn't oversee their finances. If you want to be sure what is being spent, make sure you are the one signing all checks.

Songwriters, Lyricists, and Composers

A hit song can earn a tremendous amount of money depending on how it's exploited. Similarly, so can the songs from a major Broadway musical. Let's take some time now to discuss your career as a songwriter or composer. You've written songs. You have confidence that they're good. What do you do with them now?

The number-one piece of advice is to register them for copyright protection. This not only protects you, but the people to whom you are sending your material. Once that's done you have a number of options depending on the direction you want your career to go.

You need to make a demo and pitch it in much the same manner as actors looking for representation or artists looking for a recording contract. Many artists write their own material, but others don't and need original songs for their CDs. Even artists who write their own material sometimes need *the perfect tune*, the one that will be a hit on the charts. Are you the songwriter who penned it? Perhaps, but you need to get it to the right people.

Perhaps you can "hear" an established act singing your song. What do you do? If you have access to the act, you might give them a demo and lyric sheet. If you don't have access to those people, consider contacting their management. You can find management names and contact information for most artists in directories such as the *Billboard's Annual Talent & Touring International Guide*. Write a letter introducing yourself and your music and ask for permission to send a tape and lyric sheets.

What else can you do? You might want to pitch your songs to publishers for their catalog. In turn, publishers pitch songs from their catalogs to producers, A&R personnel, record label executives, major and indie artists, advertising agencies, and production companies.

Is your dream composing the music or writing for a Broadway musical? If so you should know this: There might be a great story, there might be great acting, and there might be great singing, but the one element audiences tend to remember most from Broadway musicals is the music.

Over the years, many tunes that have become standards are songs that have emerged from Broadway musicals.

How do you go about composing the music or writing the lyrics for a musical as a career? Of course you need the talent, but in order to move ahead in this industry, you're going to have to network. Let people know what you do. Send samples of your work to producers, directors, and playwrights.

If you're still in school, begin by writing the music for college productions. Look for internships in musical theater.

If you're not in school, start composing for shows in local community theaters.

Work in summer stock, dinner, and regional theaters. If your passion is composing operatic librettos, contact opera companies to see if they have training programs and internships.

What you want to do is start building your resume and making contacts. Keep honing your craft and writing.

Continue making contacts. As you do, you will start to know producers, directors, and playwrights. You're going to have to try to get the attention of people who can use your services. You might, for example, find opportunities at smaller theaters or production companies who are willing to give a new talent a try.

What else can you do? You can work either on your own or collaborate with a lyricist, team up with a playwright, come up with an idea for a production, and develop a project. It sounds simple, but here's the catch: Unless you're independently wealthy, you will need someone to finance the project. You need an *angel*. An angel in theater is the person (or people) who financially backs a production.

How do you find angels? There are many ways. Some put together showcases to garner the attention of people who want to finance theatrical productions. Others put ads in newspapers or magazines seeking angels. Some hob-nob with wealthy people and some just get lucky.

Can you earn a living as a composer or lyricist for musical theater? You can if you're talented and lucky.

In many situations, after a musical production becomes a hit on Broadway, a soundtrack CD is put out. Can it happen to you? It can if you're talented, lucky, at the right place at the right time, and don't give up.

How do you make money as a songwriter? You might "work for hire," which means someone pays you to write a song. In this case you don't usually retain any rights to the song. It belongs to the person who paid you.

The main way you're going to make money as a songwriter is through publishing agreements. Publishing is an important part of making money if you are a composer or songwriter.

The Inside Scoop

Writer's royalties should not be confused with recording royalties that artists receive when appearing on recordings. If an individual is the songwriter and performer on the CD, he or she will receive both writer and recording royalties.

Tip from the Top

As a songwriter you want to be affiliated with one of the three performance rights agencies, ASCAP, BMI, or SESAC. These organizations collect the royalties due to you for public performance of your songs.

Let's start with the concept that you wrote the song and are the copyright holder and owner. As the copyright holder and owner of a song or composition, you have certain rights. These include, among others, the exclusive right to perform your song in public, the right to record it, the right to write down the music and lyrics and print them, and the right to use your music along with a visual image. No one else has these rights to your song, unless they pay you to do so. When that occurs, you are in effect granting them a license. This is called publishing and this is how you make money as a songwriter.

There are four main areas of publishing income. These include:

Primary sources
◎ Performance
   ▫ *Performance rights* are the rights
    to perform your song in public.
    Royalties are paid when your song is
    performed or played in public, on the
    radio, in elevators, in music services,
    or anywhere else. BMI, ASCAP,
    and SESAC are the performance
    rights organizations that collect the
    monies from people, businesses, and
    organizations who play your music.
◎ Mechanical
   ▫ *Mechanical rights* are the rights to
    reproduce your song. Royalties are

paid by the record label for the use of your song or songs on recordings. Each time someone makes a physical copy of your song on a CD, cassette, or record, you are paid a royalty.

Secondary sources

◎ Print

    ▫ A *print license* means that every time someone writes down or prints your song and publishes it, as the copyright holder and owner, you receive payment. This would include sheet music such as piano scores and music books.

◎ Synchronization

    ▫ A *synchronization license* means that every time your song is played along with a visual image you are paid. This includes things like background music used in television, films, and commercials; title songs for television, film soundtracks, and videos; and many other uses.

With all this money coming in from your songs, how do you collect it? How do you know who should pay what? Many songwriters contract with publishers. Their job is to collect the monies owed to you from all publishing agreements and licenses. In order for them to do so, you generally have to assign your copyright to the publisher. While there are exceptions, the standard publishing agreement usually gives the publisher half of the revenues collected as a fee.

There are some songwriters who administer their own publishing by creating their own publishing companies. This can be very time consuming, but they also keep the extra revenue. Which option should you take? Only you can decide.

★ The Inside Scoop

Rates for mechanical royalties are set by the U.S. Copyright Office. Currently, mechanical rates are 9.1 cents per song. That means that if one of the songs you have written is on a CD which sells 100,000 units, you would have earned $9,100. If two of the songs were on that same CD which sold 100,000 units you would have earned $18,200. Keep in mind that if the songs are used in other ways you will earn additional monies as the copyright holder.

Copyrights

If you are a songwriter, lyricist, or composer, how important is protecting yourself in the industry? If you want to enjoy the fruits of your labor, it's very important. How do you protect yourself as a songwriter? You register your songs for copyright protection.

Technically, the minute you write a song down or put it on tape it is copyrighted. Without proof, however, it's often very difficult to prove.

How do you register for copyright protection? It's simple. Contact the U.S. Copyright Office, get the forms, fill them in, and send them in with payment. As this is written, it is $45. Depending on your situation, you may want to register your printed lyrics and music as well as the recorded version of your song embedded on a tape. If you have a number of songs to register, you might want to register them all on one tape. That way while they're all registered, it will only cost one fee.

U.S. Copyright Office
Library of Congress
Washington, DC 20559
(202) 707-3000
http://www.copyright.gov

Playwrights

If you think about it, in order for any theatrical production to take place, there needs to be a play. The person responsible for this is the playwright.

Do you want to be a playwright? If the answer is yes, you should know this: Writing the play is just the first step in your quest for success. In order to be successful, you need to find a way to get your words coming out of someone's lips—live, on stage.

And that is the challenge. Finding ways to get your words turned into live productions.

If your dream is to become a successful playwright, what can you do to increase your chances? How can you break in? What can you do?

As in other parts of the industry, you're going to need to get experience. Find amateur theater companies who might be looking for a good script. Get involved in community theater. Keep plugging away and telling people what you are doing. You can never tell what can happen.

A woman I knew who had no playwriting experience wrote her first script and told everyone she talked to about it. Within a short amount of time, a local theater group asked to see the script, read it, and decided to produce the play. According to the woman, seeing her story come to life on stage and hearing the words she had written in the script coming out of the actors' mouths made it all real. It was a dream come true. It happened to her, and it can happen to you.

Look for workshops, seminars, and classes. They provide you with the opportunity to learn, write, and most importantly, be reviewed. While it's difficult, try to take any criticism as a positive thing.

What else can you do? Get together with some actors who are trying to showcase *their* talents. Consider collaborating on a project for a showcase. The actors will have the ability to showcase their talents and your script will get exposure.

In the same vein you can also arrange for a reading or produce a condensed version of the play yourself. To do this you will have to find ways to get theater companies and producers to come, but if it works, it can be well worth the trouble.

One of the best ways to get your name out there is to look for established competitions for playwrights. Many of these are sponsored by play publishers, regional and community theaters, local and national theater organizations, and colleges.

It also is useful to join dramatists associations and other professional groups. These organizations help put you in touch with others in the same field and give you the opportunity to make the contacts necessary to succeed in this field.

The New Dramatist, for example, is a service organization for scriptwriters. The Dramatist Guild offers its members assistance in a number of areas including a tremendous amount of professional support. The DG also offers internships and opportunities to have your plays read.

How do you earn money as a playwright? There are a number of different ways. You might sell your script outright for a specific sum. You might also accept an option payment on your script.

Options allow a producer to "own" a script for a specific amount of time to see if financing can be located to produce the production. If financing is found, the producer will then negotiate with the playwright (or his or her representative) for the use of the script. The playwright then receives a royalty every time the script is performed.

What you need to know is that unless you actually sell your play outright, you own it. It's much like writing a book. You might get it published, but it still belongs to you. When a producer or production company decides to use the play, they sign a contract and a licensing agreement. For the rights to use your script, you receive royalties that have been negotiated. Depending on the situation, others may also receive a percentage of royalties. For instance, you may have collaborators on the script, composers, or any other number of people involved.

If you have had your script published, the publishing company will get a percentage of the royalties and you (and any collaborators) will receive a percentage. If your script was not published, you (and your collaborators) receive all the monies.

There are a number of reasons to use a publishing company, the primary one being that in many cases, they stand a better chance of finding producers for your script than you can. Additionally, literary agents are professionals in this field and can often negotiate a better contract. They know what to look for and know what shouldn't be in your contract.

How do you find a publisher? It's similar to finding a book publisher. You can either look for one yourself or retain a literary agent to do this for you.

If you write a script and it turns into a Broadway mega hit, you can earn a great deal of money in this field. It has happened to many others and it can happen to you!

How do you get your play produced? In a nutshell, in order to get your play produced you have to get it to the people who produce plays including theaters and producers. That way they can read it over to see if they are interested.

How do you do this? You simply submit your script to theaters and producers who accept submissions. Keep in mind that not everyone accepts submissions. In many cases, submissions will only be accepted through an agent. Where do you find these? The easiest way is to look through a copy of the *Dramatist Sourcebook.*

Once you find the producers and theaters who accept new scripts, find out how they want them submitted. For example, do they want a full script? Do they want a synopsis? Do they want sample pages?

When you send out your script, be prepared to wait. Producers and theaters can receive thousands of scripts. It takes time to go through them. Don't be discouraged. It's a waiting game.

Will a producer or theater accept every script? Absolutely not. Every playwright, no matter how successful they are, has received rejection letters. But all you need to do to start is to get one acceptance letter, and you're on your way.

Protecting Yourself

I've given you a lot of advice in this book. We've covered a lot of different areas. Here is one of the most important things I have to tell you. As a creative talent, what you have to sell is *you*. You are the product. Whether you are an actor, singer, musician, songwriter, producer, arranger, or any other person on the creative talent end of the performing arts, if you don't protect yourself, you will have nothing! Do not get so caught up in what you want that you forget this fact.

If you take nothing else from this book, I hope you'll take this: I want you to protect yourself. Before you sign a contact—any contract—I want you to not only read it, but *know* and *understand* what you're reading. If you don't understand something, no matter how small, ask. Don't be embarrassed, don't feel stupid, and don't feel like someone will laugh at you. If you don't understand something—anything at all in a contract you are asked to sign, even if it is one little word—ask and get an explanation until you do understand. No ifs, ands, or buts!

If you're thinking, "Isn't that what lawyers are for?" the simple answer is yes. But that doesn't mean that you should leave your career to chance. Just because a lawyer or agent or anyone else you trust reads over a contract you have to sign, doesn't mean you shouldn't too. After you read it, ask your adviser about points you don't understand.

At some time during your career, I can almost guarantee you, someone, whether it be a manager, an agent, or a publisher will give you something to sign and say to you something to the effect of: "You can read it over if you want, but it's a standard contract. You're really wasting your time."

Should you take their word? No! Read everything. They probably are telling the truth, but perhaps their version of standard is not your version. Read every word and every line.

I can also guarantee you sometime in your career someone will say to you one or more of the following.

◎ "We don't need a contract, we trust each other."
  ▫ You need a contract.
◎ "We're friends, we don't need a contract."
  ▫ A contract will assure you will stay friends.
◎ "It's a simple gig. Don't worry about a contract. All you have to do is show up, work, and you'll get paid."
  ▫ You will have little recourse if you don't get paid. You need a contract or an agreement of sorts.
◎ "A verbal contract is as good as a written one."
  ▫ Not really. You can produce a written contract. Even if you have a witness to what was said, a written contract is better.
◎ "A contract is only as good as the paper it's written on."
  ▫ While contracts can be broken, they are still contracts.
◎ "Let's just shake on it."
  ▫ You can shake on it, after you sign a contract.

Are you getting the idea? You need to protect yourself. Do you always need a complicated contract? No, a simple agreement can sometimes suffice, but you should always have some sort of dated agreement signed by both parties stating what is expected of you, when it is expected, and what is expected in return. The best person to give you advice in this area is an attorney.

Unions

If you work in the performing arts industry, somewhere along the line you're going to have to decide if you want to belong to a union.

To begin with, you should be aware that there are a number of different unions. Each represents a different part of the entertainment industry. The main union for actors in the entertainment industry is affiliated with the AFL-CIO and called the Associated Actors and Artistes of America, which is also referred to as 4A. Under the auspices of this union are branches that relate to specific areas of acting. The most popular of these include in following:

◎ Actors' Equity Association (AEA; http://www.actorsequity.org), which is often referred to simply as Equity, represents actors and actresses who work in theater and stage managers.
◎ American Federation of Television and Radio Artists (AFTRA; http://www.aftra.org) represents performers, journalists and other artists working in the entertainment and news media.
◎ Screen Actors Guild (SAG; http://www.sag.org) represents actors involved in films.

Why join a union? There are a number of reasons. As a member of a union, you have access to a lot more casting calls. In order to work in any Broadway theater, or even any major Off Broadway production, you must be a member of the Equity. As a matter of fact most well-known regional theaters work under the rules of Equity as well. What that means is that if you want to act in those productions, you have to be a union member.

You should be aware that in order to work in television, commercials, news, broadcast journalism, film, the recording business, or a variety of other areas you must join SAG or AFTRA. You don't have a choice. So, if you are planning to act in some commercials while you are getting your stage career on track, you land a one-time role in a television series, or you get some voice-over work, you will have to become a member of the appropriate union.

Unions work hard for their members. One of the most important reasons to join a union is that they negotiate and enforce collective bargaining agreements guaranteeing minimum wages as well as working conditions. What that means to you is that if you are working under a union contract, you can be assured that you will be treated fairly and not be taken advantage of.

An important benefit of joining one of the unions is the benefits themselves. These include health insurance, retirement and pension plans, and credit unions. As a performing artist, these benefits can be very helpful.

Additionally, unions provide professional support, educational resources, seminars, and often information on casting.

Now that we've discussed why you should join a union, let's briefly discuss why you shouldn't rush out to join. Once you join Equity, you no longer are allowed to take any non-union roles. What that means is that if you don't have a lot of experience and are trying to get roles to build up your resume, you won't have the luxury of taking *any role*. If the theater isn't an Equity theater, you are out of luck. If you are searching for roles and are offered one in a non-Equity theater, you can't take it.

This doesn't mean you should never join the union. What it means is that when you are just starting out with your career, get as much experience as possible and then, when your career starts to get on track, become a member.

Becoming a union member can be expensive. Depending on the specific union, for actors, the initiation fees are over $1,000. You also are expected to pay annual dues plus a percentage of your salary, which is calculated on the specific union's jurisdiction. For example, Equity dues are approximately $100 annually. You are then expected to pay approximately 2 percent of your salary from Equity contracts.

There are a number of other unions you should be aware of depending on the specific area of the performing arts in which you are working. These include:

- American Guild of Variety Artists (AGVA) represents performers in Broadway, off-Broadway and cabaret productions, live performers in variety shows, touring productions and theme parks.
- American Guild of Musical Artists (AGMA; http://www.musicalartists.org) represents all the artists in most of the leading opera and dance companies as well as at other performing arts institutions.
- American Federation of Musicians (AFM; http://www.afm.org) represents professional musicians.

The Inside Scoop

Depending on the situation in which you are working, you may be under the auspices of a number of different unions.

- Society of Stage Directors and Choreographers (SSDC; http://www.ssdc.org) represents stage directors and chorographers who work in theater.
- Directors Guild of America (DGA; http://www.dga.org) represents film and television directors, technical coordinators, stage managers and production associates.
- Writers Guild of America (WGA; http://www.wga.org) represents writers of films and television programs.
- Internal Alliance of Theatrical Stage Employees (IATSE; http://www.iatse-intl.org) represents stagehands and projectionists among others.
- Association of Theatrical Press Agents and Managers (ATPAM; http://www.atpam.com) represents theatrical press agents.

13

SUCCESS IS YOURS FOR THE TAKING

Do You Have What It Takes?

In 1954 Ethel Merman belted out the words, "There's no business like show business," in the Hollywood musical of the same name. The film centered around the trials and tribulations of a family of vaudeville entertainers.

More than 50 years later, there *still* is no business like show business. While there have been changes in the industry, much is still the same. There are still those who want to perform; those who want to work behind the scenes; those who want to work on the business end of the industry, and, luckily, those who still want to be entertained.

I'm assuming that if you made it this far in the book, whether you want to work on the front line or behind the scenes or anywhere in between in the performing arts, this is still your dream.

One of the common characteristics you find in the majority of people who really want a career in theater or the performing arts is that they almost seem to have it in their blood. And once it's there, it's difficult to get out.

If this is you—and you know who you are—I need to ask you a very important question.

Do you have what it takes?

"What do you mean, do I have what it takes?" you ask.

Do you have what it takes to be a successful professional in the performing arts?

"Well . . . I think so," you say.

You think so? That's not good enough. You have to know so! Because if you don't believe in yourself, no one else will.

"Okay," you say. "I get it. I *know* I can be successful."

That's good! That's the attitude you need to succeed.

With that out of the way, let's go over a couple of other things that can help you in your quest for success. You have to remember that no matter what comes your way, you can't give up. Whatever you have had to deal with, when you achieve your goals you most likely will feel it was worth it. There may be stumbling blocks. You may have to take detours. There may even be times you have to choose when you reach a fork in the road. But if you give up, it's over.

Here's something else you should know. When you share your dreams and goals with others about working in the performing arts, there will always be some people who insist on telling you the statistics of the industry.

They will try to tell you how many actors aren't working; how difficult it is to succeed; how few dancers, singers, musicians, comedians, playwrights, or directors *really* make it. They might say, "It's not that you're not talented, but..."

If you listen to those people and start believing them, you probably will become one of their statistics. If you pay attention to them, then a career in theater or any of the other performing arts probably isn't for you.

However, if you have gotten to this section of the book, I'm guessing you aren't going to let anyone influence you and you are still going after your dream.

Here's something to think about. Statistically, it's difficult for most people to lose weight, yet there are many people who do. Statistically, most people who play the lottery don't win, yet there are always winners. Will it be you? Not if you don't enter.

With those things in mind, I stand behind what I have said throughout this book. No matter what the statistics are, someone has to succeed. Why shouldn't it be you? Someone has to be at the top. If you give up your dream, someone else will be there. You will be standing on the outside looking in and watching someone doing what you want. I don't think that's your dream.

Will it be easy? Not always. But the industry is huge. It is jam packed with wonderful and fulfilling opportunities. Why shouldn't you live your dream and be part it?

Whether you want to be in the forefront of the industry, behind the scenes, or somewhere in between, know this: You *can* do it and do it successfully as long as you don't give up.

Throughout your journey, always keep your eye on the prize: the great career you are working toward in the performing arts.

Sometimes your dream may change. That's okay. As long as you are following *your* dreams, not those of others, you are usually on the right road.

Whatever segment of the performing arts you select to work in, your choices are huge. What is going to be your contribution to this magical industry? Are you going to be the starring actress in a Broadway play? Are you going to be a cast member in the chorus of a Broadway musical? How about the actress starring in a touring production or regional theater?

Are you going to be the one who writes the libretto or the one who sings in the opera? Will you be the composer for the newest Broadway show? Are you going to be the songwriter, writing the words and music for other performing artists? Will you be the one who sings or plays the music? How about the one who produces or records it?

Are you going to give vocal lessons to singers, teach musicians how to play better or be a drama coach to promising actors and actresses? Is your job going to be in arts administration in an orchestra, opera or ballet company? Will you be working in the box office of a theater? Will you be working at a record label? A music publisher? A talent or booking agency? Are you the one who is going to cast the next big star?

Will you be the one who promotes and publicizes the newest play? Or will you be the one

---

⭐ **Words from the Wise**

The difference between perseverance and obstinacy is that one often comes from a strong will, and the other from a strong won't.
—Henry Ward Beecher

publicizing performing artists and helping to catapult their careers? Are you going to be working in the sales and marketing end of an opera, orchestra, ballet, or theatrical company? Will you be doing their fund raising and development?

Will you be designing or creating the costumes for productions? What about designing the sets? Will you be the production makeup artist or hair stylist?

Are you going to be a music, dance, or theater reviewer or critic? What about an entertainment industry journalist?

Will your career be managing performing artists? What about finding them work, booking them or handling their legal affairs?

What path do you want to follow? Where do you envision yourself? What do you see yourself doing? Seize your opportunity. It's there for you. Grab onto your dream to start the ball rolling.

Over the years, I've talked to many people who are extremely successful in all facets of the performing arts. One of the most interesting things about them is that most were *not* surprised at all that they were successful. As a matter of fact, they expected it.

I remember sitting backstage at a concert before a show talking to one of the singers in the act. We were discussing some of the other hot artists in the industry. The singer was telling me a story of another singer on the charts. "We

knew he was going to be a star," he said about the other artist. "When he was still in school, he told everyone he was going to be one, and that's all he talked about. "

"Doesn't everyone say that?" I asked.

"Sometimes they do," he continued, "but what made him different was he was specific about what he was going to do and when. He told everyone he was going to have a hit record before he graduated. [He hadn't even recorded anything at that time.] He started acting like a star and then dressing the part of a star. He went on and on about it so much that he almost had to be a star to save face. Funny thing was, he did have a hit before he graduated and he did turn into a huge star."

I know of at least three singers in the industry who told me that they chose outfits to wear to the Grammy's and American Music Awards the week they recorded their songs. Not only that; they wrote their acceptance speech. You know what? I later saw them pull those speeches out and read when they won.

A number of years ago a woman worked in our office who was also a trained concert violinist. When I first met her she pulled a business card out of her purse. I looked at it and it had her name, the name of a large orchestra and the position of concertmistress.

"Were you the concertmistress of that orchestra before you moved here," I asked?

"No," she replied. "But I know I will sit in the concertmistress seat at that orchestra sometime. I'm not sure when, but I know I will."

After the woman left our company, we lost touch. However, while I was doing some research on orchestras, I came across her name. She had landed that position.

I had a client who told me he had written his first acceptance speech for a Tony Award while he was still in elementary school. He revised it

---

⭐ Words from the Wise

Throughout all history, the great wise men and teachers, philosophers, and prophets have disagreed with one another on many different things. It is only on this one point that they are in complete and unanimous agreement. We become what we think about.

−Earl Nightingale

in junior high and then again in high school. He still carries around his speech in his wallet and while he hasn't yet won the award, he just landed a role which is sure to give him the opportunity to use it. The point is, when he is nominated and wins a Tony, he won't really be surprised.

Is it the planning and the work that creates the reality or is it the dream that puts them on the road to success? I think it's a combination.

Have you picked out your Tony outfit? Have your written your acceptance speech? Are you ready for success?

In case you're thinking that you're only supposed to *expect* success if your career aspirations are in the talent or creative area of the performing arts, think again. You should expect success in all areas of the performing arts from the front lines to behind the scenes, and from the talent and creative end to the business and administrative side of the industry.

Think about your success. Visualize it. Feel it. When any negative thought about your career comes into your head, replace it with a positive one.

Imagine the feeling you will have as your show ends and the audience is applauding and giving you a standing ovation. Can you hear the cheers? Can you feel the excitement? If not, visualize it until you can. That is what you're working toward.

Have you chosen the perfect suit you're going to wear when you get promoted to executive director of the orchestra? Can you see what you will be wearing when you sign the hottest actor to your roster in your talent agency? Can you picture what your office will look like? Do you know what you're going to say?

If not, you should—at least in your mind. Why? Because if you claim something, you're often closer to making it happen.

Over the years, I have heard many similar stories from people who have made it as very successful actors, singers, musicians, songwriters, dancers, composers, comedians, record company executives, publicists, journalists, and others. Was it that they knew what they wanted to do and focused on it more than others? Was it a premonition and things just worked out? Were they just lucky? Were they more talented than others? Was it visualization? Or was it that a positive attitude helped create a positive situation? No one really knows. The only thing that seems evident is that those who *expect* to be successful usually have a better chance of achieving it. Those who have a positive attitude usually have a better chance of positive things happening.

We've covered visualization earlier in the book. Whether you believe this theory or not, one thing is for sure: It can't hurt. So start planning your own party for your Tony win. Plan your own celebration for your promotion or for the career of which you've been dreaming. Plan for your own success, and then get ready for it to happen.

Creating a Career You Love

While working toward your perfect career, it's important to combine your goals with your life objectives. The trick to success in any industry is not only following your interests but following your heart. If you're working toward your dream, going that extra mile and doing that extra task won't be a chore.

And when you run into obstacles along the way, they won't be problems, just stepping-stones to get you where you're going.

By now, you have read some (if not all) of this book. You've learned that there are certain things you need to do to stack the deck in your favor whether you want your success to be on the business or talent end of the industry.

You know how to get put together your resume, bio, press kits, and more. You know how to find casting calls. You know what to do at auditions and what not to do.

You know about agents, managers, and other people on your team. You know about unions and you know how important it is to read everything before you sign a contract so you can protect yourself.

You've learned how to network and how to market yourself. You've learned some neat little tips and tricks to get your foot in the door. You've learned that you need to find ways to stand out from the crowd. You've also learned that the performing arts industry is part of show business, and that show business is a *business*, and you're ready to treat it as such.

Most of all, you've learned that it's essential to create a career you love. You've learned that you don't ever want to settle and wonder, "What if?"

Creating the career you want and love is not always the easiest thing in the world to accomplish, but it is definitely worth it. To help you focus on what you want, you might find it helpful to create a personal mission statement.

Your Personal Mission Statement

There are many people who want a career in theater and the performing arts. Some will make it and some will not. I want you to be one who makes it. I want you to be one who succeeds. Throughout the book, I've tried to give you tips, tricks, and techniques that can help. I've tried to give you the inspiration and motivation to know you can do it. Here's one more thing that might make your journey easier.

Create your personal mission statement. Why? Because your mission statement can help you define your visions clearly. It will give you a path, a purpose, and something to follow. Most important, putting your mission statement in writing can help you bring your mission to fruition.

What's a mission statement? It's a statement declaring what your mission is in your life and your career. How do you do it? As with all the other exercises you've done, sit down, get comfortable, take out a pen and a piece of paper, and start writing. What is your mission?

Remember that your mission statement is for *you*. You're not writing it for your family, your friends, or your employer. It can be changed or modified at any time.

Think about it for a moment. What do you want to do? Where do you want be? What's the path you want to take? What are your dreams? What is your mission?

There is no one right way to write your mission statement. Some people like to write it in paragraph form. Others like to use bullets or numbers. It really doesn't matter as long as you get it down in writing. The main thing to remember is to make your statement a clear and concise declaration of your long-term mission.

Your mission statement might be one sentence, one paragraph, or even fill two or three pages. It's totally up to you. As long as your mission statement is clear, you're okay.

Here are some examples of simple mission statements.

◎ An actor
  ▫ My mission is to use my skills and talent to get great leading roles and create a career as a top Broadway star.
◎ A singer
  ▫ My mission is to use my skills and talent to create a career as a top recording and performing artist.

- An opera singer
  - My mission is to use my skills and talent to create a career as a principal opera singer starring at the Metropolitan Opera and performing throughout the world.
- A dancer
  - My mission is to use my skills and talent to create a career as a modern dancer performing as a principal in Broadway shows.
- A ballet dancer
  - My mission is to use my skills and talent to create a career dancing as a principal in the New York City Ballet.
- A costume designer
  - My mission is to use my talents to create a career designing the costumes for Broadway productions.

What do you do with your mission statement? Use it! Review it to remember what you're working toward. Use it as motivation. Use it to help you move in the right direction.

You would be surprised at how many successful people have their personal mission statement hanging on their wall, taped to their computer, or in their pocket. I've seen actors who keep a copy of their mission statement taped to their dressing room mirrors, their bathroom mirrors, and their refrigerators. I've seen touring recording artists who have their mission statements hanging on the mirror in their tour bus. I've seen musicians who have their mission statement attached to the inside of their instrument case.

I've also been in the offices of press agents, publicists, journalists, casting directors, producers, and directors who have their mission statement stuck on their computer monitor, taped inside of a desk drawer, or tucked into their

---

> **Tip from the Coach**
>
> Put your personal mission statement on post-it notes and stick them up all around to keep you focused.

pocket or wallet so they can look at it on a regular basis.

Wherever you decide to place your mission statement, be sure to look at it daily so you can always keep it in mind. It makes it easier to stay focused on your ultimate goal.

Success Strategies

We have discussed marketing, promotion, and publicity. Used effectively, they can help your career tremendously. Here's what you have to remember: Don't wait for someone else to recognize your skills and talents; promote yourself. There are many keys to success in the performing arts. Self-promotion is an important one.

Don't toot your own horn in an annoying or obnoxious manner, but make sure people notice you. You want to stand out in a positive way. Don't keep your accomplishments a secret. Instead claim them proudly.

We've all been taught to be modest. "Don't boast," your mother might have said as you were growing up. But if your goal is success in your career, sometimes you can just be too quiet for your own good.

Your ultimate challenge is to create buzz. You need others to know what you've done and what you're doing in the future. Some people aren't willing or able to do what it takes. If you want to succeed, it's imperative that you get started. Buzz doesn't usually happen overnight, but every day you wait to try to get it is another day you're behind in the job.

The Inside Scoop

Don't procrastinate when an opportunity presents itself. Someone else is always on the lookout just like you, and you don't want to miss your chance.

Begin to think like a publicist even if you're lucky enough to have one. Whether you're working on the business or talent end of the industry, you need to constantly promote yourself or no one will know you exist. While others may help, the responsibility really is on *you* to make your career work and make your career successful.

No matter where you are in your career, continue to look for opportunities of all kinds. Search out opportunities to move ahead in your career and then grab hold of them.

Also know that in your life and career, on occasion, there may be doors that close. The trick here is not to let a door close without looking for the window of opportunity that is always there. If you see an opportunity, jump on it immediately.

Throughout the book we've discussed the importance of networking. Once you become successful, it's important to continue to network. Just because you have an agent does not mean that you don't want to meet other agents. Just because you landed a new job in handling the fund-raising and development at the symphony, doesn't mean you don't want to meet other arts administration executives. Just because you signed a contract with a label does not mean you don't want to meet other label executives. Just because you've signed up with a new drama coach, doesn't mean you shouldn't check out new coaches.

Whether you've landed a new job as a set designer, costume designer, prop person, publicist, journalist, or anything else in the performing arts, keep networking. Continue meeting people. Continue getting your name out there. You can never tell who knows whom and what someone might need. There are always new opportunities ahead, and if you don't keep networking, you might miss some of them.

This is especially important in the talent area where job security is difficult. If you land a role in a production, don't get so caught up in the job that you forget to network and market yourself. Make sure industry executives and insiders know about what you're doing. Send out flyers, postcards, and e-mails. Give them a call and invite them to your shows and performances. Keep nurturing your network and developing contacts.

Don't be afraid to ask for help. If you know someone who can help in your career, ask. The worst they can say is no. The best that can happen is you might get some assistance. Of course, if you can help someone else, do that as well.

Always be prepared for success. It might be just around the corner. Whatever segment of the industry you are pursuing, continue honing your craft. Rehearse until you're perfect. Keep taking classes, seminars, and workshops. Keep up with trends, read the trades, and make sure you know what is happening today.

Stay as fit and healthy as you can. Try to eat right, get sleep, exercise, and take care of yourself. After all your hard work, you don't want to finally succeed and be too sick or tired to enjoy it.

Whatever facet of the industry you're in, you are going to be selling yourself. You might be selling yourself for a role, a job, an engagement, or to have your choice of a manager or agent to represent you. You might be pitching yourself or your story for publicity or a variety of other situations. Take a lesson from others who have made it to the top and prepare ahead of time. That way when you're in a situation where you need to say something, you'll be ready. Come up with a pitch and practice it until you're comfortable.

Always be positive. Attitude is essential to your life and your professional success. People want to be around other people who are positive. If there is a choice between two people with similar talents and skills and you have a better outlook than anyone else, a more positive type of personality and passion, you're going to be chosen. You're going to get the job. You're going to succeed.

Change the way you look at situations and the situations you look at will change. What does that mean? Basically it means that the way you view a situation is the way it will be.

You can create a self-fulfilling prophecy. If you look at a situation as a problem, it will be a problem. If, on the other hand, you look at a situation as an opportunity, it becomes one. If you look at the performing arts industry and all you see are the trials and tribulations of trying to succeed, all you will have is trials and tribulations. If, on the other hand, you look at the road to success in this industry as a wonderful and exciting journey, it will be.

Climbing the Career Ladder

Generally, whatever you want to do in life, you most likely are going to have to pay your dues. Whatever part of the performing arts you have chosen to pursue, most likely you're going to have to *pay your dues* as well. Now that we've accepted that fact, the question is, how do you climb the career ladder? How do you succeed?

How do you go, for example, from a job as an assistant to the director of a department? How do you go from a coordinator to the vice president of an orchestra, ballet, or opera com-

pany? How do you go from writing plays that no one even looks at to becoming a successful playwright?

How do you go from an unknown actor to one of the hottest commodities around? How do you go from a struggling comedian to headlining in Las Vegas? How do you go from a dance student to a prima ballerina?

There are many things you're going to have to do, but it can be done. We've covered a lot of them. Work hard, keep a positive attitude, and act professionally at all times. Stay abreast of the business, network, and hone your skills and talents so you can back up your claims of accomplishments.

Look for a mentor who can help you move your career in the right direction and propel you to the top of your field. Join trade associations and unions. Read the trades; take seminars, classes, and workshops; and take part in other learning opportunities. Be the best at what you do. Keep your goal in mind.

Look at every opportunity with an open mind. When you're offered something, ask yourself:

- Is this what I want to be doing?
- Is this part of my dream?
- Is this part of my plan for success?
- Is this opportunity a stepping-stone to advancing my career?
- Will this experience be valuable to me?

Fortunately or unfortunately, job progression in the performing arts doesn't always follow the normal career path. A new assistant working in a talent agency who helps find the next big star may strike out on his or her own or be promoted to a management position before someone with seniority who has not had a similar accomplishment.

The next time you see the production assistant at a casting call, he or she might be part of the casting crew or even on stage as an actor.

A relatively new actor in a small role who gets a great review from a popular critic may be offered a leading role before an actor who has been working in the industry for years.

An understudy who steals the show might very well become a star. It all depends.

The opening act at a concert in June might be the headliner by September if their new record hits the chart with a bullet and moves up to the top 10. There are countless stories of people who have been fans in the back of an arena one year, who are the headliners the next year, or fans of a particular theatrical production who within a short amount of time are starring in the same show. If it can happen to someone else, it might happen to you.

That is one of the greatest things about a career in the performing arts. You just never know what tomorrow might bring.

You never know when your play is going to be picked up by a producer; your song is going to be recorded by a successful artist; your performance will garner major media attention; or your role as an understudy is changed to that of the leading actor or actress.

You never know when an audition is going to land you a great role, a seat in the orchestra of your dreams, a principal role in an opera, or the lead in a ballet. You never know when someone will see your costumes, set design, lighting, or choreography and your career will catapult upwards. You never know when someone will be sitting in a little club, hears your comedy, and offers you your own television show or a headlining tour. You really never know when success will come your way. It can happen at any time . . . if you don't give up.

It should be noted that success means different things to different people. There are many successful people who work in the performing arts who are not mega stars yet they earn a high income and enjoy the creativity of being a performer, whether it be an actor, singer, musician, dancer, comedian or other performing artist. You might not know their names or their faces, but they are working in the industry just the same.

And it's not just in the talent segment of the industry. It's in all aspects of the creative, business, and administrative areas. There are playwrights, directors, producers, composers, costume designers, set designers, chorographers and more. There are publicists, press agents, talent agents, booking agents, publishers, arts administrators and the list goes on. They might not work on Broadway or in one of the major orchestras, operas or ballet companies, but that doesn't preclude them from having a successful career in the performing arts.

Some actors and actresses work in regional theater, dinner theater, or a variety of other situations. Some do voice-over work or modeling or end up working in television or films. Comedians may not headline, but may work in clubs throughout the country. Some singers and musicians back-up other acts either live or in recording sessions. Some performing artists travel throughout the country or the world on either a regional or national level performing in hotels, casinos, resorts, theaters, bars, clubs, and theme parks. And in each of these situations they may need directors, producers, choreographers, set designers and more.

There are playwrights, songwriters and composers who while they haven't written one of the more popular plays or a top ten song, are earning very good livings writing scripts or composing for other projects or jingles for commercials.

Risk Taking—Overcoming Your Fears

Everyone has a comfort zone from which they operate. What's a comfort zone? It's the area where you feel comfortable both physically and psychologically. Most of the time, you try to stay within this zone. It's predictable, it's safe, and you generally know what's coming.

Many people get jobs, stay in them for years, and then retire. They know what's expected of them. They know what they're going to be doing. They know what they're going to be getting. The problem is that it can get boring, there's little challenge, and your creativity can suffer.

Stepping out of your comfort zone is especially important in the performing arts, where creativity is essential. Wanting to step out of your comfort zone is often easier said than done, but every now and then you're going to have to push yourself.

You might remember actor Jerry Orbach for his role as Detective Lennie Briscoe in *Law and Order*. What you might not know is that Orbach originally worked in theater, first as an understudy and then a star in musicals both on and off Broadway. He moved out of his comfort zone to star in television and films.

Tip from the Coach

If you're starting to feel comfortable in your career or starting to feel bored, it's time to step out of your comfort zone and look for new challenges.

Rosie O'Donnell began her career as a comedienne. She stepped out of her comfort zone to become an award-winning talk show host, to star in films and Broadway, and even to produce a Broadway production.

Lionel Ritchie and Beyonce were both part of successful groups before they stepped out of their comfort zone and became successful solo artists. Ray Romano and Kevin James were successful comedians before stepping out of their comfort zones to become major television actors.

The key to career success in the performing arts as well as your own personal growth is the willingness to step outside of your comfort zone. Throughout your career you're going to be faced with decisions. Each decision can impact your career. Be willing to take risks. Be willing to step out of your comfort zone.

Is it scary? Of course, but if you don't take risks you stand the chance of your career stagnating. You take the chance of missing wonderful opportunities.

Should you take a promotion? Should you stay at the same job? Should you go to a different company? Should you change managers? Should you change agents? Should you move to New York or stay in Chicago? What songs are best for your new CD? Should you take a chance on a new publicist?

How do you make the right decision? Try to think about the pros and cons of your choices. Get the facts, think about them, and make your decision.

"What if I'm wrong?" you ask.

Here's the good news. Usually you *will* make the right decision. If by chance you don't, it's generally not a life and death situation. If you stay at the same job and find you should have left, for example, all you need to do is look

---

> ### ⭐ Tip from the Top
>
> Try to treat everyone from subordinates to superiors to colleagues the way you want to be treated—with respect and dignity. In addition to following the golden rule, know that the way career progression sometimes works in the performing arts, you can never tell when the people who are your subordinates today, might be your colleagues or superiors tomorrow.

---

for a new job. If you change personal managers and you're not happy, either you can find a loophole or eventually your contract will end. Most things ultimately work out. Do the best you can and then go on.

If your career is stagnant, do something. Don't just stay where you are because of the fear of leaving your comfort zone and the fear of the unknown.

Some Final Thoughts

No matter where you are in your career, don't get stagnant. Always keep your career moving. Once you reach one of your goals, your journey isn't over. You have to keep moving on to the next one.

Sean "Puffy" Combs was a very successful hip-hop performer. He could have stayed where he was, but his journey wasn't over. He became a producer of hit records for other artists. Did he stop there? No! Combs went on to start a clothing line, and to star in movies and a television show. Was he done? Did he let his career become stagnant? No. Combs landed a starring role in the Broadway production of *A Raisin In The Sun*. The point is that no matter how successful your career is, you need to continually work at taking it up a level.

Are you acting in regional theater? Do you want to move up the career ladder? Keep working toward your goal. It can happen. Supporting roles on Broadway are great. A career as a lead actor or actress is better. Keep trying. Don't give up.

A career doing publicity for a midsize theater is good. A career as a theatrical press agent for Broadway productions might be better. Keep trying.

Don't get caught up in a thought pattern that at least you're working in the industry and settle for less than what you want. Every goal you meet is another stepping-stone toward an even better career in music, whether your goal is to work on the business side, talent side, or somewhere in between.

While I would love to promise you that after reading this book you will land a starring role on Broadway, direct a star-studded Broadway production, become the lead singer at the Metropolitan Opera, or be offered the job of director of an orchestra company, unfortunately I can't.

What I can tell you is that the advice in this book can help you move ahead and stack the deck in your favor in this very competitive business. I've given you the information. You have to put it into action.

> ### ⭐ Words from the Wise
>
> Whatever level you are at in your career in the talent end of the industry, always treat fans, both current and potential ones, well. They are ultimately the ones who can make your career. Fans are the ones who come see your performances, buy your CDs, help spread the word, and cheer you on.

Tip from the Coach

Persevere. The reason most people fail is because they gave up one day too soon.

—Shelly Field

Words from the Wise

Nothing in this world can take the place of persistence. Talent will not; nothing is more common than unsuccessful people with talent. Genius will not; unrewarded genius is almost a proverb. Education will not; the world is full of educated derelicts. Persistence and determination alone are omnipotent.

—Calvin Coolidge

Numerous factors are essential to your success in theater and the performing arts. To succeed in this industry, you need to be prepared. There's no question that preparation is necessary. Talent is critical as well. Being in the right place at the right time is essential, and good luck doesn't hurt.

Perseverance is vital to success in the performing arts no matter what you want to do, what area of the industry you want to enter, and what career level you want to achieve. Do you want to know why most people don't find their perfect job in the performing arts? It's because they gave up looking *before* they found it. Do you want to know why some people are on the brink of success, yet never really get there? It's because they gave up.

Do you want to know what single factor can increase your chances of success? It's perseverance! Don't give up.

Have fun reading this book. Use it to jump-start your career and inspire you to greater success and accomplishments. Draw on it to achieve your goals so you can have the career of your dreams. Use it so you don't have to look back and say, "I wish I had." Use it so you can say, "I'm glad I did."

I can't wait to hear about your success stories. Be sure to let us know how this book has helped your career in theater, music, dance, comedy, or any of the other performing arts by logging on to http://www.shellyfield.com. I would also love to hear about any of your own tips or techniques for succeeding in the performing arts. You can never tell. Your successes might be part of our next edition.

APPENDIX I

TRADE ASSOCIATIONS, UNIONS, AND OTHER ORGANIZATIONS

Trade associations, unions, and other organizations can be valuable resources for career guidance as well as professional support. This listing includes many of the organizations related to the music industry. Names, addresses, phone numbers, Web sites and e-mail addresses (when available) have been included to make it easier for you to obtain information. Check out Web sites to learn more about organizations and what they offer.

Academy of Country Music
4100 West Alemeda
Burbank, CA 91505
(818) 842-8400
info@acmcountry.com
http://www.acmcountry.com

Academy of Television Arts and Sciences (ATAS)
5220 Lankershim Boulevard
North Hollywood, CA 91601
(818) 754-2800
todd@emmys.org
http://www.emmys.org

Actors' Equity Association (AEA)
165 W. 46th Street
New York, NY 10036
(212) 869-8530
equityjobsny@actorsequity.org
http://www.actorsequity.org

Actors Studio
432 W. 44th Street
New York, NY 10036
(212) 757-0870
http://www.actors-studio.com

Alliance of Resident Theatres/New York (A.R.T./New York)
575 8th Avenue
New York, NY 10018
(212) 244-6667
artnewyork@aol.com
http://www.offbroadwayonline.com

American Alliance for Theatre and Education (AATE)
7475 Wisconsin Avenue
Bethesda, MD 20814
(301) 951-7977
info@aate.com
http://www.aate.com

American Association for Music Therapy (AAMT)

8455 Colesville Road
Silver Spring, MD 20910
(301) 589-3300
info@musictherapy.org
http://www.musictherapy.org

American Association of Community Theatre (AACT)

8402 Briar Wood Circle
Lago Vista, TX 78645
(512) 267-0711
info@aact.org
http://www.aact.org

American Ballet Competition (ABC)

2000 Hamilton
Philadelphia, PA 19130
(215) 636-9000
randy@dancecelebration.org
http://www.dancecelebration.org

American Composers Alliance

73 Spring Street
New York, NY 10012
(212) 362-8900
info@composers.com
http://www.composers.com

American Conservatory Theatre Foundation (ACTF)

30 Grant Avenue
San Francisco, CA 94109
(415) 834-3200
sfjimmy@aol.com

American Dance Guild (ADG)

PO Box 2006
Lenox Hill Station

New York, NY 10021
(212) 932-2789
americandanceguild@hotmail.com
http://www.americandanceguild.org

American Dance Therapy Association (ADTA)

2000 Century Plaza
10632 Little Patuxent Parkway
Columbia, MD 21044
(410) 997-4040
info@adta.org
http://www.adta.org

American Federation of Musicians (AFM)

1501 Broadway
New York, NY 10036
(212) 869-1330
info@afm.org
http://www.afm.org

American Federation of Teachers (AFT)

555 New Jersey Avenue NW
Washington, DC 20001
(202) 879-4400
online@aft.org
http://www.aft.org

American Federation of Television and Radio Artists (AFTRA)

260 Madison Avenue
New York, NY 10016
(212) 532-0800
info@aftra.com
http://www.aftra.com

American Guild of Music (AGM)

PO Box 599
Warren, MI 48090
(248) 336-9388
agm@americanguild.org
http://www.americanguild.org

American Guild of Musical Artists (AGMA)

1430 Broadway
New York, NY 10018
(212) 265-3687
agma@musicalartists.org
http://www.musicalartists.org

American Guild of Variety Artists (AGVA)

363 7th Avenue
New York, NY 10001
(212) 675-1003

American Mime Theatre

61 4th Avenue
New York, NY 10003
(212) 777-1710
mime@americanmime.org
http://www.americanmime.org

American Music Conference (AMC)

5790 Armada Drive
Carlsbad, CA 92008
(760) 431-9124
sharonm@amc-music.org
http://www.amc-music.org

American Place Theatre (APT)

266 W 37th Street
New York, NY 10018
(212) 594-4482
contact@americanplacetheatre.org
http://www.americanplacetheatre.org

American Society of Composers and Publishers (ASCAP)

1 Lincoln Plaza
New York, NY 10023
(212) 621-6000
info@ascap.com
http://www.ascap.com

American Society of Journalists and Authors, Inc. (ASJA)

1501 Broadway, Suite 302
New York, NY 10036
(212) 997-0947
webmaster@asja.org
http://www.asja.org

American Society of Music Arrangers and Composers (ASMAC)

PO Box 17840
Encino, CA 91416
(818) 994-4661
properimage2000@earthlink.net
http://www.asmac.org

American Symphony Orchestra League

33 W. 60th Street
New York, NY 10023
(212) 262-5161
league@symphony.org
http://www.symphony.org

American Theatre Arts For Youth (AFAFY)

1429 Walnut Street
Philadelphia, PA 19102
(215) 563-3501
atafyinfo@atafy.org
http://www.atafy.org

American Theatre Critics Association (ATCA)

c/o Theatre Service
PO Box 15282
Evansville, IN 47716
(812) 474-0549
ts@evansville.edu
http://www.americantheatrecritics.org

American Women in Radio and Television (AWRT)

8405 Greensboro Drive
McLean, VA 22102
(703) 506-3290
info@awrt.org
http://www.awrt.org

Associated Actors and Artists of America (AAAA)

165 W. 46th Street
New York, NY 10036
(212) 869-0358

Association for Theatre in Higher Education (ATHE)

PO Box 69
Downers Grove, IL 60515
(630) 964-1940
info@athe.org
http://www.athe.org

Association of Independent Music Publishers (AIMP)

PO Box 69473
Los Angeles, CA 90069
(818) 771-7301
lainfo@aimp.org
http://www.aimp.org

Association of Theatrical Press Agents and Managers, AFL-CIO (ATPAM)

1560 Broadway
New York, NY 10036
(212) 719-3666
info@atpam.com
http://www.atpam.com

Authors Guild (AG)

31 E. 28th Street
New York, NY 10016
(212) 563-5904

staff@authorsguild.org
http://www.authorsguild.org

Ballet Theatre Foundation (BTF)

890 Broadway
New York, NY 10003
(212) 477-3030
http://www.abt.org

Broadcast Music, Inc. (BMI)

320 W. 57th Street
New York, NY 10019
(212) 586-2000
newyork@bmi.com
http://bmi.com

Chamber Music America (CMA)

305 7th Avenue
New York, NY 10001
(212) 242-2022
info@chamber-music.org
http://www.chamber-music.org

Chorus America

1156 15th Street NW
Washington, DC 20005
(202) 331-7577
service@chorusamerica.org
http://www.chorusamerica.org

Costume Designers Guild (CDG)

4730 Woodman Avenue
Sherman Oaks, CA 91423
(818) 905-1557
cdgia@earthlink.net
http://www.costumedesignersguild.com

Country Music Association (CMA)

1 Music Circle South
Nashville, TN 37203
(615) 244-2840

info@cmaworld.com
http://www.cmaworld.com

Dance Critics Association (DCA)

c/o Membership Services
10592 Perry Highway
Wexford, PA 15090
(412) 363-4321
dancecritics@hotmail.com

Dance Educators of America (DEA)

PO Box 607
Pelham, NY 10803
(914) 636-3200
DEA@DEAdance.com
http://www.deadance.com

Dance Masters of America (DMA)

214-10 41st Avenue
PO Box 610533
Bayside, NY 11361
(718) 225-4013
dmamann@aol.com

Dance Theater Workshop (DTW)

219 W. 19th Street
New York, NY 10011
(212) 691-6500
dtw@dtw.org
http://www.dtw.org

Dance/U.S.A.

1156 15th Street NW
Washington, DC 20005
(202) 833-1717
http://www.danceusa.org

Directors Guild of America (DGA)

7920 Sunset Boulevard
Los Angeles, CA 90046
(310) 289-2000
http://www.dga.org

Drama Desk (DD)

244 W. 54th Street, 9th Floor
New York, NY 10019
(212) 586-2600
http://www.dramadesk.com

Dramatists Guild (DG)

1501 Broadway
New York, NY 10036
(212) 398-9366
http://www.dramatistsguild.com

Eugene O'Neill Memorial Theater Center (EOMTC)

305 Great Neck Road
Waterford, CT 06385
(860) 443-5378
info@oneilltheatercenter.org
http://www.theoneill.org

Ford's Theatre Society (FTS)

511 10th Street NW
Washington, DC 20004
(202) 638-2941
onstage@fordtheatre.org
http://www.fordstheatre.org

Friars Club (FC)

57 E. 55th Street
New York, NY 10022
(212) 751-7272
webmonk@friarsclub.com
http://www.friarsclub.com

Gospel Music Association (GMA)

1205 Division Street
Nashville, TN 37203
(615) 242-0303
info@gospelmusic.org
http://www.gospelmusic.org

Graphic Artists Guild (GAG)
90 John Street
New York, NY 10038
(212) 791-3400
http://www.gag.org

Hospital Audiences (HA)
548 Broadway
New York, NY 10012
(212) 575-7676
hai@hospaud.org
http://www.hospitalaudiences.org

Institute of Outdoor Drama (IOD)
CB 3240, 1700 Airport Road
Chapel Hill, NC 27599
(919) 962-1328
outdoor@unc.edu
http://www.unc.edu/depts/outdoor

Institute of the American Musical (IAM)
121 N. Detroit Street
Los Angeles, CA 90036
(323) 934-1221

International Alliance of Theatrical Stage Employees and Moving Picture Machine Operators of the United States and Canada (IATSE)
1430 Broadway
New York, NY 10018
(212) 730-1770

International Association of Auditorium Managers (IAAM)
635 Fritz Drive
Coppell, TX 75019
(972) 906-7441
http://www.iaam.org

International Brotherhood of Electrical Workers (IBEW)
1125 15th Street NW
Washington, DC 20005
(202) 833-7000
http://www.ibew.org

International Conference of Symphony and Opera Musicians (ICSOM)
4 W. 31st Street
New York, NY 10001
(212) 594-1636
rtl@icsom.org
http://www.icsom.org

League of American Theatres and Producers (LATP)
226 W. 47th Street
New York, NY 10036
(212) 764-1122
league@broadway.org
http://www.broadway.org

League of Historic American Theatres (LHAT)
616 Water Street
Baltimore, MD 21202
(410) 659-9533
http://www.lhat.org

League of Resident Theatres (LORT)
1501 Broadway
New York, NY 10036
(212) 944-1501
http://www.lort.org

Meet The Composer
75 9th Avenue
New York, NY 10011
(212) 645-6949
http://www.meetthecomposer.org

Metropolitan Opera Association (MOA)

Lincoln Center
New York, NY 10023
(212) 362-6000
metinfo@visionfoundry.com
http://www.metopera.org

Metropolitan Opera Guild (MOG)

70 Lincoln Center Plaza
New York, NY 10023
(212) 769-7000
http://www.metopera.org

Music Educators National Conference (MENC)

1806 Robert Fulton Drive
Reston, VA 20191
(703) 860-4000
mbrserv@menc.org
http://www.menc.org

Music Publishers Association of the United States (MPA)

PMB 246
1562 First Avenue
New York, NY 10028
(212) 327-4044
mpa-admin@mpa.org
http://www.mpa.org

Music Teachers National Association (MTNA)

441 Vine Street
Cincinnati, OH 45202
(513) 421-1420
mtnanet@mtna.org
http://www.mtna.org

Nashville Songwriters Association International (NSAI)

1701 West End Avenue
Nashville, TN 37203
(615) 256-3354
nsai@nashvillesongwriters.com
http://www.nashvillesongwriters.com

National Academy of Popular Music (NAPM)

330 W. 58th Street
New York, NY 10019
(212) 957-9230
info@songwritershalloffame.org
http://www.songwritershalloffame.org

National Academy of Recording Arts and Sciences (NARAS)

3402 Pico Boulevard
Santa Monica, CA 90405
(310) 392-3777
info@grammyfoundation.org
http://www.grammy.com

National Academy of Television Arts and Sciences (NATAS)

5220 Lankershim Boulevard
North Hollywood, CA 91601
(818) 754-2810
http://www.emmyonline.org

National Association of Broadcast Employees and Technicians (NABET)

501 3rd Street NW
Washington, DC 20001
(202) 434-1254
jclark@cwa-union.org
http://www.nabetcwa.org

National Association of Broadcasters (NAB)

1771 N Street NW
Washington, DC 20036
(202) 429-5300
nab@nab.org
http://www.nab.org

National Association of Composers USA (NACUSA)
Box 49256
Barrington Station
Los Angeles, CA 90049
(310) 838-4465
deonprice@aol.com
http://www.music-usa.org/nacusa

National Association of Dramatic and Speech Arts (NADSA)
PO Box 561
Grambling, LA 71245
(225) 216-6803
info@nadsa.com
http://www.nadsa.com

National Association of Schools of Dance (NASD)
11250 Roger Bacon Drive
Reston, VA 20190
(703) 437-0700
info@arts-accredit.org
http://www.arts-accredit.org

National Association of Schools of Music (NASM)
11250 Roger Bacon Drive
Reston, VA 20190
(703) 437-0700
info@arts-accredit.org
http://www.arts-accredit.org

National Association of Schools of Theatre (NAST)
11250 Roger Bacon Drive
Reston, VA 20190
(703) 437-0700
info@arts-accredit.org
http://www.arts-accredit.org

National Conference of Personal Managers (NCPM)
330 W. 38th Street
New York, NY 10018
http://www.ncopm.com

National Corporate Theatre Fund (NCTF)
1 E. 53rd Street
New York, NY 10022
(212) 750-6895
nctfbw153@aol.com
http://www.nctf.org

National Cosmetology Association
401 N. Michigan Avenue
Chicago, IL 60611
(312) 527-6757
nca1@sba.com
http://www.salonprofessionals.org

National Dance Association (NDA)
1900 Association Drive
Reston, VA 20191
(703) 476-3421
nda@aahperd.org
http://www.aahperd.org/nda

National Dance Council of America (NDCA)
PO Box 22018
Provo, UT 84602
(801) 422-8124
http://www.ndca.org

National Dance Institute (NDI)
594 Broadway
New York, NY 10012
(212) 226-0083
info@nationaldance.org

National Federation of Music Clubs (NFMC)

1336 N. Delaware Street
Indianapolis, IN 46202
(317) 638-4003
nfmc@nfmcmusic.org
http://www.nfmc-music.org

National Federation of Press Women (NFPW)

PO Box 5556
Arlington, VA 22205
(703) 534-2500
presswomen@aol.com
http://www.nfpw.org

National Movement Theatre Association (NMTA)

c/o Pontine Movement Theatre
PO Box 1437
Portsmouth, NH 03801
(603) 436-6660
http://www.pontine.org

National Music Publishers Association (NMPA)

475 Park Avenue South
New York, NY 10016
(646) 742-1651
pr@nmpa.org
http://www.nmpa.org

National Opera Association (NOA)

PO Box 60869
Canyon, TX 79016
(806) 651-2857
http://www.noa.org

National Orchestral Association (NOA)

245 Park Avenue
New York, NY 10167

National Performance Network (NPN)

PO Box 70435
New Orleans, LA 70172
(504) 595-8008
info@npnweb.org
http://www.npnweb.org

National Press Club (NPC)

National Press Building
529 14th Street NW
Washington, DC 20045
(202) 662-7500
info@npcpress.org
http://www.press.org

National Press Photographers Association (NPPA)

3200 Croasdaile Drive
Durham, NC 27705
(919) 383-7246
info@nppa.org
http://www.nppa.org

National Symphony Orchestra Association (NSOA)

JFK Center for the Performing Arts
2700 F Street NW
Washington, DC 20566
(202) 416-8000
http://www.nationalsymphony.org

National Theatre Conference (NTC)

School of Theatre
University of Houston
Houston, TX 77204
(713) 743-2930

National Theatre of the Deaf (NTD)

55 Van Dyke Avenue
Hartford, CT 06106
(860) 724-5179

info@ntd.org
http://ntd.org

National Theatre Workshop of the Handicapped (NTWH)

535 Greenwich Street
New York, NY 10013
(212) 206-7789
ntwhny@ntwh.org
http://www.ntwh.org

New Dramatists (ND)

424 W. 44th Street
New York, NY 10036
(212) 757-6960
newdramatists@newdramatists.org
http://newdramatists.org

New England Theatre Conference (NETC)

Northeastern University
360 Huntington Avenue
Boston, MA 02115
(617) 424-9275
mail@netonline.org
http://www.NETConline.org

North American Performing Arts Managers and Agents (NAPAMA)

459 Columbus Avenue
New York, NY 10024
info@napama.org
http://www.napama.org

Northwest Drama Conference (NDC)

Olympic College
1600 Chester Avenue
Bremerton, WA 98337
(360) 475-7315

O'Neill Critics Institute

c/o Dan Sullivan
Eugene O'Neill Theater Center

305 Great Neck Road
Waterford, CT 06385
(860) 443-5378
http://www.oneilltheatercenter.org

O'Neill National Theatre Institute (NTI)

305 Great Neck Road
Waterford, CT 06385
(860) 443-7139
http://nti.conncoll.edu

Opera America (OA)

1156 15th Street NW
Washington, DC 20005
(202) 293-4466
frontdesk@operaamerica.org
http://www.operaam.org

Organization of Professional Acting Coaches and Teachers (OPACT)

3968 Eureka Drive
Studio City, CA 91604
(323) 877-4988

Outer Critics Circle (OCC)

101 W. 57th Street
New York, NY 10019
(212) 765-8557

Paper Bag Players (PBP)

225 W. 99th Street
New York, NY 10025
(212) 663-0390
info@paperbagplayers.org
http://www.paperbagplayers.org

Playwrights Conference

534 W. 42nd Street
New York, NY 10036
(212) 244-7008

Professional Dance Teachers Association (PDTA)
PO Box 38
Waldwick, NJ 07463
(201) 652-7767
hoctordance@hoctordance.com

Public Relations Society of America (PRSA)
33 Maiden Lane
New York, NY 10038
(212) 460-1400
http://www.prsa.org

Radio Television News Directors Association (RTNDA)
1600 K Street NW
Washington, DC 20006
(202) 659-6510
rtnda@rtnda.org
http://rtnda.org

Recording Industry Association of America (RIAA)
1330 Connecticut Avenue NW
Washington, DC 20036
(202) 775-0101
http://www.riaa.com

Screen Actors Guild (SAG)
5757 Wilshire Boulevard
Los Angeles, CA 90036
(323) 954-1600
http://www.sag.org

Screen Extras Guild (SEG)
3253 North Knoll Drive
Los Angeles, CA 90068

SESAC, Inc.
152 W. 57th Street
New York, NY 10019

(212) 586-3450
http://www.sesac.com

Society of American Fight Directors (SAFD)
School of Theatre
6321 North Lakewood
Chicago, IL 60660
(773) 764-3825
president@safd.org
http://www.safd.org

Society of Stage Directors and Choreographers (SSDC)
1501 Broadway
New York, NY 10036
(212) 391-1070
info@ssdc.org
http://www.ssdc.org

Songwriters Guild of America
1500 Harbor Boulevard
Weehawken, NJ 07086
(201) 867-7603
songwritersnj@aol.com

Theatre Communications Group (TCG)
520 Eighth Avenue
New York, NY 10018
(212) 609-5900
tcg@tcg.org
http://www.tcg.org

Theatre Development Fund (TDF)
1501 Broadway
New York, NY 10036
(212) 221-0885
info@tdf.org
http://www.tdf.org

Theatre Guild (TG)
135 Central Park West
New York, NY 10023
(212) 873-0676

United Scenic Artists (USA)
29 W. 38th Street
New York, NY 10018
(212) 581-0300
usa829@aol.com
http://www.usa829.org

United States Institute for Theatre Technology (USITT)
6443 Ridings Road
Syracuse, NY 13206
(315) 463-6463
info@office.usitt.org
http://www.usitt.org

United States National Institute of Dance (USNID)
38 S. Arlington Avenue
PO Box 245
East Orange, NJ 07019
(973) 673-9225

University Resident Theatre Association (URTA)
1560 Broadway
New York, NY 10036
(212) 221-1130
urta@aol.com

Up With People (UWP)
1675 Broadway
Denver, CO 80202
(303) 460-7100
anarans@upwithpeople.org
http://www.upwithpeople.org

Women In Communications Foundation
355 Lexington Avenue
New York, NY 10017
(212) 297-2133
http://www.nywici.org/foundation

World Congress of Teachers of Dancing (WCTD)
c/o United States National Institute of Dance
38 S. Arlington Avenue
PO Box 245
East Orange, NJ 07019

Writers Guild of America East (WGA)
555 W. 57th Street
New York, NY 10019
(212) 767-7800
info@wgaeast.org
http://www.wgaeast.org

Writers Guild of America West (WGA)
7000 W. Third Street
Los Angeles, CA 90048
(323) 951-4000
website@wga.org
http://www.wga.org

Yiddish Theatrical Alliance (YTA)
31 E. 7th Street
New York, NY 10003
(212) 674-3437

Young Concert Artists (YCA)
250 W. 57th Street
New York, NY 10107
(212) 307-6655
yca@yca.org
http://www.yca.org

APPENDIX II

THEATER AND PERFORMING ARTS WEB SITES

The Internet is a premier resource for information, no matter what you need. Surfing the Web can help you locate almost anything you want, from information to services and everything in between.

This listing contains an assortment of various theater and other performing arts related sites that may be of value to you in your career. Use this list as a start. There are literally thousands of Web sites related to the performing arts and more emerging every day.

This listing is for your information. The author is not responsible for any site content. Inclusion or exclusion in this listing does not imply any one site is endorsed or recommended over another by the author.

Academy of Motion Pictures and Sciences
http://www.oscars.org

Actor News
http://www.actornews.com

Actors' Equity Association
http://www.actorsequity.org/home.html

Actors Equity Casting Call
http://web.actorsequity.org/CastingSearch

Actors Site.com
http://www.actorsite.com

Aisle Say
http://www.aislesay.com

Amazon.com
http://www.amazon.com

American Association of Community Theatre
http://www.aact.org

American College Dance Festival Association
http://www.acdfa.org

American Federation of Musicians
http://www.afm.org

American Theatre Wings
http://www.tonyawards.com/en_US/index.html

Andrew Lloyd Webber
http://www.reallyuseful.com/rug/html/index.htm

Answers 4 Dancers
http://www.answers4dancers.com

ARTISTdirect
http://www.artistdirect.com

Arts Jobs
http://www.artslynx.org/jobs.htm

ASCAP
http://www.ascap.com

Auditions.com
http://www.auditions.com

Backstage
http://www.backstage.com

Backstage Jobs
http://backstagejobs.com

Backstage World
http://www.backstageworld.com

Baker's Plays
http://bakersplays.com

Berklee Music
http://www.berkleemusic.com

Billboard
http://www.billboard.com

BMI
http://www.bmi.com

Broadway World.com
http://www.broadwayworld.com

CastingAudition.com
http://www.castingaudition.com

Cirque du Soleil
http://www.cirquedusoleil.com

Comedy Club Circuit
http://www.comedy-club-comics.com

Costume Society of America
http://www.costumesocietyamerica.com

Curtain Up
http://www.curtainup.com

Directory of Summer Theater
http://www.summertheater.com/directory.html

Disneyland Resort Auditions
http://corporate.disney.go.com/careers/
auditions_disneyland.html

Disney On Broadway
http://disney.go.com/disneytheatrical/index.html

Disney On Broadway: The Lion King
http://disney.go.com/disneytheatrical/thelionking

Disney On Broadway: Tarzan
http://disney.go.com/disneytheatrical/tarzan

Dramatists Guild of America
http://www.dramatistsguild.com

Educational Theatre Association
http://www.edta.org/

Emmyonline Job Bank
http://jobbank.emmyonline.org

Entertainment Careers.net
http://www.entertainmentcareers.net

Entertainment Jobs.com
http://www.entertainmentjobs.com

**Entertainment Services and Technology
Association**
http://www.esta.org/jobs/index.php

Gershwin Fan
http://www.gershwinfan.com

Harry Fox Agency, Inc.
http://www.harryfox.com

Hershey Park Auditions
http://www.hersheypa.com/attractions/
hersheypark/entertainment/auditions.html

IATSE
http://www.iatse-intl.org

Inside Broadway
http://www.insidebroadway.org

International Dance Festival
http://www.internationaldancefestival.org

Internet Broadway Database
http://www.ibdb.com

Irving Berlin
http://www.irvingberlin.com/irving_berlin

League of Historic American Theaters
http://www.lhat.org

League of Resident Theatres
http://www.lort.org

Leonard Bernstein
http://www.leonardbernstein.com

Live Broadway
http://www.livebroadway.com

Lyrical Line
http://www.lyricalline.com

Lyrics.com
http://www.lyrics.com

Marketing Your Music
http://www.marketingyourmusic.com

Metropolitan Opera
http://www.metoperafamily

Metropolitan Opera Guild
http://www.metoperafamily.org/guild

Muse's Muse Songwriting Resource
http://www.musemuse.com

Museum of Costume
http://www.usitt.org

Musical Cast Album Database
http://www.castalbumdb.com

Musical Theatre International
http://www.mtishows.com

Music Biz Advice
http://www.musicbizadvice.com

MusicContracts.com
http://www.musiccontracts.com

Musician's Assistance Program
http://www.map200.org

Musicians National Referral
http://www.musicianreferral.com

National Alliance For Musical Theater
http://namt.org

National Broadway Theatre Awards
http://www.nationalbroadwaytheatreawards.com

National Music Publishers Association
http://www.nmpa.org

New York City Ballet
http://www.nycballet.com

New York Theatre Experience
http://www.nytheatre.com

New York Times **Theater Reviews**
http://theater.nytimes.com/pages/theater

Opera News Online
http://www.metoperafamily.org/operanews/index.aspx

Pioneer Drama Service
http://www.pioneerdrama.com

The Phantom of the Opera
http://www.thephantomoftheopera.com

Playbill **Job Listings**
http://www.playbill.com/jobs/find/category_listing/1.html

Playbill **Online**
http://www.playbill.com

Pollstar.com
http://www.pollstar.com

PowerGig
http://www.powergig.com

Professional Musicians Referral
http://www.pmr-musicians.com

Radio and Records
http://www.radioandrecords.com

Rent—The Broadway Musical
http://www.siteforrent.com

Samuel French, Inc.
http://samuelfrench.com

Screen Actors Guild
http://www.sag.org

SESAC, Inc.
http://www.sesac.com

Shelly Field
http://www.shellyfield.com

Showbizjobs.com
http://www.showbizjobs.com

Showbizltd.com
http://www.showbizltd.com

Stage Managers Association
http://www.stagemanagers.org

Stress Free Success
http://www.shellyfield.com

Theater Communications Group
http://www.tcg.org

Theater Jobs
http://theatrejobs.com

Theater Mania
http://www.theatermania.com

Tony Awards
http://www.tonyawards.com

United Scenic Artists Local 829
http://www.usa829.org

United States Institute for Theater Technology
http://www.usitt.org

USA International Ballet Competition
http://www.usaibc.com

USA Musician
http://www.usamusician.com

U.S. Copyright Office
http://www.copywright.gov

U.S. Patent and Trademark Office
http://www.uspto.gov

U.S. Small Business Administration (SBA)
http://www.sba.gov

Variety
http://www.variety.com

BIBLIOGRAPHY

A. Books

There are thousands of books on all aspects of theater and the performing arts. Sometimes just reading about someone else's success, inspires you, motivates you or just helps you to come up with ideas to help you attain your own dreams.

Books can be a treasure trove of information if you want to learn about a particular aspect of a career or gain more knowledge about how something in the industry works.

The books listed below are separated into general categories. Subjects often overlap. Use this listing as a beginning. Check out your local library, bookstore, or online retailer for other books about the industry.

Acting and Directing

Barton, Robert. *Acting: Onstage and Off.* Belmont, CA: Wadsworth Publishing, 2005.

Blumenfield, Robert. *Accents: A Manual For Acting.* New York: Limelight Editions, 2002.

Caldarone, Marina. *Actions: The Actor's Thesaurus.* New York: Theatre Communications Group, Inc., 2004.

Chubbuck, Ivana. *The Power of The Actor.* East Rutherford, NJ: Penguin Group, 2005.

Cohen, Robert. *Acting Professionally: Raw Facts about Careers in Acting.* Burr Ridge, IL: McGraw-Hill Higher Education, 2003.

Elgin, Kathy. *Theatre and Entertainment: Shakespeare's World.* Minneapolis: Compass Point, 2004.

Greene, Alexis. *Lucille Lortel: The Queen of Off Broadway.* New York: Limelight Editions, 2004.

Gussow, Mel. *Micahel Gambon: A Life In Acting.* New York: Applause Theatre Book Publishers, 2005.

Hester, John. *Stage Acting Techniques: A Practical Guide.* Ramsbury, UK: Crowood Press, Limited, 2004.

Jazwinski, Peter. *Act Now!: A Step-by-Step Guide to Becoming a Working Actor.* New York: Crown Publishing Group, 2003.

Jones, Robert Edmond. *The Dramatic Imagination: Reflections and Speculations of the Arts of the Theatre.* New York: Routledge, 2004.

Kanner, Ellie. *How Not To Audition: Avoiding The Common Mistakes Most Actors Make.* Hollywood, CA: Lone Eagle Publishing, 2003.

Kellow, Brian. *The Bennetts: An Acting Family.* Lexington: University Press of Kentucky, 2004.

Kohlhaas, Karen. *The Monologue Audition: A Practical Guide For Actors.* New York: Limelight Editions, 2000.

Levy, Gavin. *112 Acting Games: A Comprehensive Workbook of Theatre Games For Developing*

Acting Skills. Colorado Springs, CO: Meriwether Publishing, Limited, 2005.

Martinez, Tony. *An Agent Tells All: An Uncensored Look at the Business of Acting.* Beverly Hills, CA: Hit Team Publishing, 2005.

Moss, Larry. *The Intent To Live: Achieving Your True Potential As An Actor.* Westminster, MD: Bantam Books, 2004.

Salt, Chrys. *Make Acting Work.* London: Methuen Publishing Limited, 2004.

Schulman, Michael. *Play The Scene: The Ultimate Collection of Contemporary and Classic Scenes and Monologues.* New York: St. Martins Press, 2005.

Simon, Ali. *Masking Unmasked: Four Approaches To Basic Acting.* New York: Palgrave Macmillan, 2004.

Watson-Guptill Publications Staff. *Living On Stage.* New York: Watson-Guptill Publications, 2004.

Wienir, David. *Making It on Broadway: Actors' Tales of Climbing to the Top.* New York: Allworth Press, 2004.

Wroe, Craig. *An Actor Prepares…To Live In New York City: How To Live Like A Star Before You Become One.* Pompton Plains, NJ: Amadeus Press, 2004.

Ballet

Cooper, Bill. *The Royal Ballet: In House.* New York: Theatre Communications Group, Inc., 2004.

Gottlieb, Robert. *George Balanchine: The Ballet Maker.* New York: Harper Trade, 2004.

Teachout, Terry. *All in the Dances: A Brief Life of George Balanchine.* San Diego: Harcourt Trade Publishers, 2004.

Classical Musicians and Orchestras

Drew, Lucas. *Everything You Always Wanted To Know About The Symphony Orchestra.* Boca Raton, FL: Edwin F. Kalmus & Company, Inc., 1992.

Getzinger, Donna and Daniel Feldsenfeld. *Johannes Brahms and The Twilight of Romanticism.* Greensboro, NC: Morgan Reynolds Incorporated, 2004.

Hirzy, Ellen C. *Working with the Music Director: A Handbook for Board Members, Executive Directors, and Music Directors.* New York: American Symphony Orchestra League, 1999.

Morrison, Richard. *Orchestra: The LSO: A Century of Triumphs and Turbulence.* New York: Faber & Faber, Inc., 2004.

Todd, Larry R. *Mendelssohn: A Life in Music.* New York: Oxford University Press, 2005.

Whiting, Jim. *The Life and Times of Igor Stravinsky.* Hockessin, DE: Mitchell Lane Publishers, Inc., 2004.

————. *The Life and Times of George Frederic Handel.* Hockessin, DE: Mitchell Lane Publishers, Inc., 2003.

Zannos, Susan. *The Life and Times of Ludwig Van Beethoven.* Hockessin, DE: Mitchell Lane Publishers, Inc., 2003.

Comedy

Benjava, Gustav. *The Divine Comedian.* Philadelphia: Xlibris Corporation, 2004.

Hentzell, Tim. *So, You're A Comedian, Tell Me A Joke.* Morrisville, NC: Lulu.com, 2004.

Makinson, Robert. *How to Be a Comedian Handbook.* Brooklyn, NY: R. B. Makinson, 2002.

Murray, Ken. *Life on a Pogo Stick: Autobiography of a Comedian.* Temecula, CA: Textbook Publishers, 2003.

Vance, Jeffrey. *Harold Lloyd: Master Comedian.* New York: Harry N. Abrams, Inc., 2002.

White, Karyn Ruth. *Your Seventh Sense: How to Think Like a Comedian.* Denver: LifeStar, 2004.

Dance

Cruz, Barbara C. *Alvin Ailey: Celebrating African-American Culture In Dance.* Berkeley Heights, NJ: Enslow Publishers, 2004.

Garafola, Lynn. *Legacies of Twentieth-Century Dance.* Middletown, CT: Wesleyan University Press, 2005.

Directing

Baldwin, Chris. *Stage Directing: A Practical Guide.* Ramsbury, UK: Crowood Press, 2003.

Braun, Kazimierz. *Theatre Directing - Art, Ethics, Creativity.* Lewiston, NY: Edwin Mellen Press, 2000.

Frerer, Lloyd Anton. *Directing for the Stage.* Burr Ridge, IL: McGraw-Hill Higher Education, 2003.

Hodge, Francis. *Play Directing: Analysis, Communication, and Style.* Boston: Allyn & Bacon, Inc., 2004.

Reich, Russell. *Notes On Directing.* New York: RCR Creative Press, 2003.

Entertainment Law

Butler, Joy R. *The Musician's Guide Through the Legal Jungle: Answers to Frequently Asked Questions about Music Law.* Arlington, VA: Sashay Communications, 2002.

Isaacs, Sidney C. *The Law Relating to Theatres, Music-Halls and Other Public Entertainments and to the Performers Therein, Including the Law of Musical and Dramatic Copyright, No. 1.* Holmes Beach, FL: Gaunt, Inc., 1999.

Parker, Nigel. *Music Business: A Professional Guide to Infrastructure, Practice and Law of the Industry.* Poole, UK: Palladian Law Publishing, Ltd., 2004.

Platinum Millennium Publishing Staff. *101 Music Business Contracts - Updated Edition - Preprinted Binder / CD-ROM Set: Containing over 100 Contracts and Agreements for Recording Artist, Musicians, Record Companies, Managers, Songwriters, Labels, Producers, Indies and Any and All Others in the Music Industry: Entertainment Law at Its Best!* Bridgeport, CT: Platinum Millennium, 2002.

Settle, Alfred Towers, and Frank H. Baber. *The Law of Public Entertainments: Theaters, Music and Dancing, Stage Plays, Cinematographs, Copyright, Sunday Performances, Children, Theatrical Cases, and Specimen Contracts.* Buffalo, NY: William S. Hein & Company, Incorporated, 2003.

Soocher, Stan. *They Fought the Law: Rock Music Goes to Court.* New York: Music Sales Corporation, 2004.

Music Business

Brabec, Jeffrey. *Music, Money, and Success: The Insider's Guide to Making Money in the Music Industry.* New York: Music Sales Corporation, 2004.

Colley, Craig W. *You Can Make Money In Music: Everything a Musician Needs to Know to Become Steadily Employed as a Live Performer.* Milwaukee, WI: Hal Leonard Corporation, 1991.

Curran, Mark. *Getting Gigs!: The Musician's and Singer's Survival Guide to Booking Better Paying Jobs With or Without an Agent.* Simi Valley, CA: New Media Digital, Inc., 2004.

Field, Shelly. *Career Opportunities In The Music Industry.* New York: Facts On File, 2004.

Frascogna, Xavier M. *This Business of Artist Management.* New York: Watson-Guptill Publications, 2004.

Grant, A. *Music Business: It's all about the Music, Right?* Lincoln, NE: iUniverse, 2005.

Harris, Kevin. *Inside Music 2005: The Insider's Guide to the Industry.* London: Ebury Press, 2004.

Kusek, David. *The Future of Music.* Boston: Berklee Press Publications, 2005.

Moore, Steve. *The Truth about the Music Business: A Grassroots Business and Legal Guide.* Boston: Course Technology, Inc., 2005.

Platinum Millennium. *How to Make A Fortune in the Music Industry by Doing It Yourself: Your Personal Step-by-Step Guide to Having A Successful Career in the Music Business. A-K-A How to Sell Music, Book Shows and Get Noticed!* Waterbury, CT: Platinum Millennium, 2005.

———. *The Music Business: How YOU Can Make $500,000 or More a Year in the Music Industry by Doing It Yourself!* Bridgeport, CT: Platinum Millennium, 2005.

Rudsenske, J. Scott. *Music Business Made Simple: A Guide to Becoming a Recording Artist.* New York: Music Sales Corporation, 2004.

———. *Music Business Made Simple: A Guide to Becoming a Recording Artist.* Music Sales Corporation, 2004.

Wilson, Lee. *Making It in the Music Business: The Business and Legal Guide for Songwriters and Performers.* New York: Allworth Press, 2004.

Music Publishing

Beall, Eric. *Making Music Make Money: An Insider's Guide to Becoming Your Own Music Publisher.* Boston: Berklee Press Publications, 2003.

Howard, George. *Music Publishing 101.* Milwaukee, WI: Hal Leonard Corporation, 2004.

Kashif. *Kashif's Music Publishing Source Guide.* Venice, CA: Brooklyn Boy Books, 1998.

Sellars, Paul. *Publishing Music Online.* New York: Music Sales Corporation, 2004.

Smith, Regina. *Music Publishing 101: Crash Course.* Miami: No Walls Production & Publishing, 2001.

Whitsett, Tim. *Music Publishing: The Real Road to Music Business Success.* Vallejo, CA: Artistpro.com, 2001.

Music and Theater Criticism

Billington, Michael. *One Night Stands: A Critic's View of Modern British Theatre.* New York: Theatre Communications Group, Inc., 2002.

Hornby, Richard. *Mad about Theatre.* New York: Applause Theatre Book Publishers, 2000.

Wingell, Richard. *Writing About Music.* East Rutherford, NJ: Prentice Hall, 2001.

Opera

Bradley, Ian. *Oh Joy! Oh Rapture.* New York: Oxford University Press, 2005.

Douglas, Nigel. *The Joy of Opera.* London: Andre Deutsch: 2005.

Kopp, Richard. *Notes On This Evening's Opera.* Bloomington, IN: Authorhouse, 2005.

Kramer, Lawrence. *Opera and Modern Culture: Wagner and Strauss.* Berkeley: University of California Press, 2004.

Russell, P. Craig. *The P. Craig Russell Library of Opera Adaptations, Vol. 3.* New York: NBM Publishing Company, 2004.

Ottenberg, Eve. *The Widow's Opera.* Bloomington, IN: AuthorHouse, 2005.

Playwriting

Cassady, Marsh. *Playwriting Step by Step.* San Jose, CA: Resource Publications, Inc., 2003.

Catron, Louis E. *The Elements of Playwriting.* Prospect Heights, IL: Waveland Press, Inc., 2001.

Dromgoole, Dominic. *The Full Room: An A-Z of Contemporary Playwriting.* London: Methuen Publishing Limited, 2004.

Greig, Noel. *Playwriting: A Practical Guide.* New York: Routledge, 2005.

Hatcher, Jeffrey. *The Art and Craft of Playwriting.* Cincinnati: F & W Publications, Incorporated, 2000.

Macgowan, Kenneth. *A Primer of Playwriting.* Temecula, CA: Textbook Publishers, 2003.

Shamas, Laura A. *Playwriting for Theater, Film and Television.* Cincinnati: F&W Publications, 2003.

Publicity, Public Relations, and Promotion

Alterman, Glenn. *Promoting Your Acting Career: A Step-by-Step Guide To Opening The Right Doors.* New York: Allworth Press, 2004.

Austin, Pam, and Bob Austin. *Getting Free Publicity: The Secrets of Successful Press Relations.* Oxford, UK: How To Books, 2005.

Baker, Bob. *Guerrilla Music Marketing Handbook: 201 Self-Promotion Ideas for Songwriters, Musicians & Bands.* Colorado Springs, CO: Spotlight Publishing, 2001.

Britt, Shawnassey Howell. The Independent Record Label's Plain and Simple Guide to Music Promotion. Jackson, MS: One Horse Publishing, 2004.

Fletcher, Tana and Julia Rockler. *Getting Publicity.* Bellingham, WA: Self-Counsel Press, Inc., 2004.

Hamilton, Joni. *The Beginner's Guide to Publicity.* Wheaton, IL: Synoia Digital Press, 2005.

Kalmar, Veronika. *Label Launch: A Guide to Independent Record Recording, Promotion, and Distribution.* New York: St. Martin's Press, 2002.

Kolb, Bonita. *Marketing for Cultural Organisations: New Strategies for Attracting Audiences to Classical Music, Dance, Museums, Theatre and Opera.* London: International Thomson Business Press, 2004.

Lathrop, Ted. *This Business of Music Marketing and Promotion, Revised and Updated Edition.* New York: Billboard Books, 2003.

McArthur, Nancy. *How to Do Theatre Publicity.* Berea, OH: Good Ideas Company, 1978.

Reilly, Andrew. *An Actor's Business: How To Market Yourself As An Actor No Matter Where You Live.* Boulder, CO: Sentient Publications, 2004.

Sinnett, Clair. *Actors Working: The Actor's Guide To Marketing Success.* El Segundo, CA: Actors Working Books, 2004.

Summers, Jodi. *Making and Marketing Music.* New York: Allworth Press, 2004.

Songwriting and Composing

Blume, Jason. *6 Steps to Songwriting Success: The Comprehensive Guide to Writing and Marketing Hit Songs.* New York: Watson-Guptill Books, 2004.

Byers, Dave. *Songwriting Fundamentals: Discover The Joy of Songwriting.* New York: Billboard Books, 2004.

DeMain, Bill. *In Their Own Words: Songwriters Talk About The Creative Process.* Westport, CT: Greenwood Publishing Group, 2004.

Dion, Frank. *Fingers Bleed: Learn How to Write a Song In About 15 Minutes and Increase Your Chances of Becoming A Rock-n-Roll Superstar.* North Charleston, SC: BookSurge, 2004.

Dominic, Serene. *Burt Bacharach: Song by Song.* New York: Music Sales Corporation, 2004.

Hirschhorn, Joel. *Complete Idiot's Guide To Songwriting 2.* East Rutherford, NJ: Penguin Group, 2004.

Hooper, Caroline. *Learn Songwriting.* Tulsa, OK: EDC Publishing, 2004.

Pincus, Lee. *The Songwriter's Success Manual.* Mattituck, NY: Amereon, Limited, 2004.

Rooksby, Rikky. *Melody: How To Write Great Tunes.* San Francisco: Backbeat Books, 2004.

Stagecraft

Civardi, Giovani. *Drawing Scenery: Landscapes, Seascapes and Buildings.* Turnbridge Wells, UK: Search Press, Limited, 2004.

Crabtree, Susan. *Scenic Art for the Theatre: History, Tools, and Techniques.* San Diego: Elsevier Science & Technology Books, 2004.

Essig, Linda. *Lighting and the Design Idea*. Belmont, CA Wadsworth Publishing, 2004.

Gillette, J. Michael. *Theatrical Design and Production: An Introduction to Scene Design and Construction, Lighting, Sound, Costume, and Makeup*. New York: McGraw-Hill Companies, 2004.

Gustafson, David Eldon. *Position: Anchoring Yourself and Mastering Stagecraft*. Upland, CA: InfoDynamics Publication, 2003.

Kramer, Wayne. *The Mind's Eye: Theatre and Media Design from the Inside Out*. Portsmouth, NH: Heinemann, 2004.

Maccoy, Peter. *Essentials of Stage Management*. New York: Routledge, 2004.

McDonagh, Joe. *Opening Night*. Studio City, CA: Players Press, 2003.

Orton, Keith. *Model Making for the Stage: A Practical Guide*. Ramsbury, UK: Crowood Press, Limited, 2005.

Pallin, Gail. *Stage Management: The Essential Handbook*. New York: Theatre Communications Group, 2004.

Richmond, Susan. *Further Steps In Stagecraft*. Studio City, CA: Players Press, 2003.

Sofer, Andrew. *The Stage Life of Props*. Ann Arbor: University of Michigan Press, 2003.

Swift, Charles I. *Introduction to Stage Lighting: The Fundamentals of Theatre Lighting Design*. Colorado Springs, CO: Meriwether Publishing, Limited, 2004.

White, Christine A. *Computer Visualization for the Theatre: 3D Modeling for Designers*. San Diego: Elsevier Science & Technology Books, 2003.

Wilson, Andy. *Making Stage Props: A Practical Guide*. Ramsbury, UK: Crowood Press, Limited, 2003.

Theatrical Makeup

Hawker, Yvonne. *Make-up Designory's Beauty Make-up*. Burbank, CA: Make-up Designory, 2004.

Vinther, Janus. *Special Effects Make-Up*. New York: Routledge, 2003.

B. Periodicals, Publications, and Webzines

Magazines, newspapers, membership bulletins and newsletters help keep you up to date with industry happenings and abreast of new trends. There are various periodicals geared towards different parts of the music industry. Use this listing as a beginning.

Check out your local library, bookstore or newsstand for additional titles of interest. Don't forget to look for Web versions of many popular music periodicals.

CHAMBER MUSIC

Chamber Music
Chamber Music America
305 Seventh Avenue
New York, NY 10001
(212) 242-2022
info@chamber-music.org
http://www.chamber-music.org

CIRCUS AND MAGIC

Circus Magazine
Circus Enterprise Corporation
6th West 18th Street
New York, NY 10011
(212) 633-9042
(212) 242-5734 (fax)
circusmhe@aol.com

Magic: An Independent Magazine for Magicians
Stagewrite Publishing Incorporated
6220 Stevenson Way
Las Vegas, NV 89120

(702) 789-0099
(702) 798-0220 (fax)
publisher@magicmagazine.com
http://www.magicmagazine.com

The Magic Magazine
Magic Industries
20 East 46th Street
New York, NY 10017

CRITICS, REVIEWS, AND NEWS

Entertainment Weekly
Time & Life Building
Rockefeller Center
New York, NY 10020
(212) 522-1212
(212) 467-1396 (fax)
http://www.ew.com/ew

Rolling Stone
Wenner Media Incorporated
1290 Avenue of The Americas
New York, NY 10104
(212) 484-1616
(212) 767-8209
http://www.rollingstone.com

Victory Music Review
PO Box 2254
Tacoma, WA 98401
(253) 428-0832
(253) 660-3263 (fax)
victory@nwlink.com
http://www.victorymusic.org

DANCE AND CHOREOGRAPHY

Attitude: The Dancers Magazine
1040 Park Place
Brooklyn, NY 11213

(718) 773-3046
dancegiantsteps@hotmail.com
http://www.geocities.com/danceattitude

Ballet Dance Magazine
37 West 12th Street
New York, NY 10011
(212) 924-5183
http://www.ballet-dance.com

Ballet Review
http://www.balletreview.com
Dance Chronicle
270 Madison Avenue
New York, NY 10016
(212) 696-9000
http://www.dekker.com

Dance Magazine
333 Seventh Avenue
New York, NY 10001
(212) 979-4803
http://www.dancemagazine.com

Studies In Dance History
Dance Program
University of Minnesota
108 Norris Hall
Minneapolis, MN 55455

DANCE THERAPY

American Journal of Dance Therapy
American Dance Therapy Association
2000 Century Plaza
10632 Little Patuxent Parkway
Columbia, MD 21044
(410) 997-4040
(410) 997-4048 (fax)
info@adta.org
http://www.adta.org

HALLS, ARENAS, CLUBS, AND OTHER VENUES

Amusement Business
PO Box 24970
Nashville, TN 37202
(615) 321-4250
(615) 327-1574 (fax)
http://www.amusementbusiness.com

Facility Magazine
4425 West Airport Freeway
Irving, TX 75062
(972) 255-8020
(972) 255-9582 (fax)

MUSICIANS

The American Organist Magazine
American Guild of Organists
475 Riverside Drive
New York NY 10115
(800) AGO-5115

Guitar Player
460 Park Avenue South
New York, NY 10016
(212) 378-0400
(212) 378-2149 (fax)
http://www.guitarplayer.com

Guitar World
1115 Broadway
New York, NY 10010
(212) 807-7100
http://www.guitarworld.com

Harp Magazine
8737 Colesville Road
Silver Springs, MD 20910
(301) 588-4114

(301) 588-5531 (fax)
http://www.harpmagazine.com

Hit Parader
210 Route 4
Paramus, NJ 07652
(973) 843-4004
http://www.hitparader.com

Independent Musician Magazine
1067 Market Street
San Francisco, CA 94103
(415) 503-0340
http://www.immagazine.com

International Musician
American Federation of Musicians
1501 Broadway
New York, NY 10036
(212) 869-1330
http://www.afm.org

JazzTimes
8737 Colesville Road
Silver Spring, MD 20910
(301) 588-4114
(301) 588-2009 (fax)
http://www.jazztimes.com

Keyboard Magazine
2800 Campus Drive
San Mateo, CA 94403
(650) 513-4300
(650) 513-4642 (fax)
http://www.keyboardonline.com

Music Trades
PO Box 432
Englewood, NJ 07631
(201) 871-1965
http://www.musictrades.com

OPERA

Opera Journal
National Opera Association
PO Box 60869
Canyon, TX 79016
(806) 651-2857
(806) 651-2958 (fax)
http://www.noa.org

Opera News
Metropolitan Opera Guild
70 Lincoln Center Plaza
New York, NY 10023
(212) 769-7080
http://www.metopera.org

ORCHESTRAS

Symphony
American Symphony Orchestra League
33 W. 60th Street, 5th Floor
New York, NY 10023
(212) 262-5161
(212) 262-5198 (fax)
http://www.symphony.org

PERFORMING ARTS—GENERAL

Arts Management
Radius Group, Inc.
110 Riverside Drive
New York, NY 10024
(212) 579-2039
(212) 579-2049 (fax)
http://www.artsmanagementnews.com

BCA News
Business Committee for the Arts, Inc.
29-27 Queens Plaza North
Long Island City, NY 11101

(718) 482-9901
(718) 482-9911 (fax)
info@bcainc.org
http://www.bcainc.org

IEG Sponsorship Report
IEG, Inc.
640 North LaSalle
Chicago, IL 60610
(312) 944-1727
(312) 944-1897 (fax)
ieg@sponsorship.com

Journal of Arts Management Law and Society
Heldref Publications
1319 18th Street NW
Washington, DC 20036
(202) 296-6267
(202) 296-5149 (fax)
tch@heldref.org
http://www.heldref.org/jamls.php

Performing Arts Journal
MIT Press
PO Box 260
Village Station
New York, NY 10014
(212) 243-3885
journals-info@mit.edu
http://mitpress.mit.edu/PAJ

Performing Arts Magazine
Performing Arts Network
10350 Santa Monica Boulevard
Los Angeles, CA 90025
(310) 551-1115
(310) 551-2079 (fax)
info@performingartsmagazine.com
http://www.performingartsmagazine.com

PUBLIC RELATIONS, PUBLICITY, AND PROMOTION

Contacts: The Media Pipeline for PR People
Mercomm, Inc.
550 Executive Boulevard
Ossining, NY 10562
(914) 923-9400
(914) 923-9484 (fax)

Public Relations Journal
PRSA
33 Maiden Lane
New York, NY 10038
(212) 460-1400
(212) 995-0757 (fax)
http://www.prsa.org

TALENT AND WRITING

Acoustic Guitar Magazine
220 West End Avenue
San Rafael, CA 94901
(415) 485-6946
(415) 485-0831 (fax)
http://www.acousticguitar.com

American Songwriters Magazine
50 Music Square West
Nashville, TN 37203
(615) 321-6096
(615) 321-6097 (fax)
http://www.americansongwriter.com

ASCAP In Action
American Society of Composers and Publishers
(ASCAP)
1 Lincoln Plaza
New York, NY 10023
(212) 621-6000
http://www.ascap.com

BMI: The Many Worlds of Music
Broadcast Music Inc. (BMI)
320 W. 57th Street
New York, NY 10019
(212) 586-2000
http://www.bmi.com

Downbeat Magazine
102 North Haven Road
Elmhurst, IL 60126
(800) 535-7496
http://www.downbeat.com

Songwriter's Market
Writer's Digest Books
4700 E. Galbraith Road
Cincinnati, OH 45236
(513) 531-2690
songmarket@fwpubs.com

TEACHING

American Music Teacher
441 Vine Street
Cincinnati, OH 45202
(513) 421-1420
(513) 421-2503 (fax)
mtnanet@mtna.org

Music Educators Journal
MENC: The National Association for Music Education
1806 Robert Fulton Drive
Reston, VA 20191
(703) 860-4000
mbrserv@menc.org
http://www.menc.org

Teaching Music
MENC: The National Association for Music Education
1806 Robert Fulton Drive
Reston, VA 20191

(703) 860-4000
mbrserv@menc.org

THEATER

American Alliance for Theater & Education Newsletter
American Alliance for Theater & Education
Theatre Department
Arizona State University
PO Box 872002
Tempe, AZ 85287
(480) 965-6064
(480) 965-5351 (fax)
aate.info@asu.edu
http://www.aate.com

American Drama
American Drama Institute
University of Cincinnati
Cincinnati, OH 45221
(513) 556-3914
(513) 556-5960 (fax)
american.drama@uc.edu

American Theater
Theatre Communications Group
520 Eighth Avenue
New York, NY 10018
(212) 609-5900
(212) 609-5901 (fax)
tcg@tcg.org, orders@tcg.org
http://www.tcg.org

Curtains Up
http://www.curtainup.com

The Drama Review
The MIT Press
5 Cambridge Center
Cambridge, MA 02142

(800) 405-1619
(617) 258-6779 (fax)
journals-info@mit.edu
http://mitpress.mit.edu

Dramatics Guild Quarterly
Dramatists Sourcebook
Eugene O'Neill Review
Suffolk University
Department of English
Boston, MA 02114
(617) 573-8272
(617) 624-0157 (fax)
istrange@acad.suffolk.edu

Dramatics Magazine
Educational Theatre Association
2343 Auburn Avenue
Cincinnati, OH 45219
(513) 421-3900
(513) 421-7077 (fax)
info@edta.org, pubs@edta.org

Dramatists Guild Resource Directory
The Dramatists Guild of America Inc.
1501 Broadway
New York, NY 10036
(212) 398-9366
(212) 944-0420 (fax)

Institute of Outdoor Drama Newsletter
CB 3240
1700 Airport Road
Chapel Hill, NC 27599
(919) 962-1328
(919) 962-4212 (fax)
outdoor@unc.edu
http://www.unc.edu/depts/outdoor

Playbill
http://www.playbill.com

Preview Theater Magazine

Hogan Communications
150 E. Olive Avenue
Burbank, CA 91502
(818) 848-4876
(818) 848-4995 (fax)

Stage Directions

Lifestyle Ventures L.L.C.
250 W. 57th Street
New York, NY 10107
(212) 265-8890
(212) 265-8908 (fax)
stagedir@aol.com
http://www.stage-directions.com

Stages

Curtains Inc.
301 W. 45th Street
New York, NY 10036
(212) 245-9186

Theatrical Index

888 Eighth Avenue
New York, NY 10019
(212) 586-6343

THEATER—PRODUCTION

Entertainment Design

Primedia Business
249 W. 17th Street
New York, NY 10011
(212) 462-3300
(212) 367-8345 (fax)
http://www.etecnyc.net

Lighting Dimensions Magazine

Primedia Business
32 W. 18th Street
New York, NY 10011

(212) 229-2084
(212) 229-2084 (fax)
http://www.lightingdimensions.com

Make-Up Artist Magazine

4018 NE 112th Avenue
Vancouver, WA 98682
(360) 882-3488
(360) 885-1836 (fax)
http://www.makeupmag.com

Stage Directions

Lifestyle Ventures L.L.C.
250 W. 57th Street
New York, NY 10107
(212) 265-8890
(212) 265-8908 (fax)
stagedir@aol.com
http://www.stage-directions.com

Stages

Curtains Inc.
301 W. 45th Street
New York, NY 10036
(212) 245-9186

Theatre Crafts International

Amusement Business
PO Box 24970
Nashville, TN 37202
(615) 321-4250
(615) 327-1574 (fax)
http://www.amusementbusiness.com

Theatre Design and Technology

U.S. Institute for Theatre Technology
3001 Springcrest Drive
Louisville, KY 40241
(502) 426-1211
(502) 423-7467 (fax)
info@office.usitt.org
http://www.usitt.org

TOURING

Pollstar
4697 W. Jacquelyn Avenue
Fresno, CA 93722
(559) 271-7900
(559) 271-7979 (fax)
info@pollstar.com
http://www.pollstar.com

TRADES

Back Stage
VNU Business Media
770 Broadway
New York, NY 10003
(646) 654-5000
http://www.backstage.com

Billboard
770 Broadway
New York, NY 10003
(646) 654-4400
(646) 654-4681 (fax)
http://www.billboard.com

Daily Variety
Reed Business Information
249 W. 17th Street
New York, NY 10011
(212) 337-6900
(212) 337-6977 (fax)

The Hollywood Reporter
5055 Wilshire Boulevard
Los Angeles, CA 90036
(323) 525-2000
(323) 525-2377 (fax)
http://www.hollywoodreporter.com

Variety
Reed Business Information
5700 Wilshire Boulevard
Los Angeles, CA 90036
(323) 857-6600
(323) 965-2475 (fax)
http://www.variety.com

INDEX

A

accents 181–182
accomplishments 241
   resume component 98–99
   special 67, 68
accountability in the workplace 203–204
accountants 225
accounting skills 77–78
Ace Award 24
achievements, resume component 98–99
acting coach 225
action, positive 12–13, 46, 52
action journal 52, 53–54
action plan 12
   described 38–39
   designing 46
   examples of 47–51
   how to use 52
   using, for specific jobs 49–51
   using, to succeed 39–40
   what to include in 45–46
      career goals 45
      what you need to reach goals 45–46
      your actions 46
      your timetable 46
   your personal 40–45
      differentiate yourself 42, 44
      getting noticed 44
      what you need 42
      your market 41–42
actor 41
   resume for 100–103
Actors Equity Association (AEA) 174, 212, 232

administrative end of performing arts 177
advertisements
   to get gigs 221
   importance of keeping 55
   job 29, 81–84, 94, 149–160, 194
   press releases vs. 184
advocate, finding 146–147
AEA. *See* Actors Equity Association
AFL-CIO 232
AFM. *See* American Federation of Musicians
AFTRA. *See* American Federation of Television and Radio Artists
agents 39, 41–42, 101, 127, 210, 230
AGMA. *See* American Guild of Musical Artists
AGVA. *See* American Guild of Variety Artists
Alda, Alan 24
American Ballet Theatre 33
American Federation of Musicians (AFM) 214, 233
American Federation of Television and Radio Artists (AFTRA) 232
American Guild of Musical Artists (AGMA) 233
American Guild of Variety Artists (AGVA) 233
American Idol 58, 146
American Music Awards 236
American Society of Composers, Authors, and Publishers (ASCAP) 227
American Symphony Orchestra League 148, 213
angel 227
apprenticeships 147–148, 213, 215
ASCAP. *See* American Society of Composers, Authors, and Publishers
Associated Actors and Artistes of America (4As) 232

Association of Theatrical Press Agents and
    Managers (ATPAM) 233
associations. *See* trade associations
Atlanta, GA 72, 211
Atlantic City, NJ 82
attire. *See* wardrobe
attitude, positive 12–13, 183, 189, 196
attorneys. *See* lawyers
audition 150, 214. *See also* theatrical audition;
    unified auditions

B

background sheets 55
Backstage 81, 82, 104, 149, 174, 194
ballet companies 72, 148, 215
Barr, Roseanne 216
benefit performances 224
Berkshires (Massachusetts) 148
Better Business Bureau 69
Beyoncé 243
billboard advertisements 221
Billboard 81, 82, 149, 195
    Annual Talent & Touring International Guide 226
bio 18, 55
    group 123
    tool for success 92, 122–123
biography. *See* bio
BMI. *See* Broadcast Music, Inc.
body language 182
booking agencies 221–222
booking agents 221–222, 225
booking gigs
    by yourself 219–221
    using agents 221–222
books, as learning tool 194, 209
bookstores and open job market 81
Boston, MA 72, 211
branding 177
breakdown services 174
Broadcasting 82
Broadcast Music, Inc. (BMI) 227
Broadway 41, 70, 167, 243
brochures 45, 92, 114–116
business and networking cards 14, 18, 84, 136–137,
    189
    interviews and 155
    styles of 111–113
    tool for success 92, 110–114

business end of performing arts 41–42, 177, 197
business managers 18, 41–42, 225

C

cable station guest 190
callbacks 163, 171
candy bars to get call back 134
career, changing 77–80
career, creating 90–91
career, theater and performing arts
    changing 77–80
    creating 237–238
    determining 13–16
    finding job you want 80–84
    getting what you want 33–34
    vs. job 16–17
    ladder 241–243
    moving into 77–80
    preparation 56–75
    setting goals 34–36
    using job to create 76–77
    visualization 36–37
    what's stopping you 27, 29–30
    what you want to do 19–24
    your dream 24–27, 28
    your joy/happiness 30–32
    your talents 32–33
career coach 7–10
    determining right career 13–16
    personal coach 10–12
    positive attitude and actions 12–13
career fair 58
career vs. job 16–17
career objective, resume component 97
career portfolio. *See* portfolio
career success book. *See* personal career success book
career summary, resume component 96–97
Carlin, George 216
Cashbox 89
casinos 212
cast breakdowns. *See* character breakdowns
casting agents 127
casting directors 174
casting notice 169, 174, 194
casting panel 171–172, 175
CDs
    for storage 93
    tool for success 121

cell phone 201
character breakdowns 169, 171
charity auction 190–191
Chicago, IL 72, 211
children's theater 167
chocolate chip cookies to get call back 133–134
choruses 209
circus performers 219
civic groups 141, 188, 190
classes. See courses
classical music 213–215
clippings 55, 189
clothing for head shot 104
clubs, going to 29
cold calls 29, 87–90, 130
cold reading 167–168, 175
colleagues, dealing with 198–199
Combs, Sean "Puffy" 244
comedian 42, 72, 73
comedy 215–219
commercial agents 210
communication skills 181–183
community service, resume component 99
community theaters 33, 209
compensation 161
competitions 213, 215
composers 41, 226–228
conferences 58, 85–86, 137
confidential issues 117
contacts, theater and performing arts 18. See also
   networking
      making and using 144–146
      meeting the right people 136–138
      who you know 135–136
      worksheets 145
contracts 231
conventions 85–86, 137
copyrights 146, 226–228
correspondence, importance of keeping 53–55
Cosby, Bill 216
costume design 41
courses
      as networking opportunity 69
      as workplace learning tool 195
      taking 29, 60, 209
      teaching 45

cover letter 18
      interviews 150–152
      tool for success 107–110
coworkers, dealing with 198–199

D

daily action journal. See action journal
dance auditions 169–170
Dance Magazine 148, 195
dancer 42
dancing 215
demo 45, 226
DG. See Dramatist Guild
DGA. See Directors Guild of America
differentiate yourself 42, 44
dinner theaters 33, 72, 167, 209, 211, 226, 242
directors 101, 127, 175
Directors Guild of America (DGA) 233
discrimination 8–9
disks, for storage 103
Disney 177
drama coach 225
Dramatist Guild (DG) 229
Dramatist Sourcebook 230
dress policy 181
DVDs 93, 122

E

earnings. See salary
education
      requirements 29
      resume component 97–98
      succeeding in the workplace 194
      training and 69–70, 71
educational symposiums as networking opportunity
      136
egg idea to get call back 130–132
e-mailing
      company policies on 195, 201
      confidentiality of 201
      copies of 53
Emmy Award 24
employment agencies 81
entertainment reporter 77
Equity. See Actors Equity Association
ethics in the workplace 202–203
examples
      action journal 53

action plan for specific job 49–51
basic action plan 47–48
bios 122, 123
business and networking cards 111–113
cover letter 108–110
mission statements 238–239
networking worksheet 140
opportunities worksheet 59
pitch letter 190
quote sheet 121
reference sheet 106
resume 102
talent worksheet 65
thank-you notes 163
experience (professional and work), resume component 98
expert, becoming an 187–189
exposure, getting 223–224

F

fan mail 55
fans, dealing with 201–202
faxing resume 152, 153
feature story 191
fees 222
Fierstein, Harvey 25
finances, keeping track of 225
five Ps of marketing 178–179
fortune cookie to get call back 132–133
fund-raiser performances 224

G

Garland, Judy 57
gatekeepers 125
general work-related goals 35
Getty, Estelle 22, 25
gigs, getting 219–222
Glengarry Glen Ross 24
goals
    general work-related 35
    long-term 35, 39, 45
    passions and 74–75
    setting 34–36
    short-term 35, 39, 45
    specific work-related 35
Goldberg, Whoopi 216
The Golden Girls 22, 25

gossip, office 196–197
Grammy award 24, 236
Grease 146
grooming, personal 180–181
guilt factor and persistence 129–130

H

hairstyle for head shot 104–105
handouts 55
head shots 55, 92, 101, 103–105, 175
help wanted ads. *See also* advertisements, job
hidden job market 83–84
hobbies 31, 63
Hotjobs.com 83
HR department. *See* human resources department
human resources (HR) department 89
hypnotists 219

I

IATSE. *See* Internal Alliance of Theatrical Stage Employees
industry publications 81–83
information technology 78
interests, resume component 110–111
Internal Alliance of Theatrical Stage Employees (IATSE) 233
International Musician 214
Internet
    casting notices and auditions 174
    exposure through 224
internships 58, 147–148, 194, 215, 226
interviews
    environments 155–157
    follow-up 163–164
    getting 149–155
    process 155
        what to bring 155
        what to wear 155
    questions
        from interviewer 157–160
        for you to ask 160–161
    salary and compensation 161
    talent area 150
    thank-you notes 162–163
    tips for 60, 61, 63, 163
inventory and self-assessment 58, 60

J

Jackie Mason: Freshly Squeezed 24
James, Kevin 216, 243
job
    career vs. 16–17
    finding 80–84
    related skills 63
    search strategies 76–91
    using to create career 76–77
job market
    hidden 83–84
    open 81
journal. *See* action journal

K

Kellogg's 177
Kiss (band) 44

L

Last Comic Standing 146
Las Vegas, NV 72, 82
Law and Order 243
lawyers 225, 231
learning tools in the workplace 193–195
legitimate agents 210
legitimate theater 167
leisure time skills 63
Leno, Jay 216
Letterman, David 216
letters of recommendation 55, 107
libraries and open job market 81
lies on resume 100
life skills 63
lighting design 41
Lincoln Center 215
lists, making 205
locations
    audition 171
    job 18, 27, 41, 70–73
long-term goals 35, 39, 45
Los Angeles, CA 72, 104, 211
lyricists 226–228

M

magazines 189–190, 191
magicians 42, 219

makeup for head shot 104–105
Making It in Music 12
Making It in the Performing Arts seminars 12
Making It in Theater seminars 12
managers. *See* business managers; personal managers
market, determining 41–42
marketing skills 78
marketing yourself 18, 55, 124–125
    contacts, making and using 144–146
    expert, becoming an 187–189
    finding a mentor/advocate 146–147
    five Ps 178–179
    getting gigs 220
    getting noticed 44
    importance of 177–178
    internships/apprenticeships 147–148
    meeting the right people 136–138
    networking basics 138–144
    new opportunities 191–192
    on the phone 124–135
    like a pro 183–187
    putting together your package 179–181
    resume and 92
    other strategies 189–190
    for success 177–192
    visibility and 183–187
    who you know 135–136
Martin, Steve 216
M*A*S*H 24
Mason, Jackie 22, 24
McDonalds 177
meal, interview during 156
mechanical rights 227–228
media
    contacting 45, 184
    possibilities lists 55
media kit. *See* press kit
mentor 146–147, 213
Metropolitan Opera 148
    Young Artists Program 215
mimes 219
mission statement, personal 238–239
modeling 242
monologue 165–167, 175
Monster.com 83
morals in the workplace 202–203
mugs to get call back 135

musical theater audition 168–169
music industry 72–73, 212–215

N

Nabisco 177
Nashville, TN 72
National Association of Schools of Theatre 69
NETC. *See* New England Theater Conference
networking. *See also* contacts, theater and performing
   arts
      auditions and 174
      basics 138–140
      cards. *See* business and networking cards
      contact information sheet 145
      expanding 140–142
      how to 14–16
      opportunities 58, 84–85, 136–137
      savvy 142–144
      ways of 29
      worksheets 140, 141
New Dramatist 229
New England Theater Conference (NETC) 212
newsletters and job advertisements 81–83
newspaper
      advertisements 81, 150, 174
      writing for 189–190, 191
news releases. *See* press releases
New York City, NY 41, 70, 72, 82, 104, 211, 212
New York City Ballet 147
notebook, keeping 205
not-for-profit groups 141, 188
noticed, getting 44–45

O

O'Donnell, Rosie 243
off Broadway 41, 70, 167
office skills 78
off-off Broadway 41, 70, 167
open casting calls 174
open job market 81
Opera America 148, 214–215
operas 72, 209, 214–215, 226
opportunities 56–58
      looking for 58, 59
Orbach, Jerry 243
orchestras 209, 214
organization in the workplace 204–205

organizations. *See* trade associations; unions
Outer Critics Circle Award 24

P

packaging
      marketing and 178, 179
      putting together 179–181
Paltrow, Gwyneth 148
passions and goals 74–75
past
      reviewing 73–74
      using to create future 74, 75
patience and phone calls 130
performance rights 227
performers. *See* talent end
performing arts industry. *See* theater and performing
   arts industry
persistence 129–130, 152
personal action plan. *See* action plan
personal career success book 52–55
personal coach 10–12
personality traits 66–67
      marketing for success 182
      resume component 98
personal managers 41–42, 225
personal references 106–107
Philadelphia, PA 72, 211
phone
      cell phone 201
      etiquette 201
      selling yourself
            getting someone to call you 130–145
            getting through 125–129
            persistence and guilt 129–130
            three Ps 129
            timing 128–129
photographers, finding 103–104
pitch
      demo 226
      letter 190
Playbill 81, 82, 194–195
playwrights 239–230
politics, workplace 18, 195–196
portfolio 18
      confidential issues 117
      contents of 117–118
      interviews and 155
      tool for success 92, 116–118

positioning and marketing 178, 179
positive attitude and actions. *See* attitude, positive
prepared reading 167–168
press agents 223, 225
press kit 18, 92, 119–121, 122
press pack. *See* press kit
press releases 184–187
price and marketing 178–179
print license 228
producers 101
product and marketing 178
professional experience, resume component 98
professionalism 208
professional references 105–106
professional support team. *See* talent support team
promo kit. *See* press kit
promotion and marketing 178, 179, 220
proofreading 116, 186
proof sheets for head shots 105
protecting yourself 230–231
publications 77, 81–83. *See also* trade associations,
    publications
publicists 223, 225
publicity firm 77
public relations
    careers 77
    counselors 223, 225
publishing companies 230
publishing income 227–228
puppeteers 219

Q

quote sheets 92, 121

R

radio 190
A Raisin in the Sun 244
reading, as learning tool 209
reading, prepared. *See* prepared reading
references
    interviews and 155
    letters of recommendation 107, 155
    personal 106–107
    professional 105–106
    resume component 99
    tool for success 92, 105–107
regional theaters 33, 72, 167, 211, 212, 226, 242
rejection 90, 124

repertory theater 167, 211
resorts 212
resume 18, 55
    audition and 175
    contents of 96–99, 101–103
        accomplishments and achievements 98–99
        career objective 97
        career summary 96–97
        community service and volunteer activities 99
        education 97–98
        professional and work experience 98
        references 99
        skills and personality traits 98
    home address on 101
    interview and 150–152, 155
    length 100, 101
    lies on 100
    paper 95, 151–152
    redefining 95–96
    as selling tool 92–95
    storing updated copies 93
    tailoring to job advertisement 93, 94, 151–152
    theatrical 100–103
    traditional 100
    writing style 99–100
risks, taking 206, 243–244
Ritchie, Lionel 243
Rock, Chris 216
romance, office 196
Romano, Ray 216, 243
Rooney, Mickey 210
roses to get call back 135
royalties 227, 230

S

SAG. *See* Screen Actors Guild
salary 161, 197–198
sales skills 78
Santa Fe Opera 148
scenic design 41
School of American Ballet 147
scrapbook 142
Screen Actors Guild (SAG) 232
scripts
    auditions 167–168, 175, 211
    cold calls 87
    interviews 157

search strategies 18
Seattle, WA 72
Seattle Opera 148
Seinfeld, Jerry 216
self-assessment 58, 60
selling yourself. *See* marketing yourself
seminars
    attending 29, 55, 209
    as networking opportunity 69, 85, 136
    as workplace learning tool 195
SESAC 227
SETC. *See* Southeastern Theatre Conference
sexual discrimination 8–9
short-term goals 35, 39, 45
sides 167, 175, 211
Simmons, Gene 44
singers 42
singing coach 225
skills
    changing careers 77–78
    determining 63–65
    marketing for success 182–183
    resume component 98
    types of 63, 126
Society of Stage Directors and Choreographers
    (SSDC) 233
songwriters 41, 226–228
sound design 41
Southeastern Theatre Conference (SETC) 212
special accomplishments. *See* accomplishments,
    special
specialized action plan. *See* action plan, specialized
SSDC. *See* Society of Stage Directors and
    Choreographers
Staples 115
stock theater 72, 211
straight theater 167
Strawhat Auditions 212
street performers 219
strengths 60–63, 158
success
    creating your career 237–238
    marketing yourself for 177–192
    planning for
        action journal 52, 53
        action plan 38–52
        be your own career manager 38
        career success book 52–53

strategies 239–241
on the talent end 207–233
tools for 92–123
    bio 122–123
    brochures 114–116
    business and networking cards 110–114
    CDs 121
    cover letters 107–110
    DVDs 122
    head shots 103–105
    portfolio 116–118
    press kits 119–121, 122
    quote sheets 121
    references 105–107
    resume 92–103
    Web site 123
in the workplace 193–206
summer stock theaters 209, 226
superiors, dealing with 199–201
support team. *See* talent support team
symphonies 72
Symphony 82
symposiums, making contact through 136
synchronization license 228

T

talents 210
talent brokers 225
talent end
    audition 150
    breaking into theater and performing arts 78–80,
        208–209
    classical music 213–215
    comedy 215–219
    copyrights 228
    dancing 215
    getting exposure 223–224
    getting gigs 219–222
    interview 150
    market 41
    marketing for 177
    moving up in the business 209–212
    music industry 212–213
    office gossip 197
    playwrights 229–230
    portfolio 118
    professional support team 224–225

protecting yourself 230–231
songwriters, lyricists and composers 226–228
succeeding on 207–233
trusting people 231
unified auditions 212
unions 232–233
wardrobe 181
workplace politics 196
talents 24, 32–33, 63, 65–66, 182–183
talent support team 224–225
talk show circuit 190
tasks, breaking up 40
teaching classes 45, 85
technical skills 63
television station, talk show circuit 190
thank-you notes 163
theater and performing arts industry
    moving into 77–80
    networking in 84–85
    publications 81–83
theatrical audition 175–176. *See also* audition
    casting panel 171–172
    character breakdowns 171
    dance 169–170
    finding 173–175
    locations 171
    musical theater 168–169
    process 165–168, 175–176
    tips 172–173
    wardrobe 170–171
    what to bring 172
theatrical resume 100–103. *See also* resume
three Ps of phone calls 129
time in the workplace 204–205
time management in the workplace 204–205
timetable for reaching career goals 46
Tony (award) 24, 71, 236–237
tools for success. *See under* success
Torch Song Trilogy 25
tour coordinators 225
touring productions 72
tour managers 225
trade associations 18, 58
    casting notices and auditions 174, 194
    job advertisements 81–83, 149, 194
    joining 190
    making contacts through 136–137
    publications 89, 194–195

trade shows 85–86
training programs 69–70, 71, 194, 215
transferable skills 63, 126
Trump, Donald 177

U

unified auditions 212
unions 174, 222, 232–233. *See also specific union*
United Professional Theatre Auditions (UPTA) 212
UPTA. *See* United Professional Theatre Auditions
U.S. Copyright Office 228

V

Variety 81, 104, 149
verbal communication skills 181–182
videos 45, 120
visible, making yourself 183–187
visualization 35–37, 237
vocal coach 225
voice mail 129–130
voice-over work 242
volunteer activities 31, 190
    generate visibility through 190
    portfolio component 142
    resume component 99
    succeeding in the workplace 194
    way to network 29, 143–144

W

wardrobe
    audition 170–171
    dressing for success 179–181
    interviewing 155
Washington, D.C. 72
Washington National Opera 148
WGA. *See* Writers Guild of America
weaknesses 60–63, 158
Weaver, Sigourney 148
Web sites
    casting notices and auditions 174
    internships/apprenticeships 147
    job advertisements 81–83, 149
    personal 92, 123, 224
    source of contact information 89
Williams, Robin 216
Williamstown Theatre Festival 148
work experience, resume component 98

workplace, succeeding in
    accountability 203–204
    colleagues dealing with 198–199
    dress policy 181
    ethics and morals 202–203
    fans, dealing with 201–202
    learning tools in 193–195
    office romance 196
    office gossip 196–197
    politics 195–196
    positive attention in 199
    salary issues 197–198
    superiors, dealing with 199–201
    time, time management, organization 204–205
    tips on 205–206
work-related goals 35
worksheets
    cold call tracking 88
    education and training 70, 71
    focus on job of your dream 28
    location 72
    networking 140, 141
    networking contact information sheet 145
    opportunities 59
    personal action plan 48

    personality traits 67
    skills 64
    special accomplishments 68
    strengths and weaknesses 61, 62
    talents 65, 66
    things you don't want to do 21
    things you enjoy doing 23
    using past to create future 75
    what stands between you and dream 43
workshops
    attending 29, 55, 209
    as networking opportunity 69, 85, 136
    as workplace learning tool 195
The World According to Me 22, 24
Writers Guild of America (WGA) 233
writing
    magazine/newspaper articles/columns 127–128, 189–190
    skills. *See* written communication skills
    style for resume 99–100
written communication skills 77, 137–138, 182

Y

Yang, Fan 219
"You're the One That I Want" 146